SHOCK ARMY OF
THE BRITISH EMPIRE

SHOCK ARMY OF THE BRITISH EMPIRE

*The Canadian Corps in
the Last 100 Days of the Great War*

Shane B. Schreiber

Foreword by John A. English

Vanwell Publishing Limited
St. Catharines, Ontario

Published in paperback 2004 by Vanwell Publishing Limited. No part of this book may be reproduced or used in any form or by any means, electronic or mechanical, including photocopying, recording, or in any information storage and retrieval system, without permission in writing from the publisher.

Shock Army of the British Empire/ The Canadian Corps in the Last 100 Days of the Great War by Shane Schreiber originally published by Praeger, an imprint of Greenwood Publishing Group, Inc, CT , USA. © Copyright 1997. Published in paperback by arrangement with Greenwood Publishing Group Inc. All rights reserved.

Vanwell Publishing acknowledges the financial support of the Government of Canada through the Book Publishing Industry Development Program for our publishing activities.

Cover Design: Vanessa Kooter
Cover: Bastien, *Over the Top: Neuville-Vitasse* (CWM 19710261-0056, Beaverbrook Collection of War Art, © Canadian War Museum)

Vanwell Publishing Limited
1 Northrup Crescent
P.O. Box 2131
St. Catharines, Ontario L2R 7S2
sales@vanwell.com
tel: 905-937-3100
fax: 905-937-1760

Printed in Canada

Library and Archives of Canada Cataloguing in Publication Data

Schreiber, Shane B., 1966-
    Shock army of the British empire: the Canadian Corps in the last 100 days of the Great War/Shane B. Schreiber; foreword by John A. English.

Includes bibliographical references and index.
ISBN 1-55125-096-9

    1. World War, 1914-1918--Campaigns--Western Front. 2. Canada. Canadian Army. Canadian Corps--History. I. Title.

D547.C2S27 2004   940.4'35
C2004-906836-9

To Kelly, Matthias and Seth

CONTENTS

FIGURES AND MAPS

FOREWORD BY JOHN A. ENGLISH

Seventy-three years separate the 100-hour ground campaign of the Gulf War from the 100 Days of victory in the Great War. Yet, for all the difference of time and space, substantial similarities can be seen in both campaigns. Indeed, one could argue that the 100 Days were the original crucible for the 100 hours of *Desert Saber*, particularly in respect to sophisticated planning, logistical preparations, chemical warfare countermeasures, and the detailed coordination of all arms ground and air action. From the surprise attack at Amiens on 8 August 1918, "the black day of the German army," the field forces of the British Empire advanced relentlessly over some 100 kilometers, using techniques later refined in *Blitzkrieg*, to break the back of the German Army on the Western Front. To an extent greater perhaps than any other fighting formation, the Canadian Corps spearheaded this last Allied offensive of the war. In a series of actions from the breaking of the Drocourt-Queant switch in the Hindenberg Line in early September to the capture of Mons on 11 November, the German Army was sent reeling back, to be saved from ultimate destruction only by the eleventh-hour Armistice.

Never before or since have Canadian troops played such a crucial and decisive role in land operations. The exemplary fighting performance of the Canadian Corps was enough to persuade Canada's foremost military historian, the late Colonel C.P. Stacey, that the "creation of the Canadian Corps was the greatest that Canada had ever done." World War Two, he noted with some irony, was but the second-greatest event in Canadian history. In terms of lives lost this was most certainly the case, and by such a yardstick the Great War remains Canada's greatest war. The conflict cost the dominion over 60,000 dead, a greater price for such a tiny nation than the 48,000 Americans killed in the Great War. Indeed, the Canadian death toll in this far-distant war exceeded that of the United States in Vietnam; but whereas the latter drew its soldiers from a population base of more than 200 million, the Dominion of Canada in the summer of 1914 boasted fewer than 8 million souls. Proportionally, although rarely recognized, Canadian Great War battlefield losses can be equated to the 600,000 soldiers of both sides who perished in the American Civil War.

   Shock Army of the British Empire is not, however, a laudatory nationalist
work of history. It presents rather a critical analysis of Canadian Corps operations
during the 100 Days, which by any measure of indirect fire, mechanization, tactical air
support, chemical weaponry, electronic deception, or command and control,
challenges were thoroughly modern in nature. How the Canadian Corps managed to
turn a tactical victory into a continuous string of consecutive successes in a sustained
campaign remains the central focus of this detailed study based on primary sources,
maps, and other practical considerations affecting modern military operations.
Obviously, there are lessons to be gleaned from the examination of how this one corps,
which was as large as a small British field army, adjusted to new battlefield realities
by adopting and generating highly innovative fighting approaches to war. That this
was not easily accomplished without "hard pounding" is additionally evident, for the
ferocious fighting of the 100 Days accounted for roughly 20% of all Canadian
casualties during the entire war.

   From an operational perspective, the Great War still lies heavily on the
military landscape, shrouded in the mists of history and myth that becloud the true
dimensions of its salience. The forlorn images of the Somme and Passchendaele
regrettably continue to overshadow the fire and movement victories of 1918. Yet, the
more one studies later wars and military operations, the more one is inexorably drawn
back to this watershed in war fighting which witnessed unparalleled technological
change, and for the first time in history saw more soldiers perish by fire than disease.
Unfortunately, too few historians have dared or deigned to peer behind the broad
arrows and rough outlines of the grand strategic picture.

   The critical question remains, however, what do reasonably matched armies
do when strategic alternatives have been exhausted and there are no flanks around
which to maneuver? Had the Cold War turned hot on the European Central Front,
where similar conditions prevailed, it would doubtless have been characterized by
reciprocal hard pounding, for the relatively easy one-sided success of Western arms
in the Gulf could hardly have been repeated in the closer country of Germany. The
great-grandsons of those who served on the Western Front, where solutions had to be
found in bloody actions fought from the bottom up, might well in such circumstances
have been forced to rediscover what their forefathers had already learned at such a
brutal cost. I can think of no study that better describes the tribulations of the latter in
their Great War trial by fire than *Shock Army of the British Empire*.

ACKNOWLEDGMENTS

A wise old army Warrant Officer once told me, "Sir, you're not successful unless a lot of other people want you to be." For whatever success I may have attained with this work, I would be remiss if I did not thank "a lot of other people."

First and foremost, I need to thank Lt. Col. Dr. Jack English for encouraging me to write this work. He was a constant inspiration, and was very often more enthusiatic about my research than I was. His interest and belief not only in my subject, but also in my abilities to do it justice, went a long way in helping me shape the final product.

I would also like to thank Dr. Michael Hennessy, and Dr. Ron Haycock of the History Department at the Royal Military College (RMC) for reading (and grilling me on) drafts of the manuscript. I am especially grateful to Dr. A.M.J. Hyatt for his contributions, and would like to thank him for taking time out of his busy schedule to read and make detailed comments on the draft. Bruce Gudmundsson was particularly kind in letting me vent my ideas to him, and in sending me research material that I might have otherwise overlooked. Major Bill Philbin, USMC, and other members of the War Studies Program at RMC are also due some appreciation for reading various parts of the work in progress, and for putting up with my constant digressions into late World War One history. I need to also thank Chris Ankersen for his critique of the final draft, and for all his excellent suggestions.

Beniot Cameron and the staff at RMC's Massey Library were very kind to me throughout the research, especially with respect to access to the archives (sorry about the overdue books.) I would also like to thank the extremely helpful staff at the National Archives of Canada for putting up with my endless inquiries and for their expert assistance. I also need to thank Laura Haycock, the War Studies Program Administrative Genius, for all her help and good humour.

Marcia Goldstein at Greenwood Publishing was a paragon of patience and advice as she herded me towards completion of all the adminsitrative details in preparation of the book. My wish for her is that she never again be afflicted with such a disorganized would-be author. Likewise I must thank Katie Chase, whose expert copyediting has helped me cull the manuscript of its many errors; any that are left are my responsibility alone.

Lastly, I need to thank Emilie for putting up with me while I was too engrossed in events of eighty years ago to pay attention to what was happening today, and Kelly, who was the very model of patience and understanding while I worked to finish the final stages of the book.

Thanks, again, to all.

ABBREVIATIONS

AIB	Australian Infantry Brigade
AIF	Australian Imperial Force
Bde	Brigade; an army formation made up of 3-4 battalions, plus ancillary support arms such as artillery and logistical units.
BEF	British Expeditionary Force
BGGS	Brigadier General, General Staff; usually the Chief of Staff in a corps.
Bn	Battalion; an army organization of between 600-1000 soldiers.
Brig.-Gen.	Brigadier General
C3	Military jargon for "Command, Control, and Coordination."
C3I	Military jargon for "Command, Control, Cordination, and Intelligence."
CAPC	Canadian Army Pay Corps
CASC	Canadian Army Service Corps
CBSO	Counter-Battery Staff Office
CCGS	Canadian Corps General Staff
CE	Corps Engineer
CEF	Canadian Expeditionary Force
CIB	Canadian Infantry Brigade
CMR	Canadian Mounted Rifles
CO	Commanding Officer
Coy	Company; a suborganization of a battalion made up of between 90-150 soldiers.
CWNS	Canadian War Narrative Section
DA & QMG	Deputy Adjutant and Quartermaster General
Div	Division; a military formation made up of a number of brigades.
GHQ	General Headquarters; i.e. Field Marshall Haig's Headquarters.

GOC	General Officer Commanding
GOCRA	General Officer Commanding, Royal Artillery; an artillery officer in command of a division's, corps', or Army's artillery assets.
GS	General Staff
GSO	General Staff Officer
HE	High Explosive
HQ	Headquarters
MG	Machine Gun [or **M**anuscript **G**roup (NAC)]
MGGS	Major-General, General Staff; the Chief of Staff of an Army formation.
NAC	National Archives of Canada, Ottawa, Ontario
OR	Other ranks; soldiers below the rank of Sergeant.
Pl	Platoon; a suborganization of the company, usually made up of 25-45 soldiers.
RAF	Royal Air Force (as of 1 April 1918).
RG	Record Group (NAC)
RMC	Royal Military College of Canada
SAA	Small Arms Ammunition
Sect	Section; a suborganization of the platoon, usually of about 8-12 soldiers.
TM	Trench Mortar

SHOCK ARMY OF
THE BRITISH EMPIRE

INTRODUCTION

Hard pounding, this, gentlemen; try who can pound the longest.[1]
Wellington, at Waterloo 18 June 1815

It is a sublime irony of history that the above words, uttered by Wellington on the battlefield of Waterloo just as he was bringing Napoleon's "100 Days" to an ignominious end, could almost as easily describe the culminating battles of the British Expeditionary Force's (BEF) 100 Days campaign of the Great War, fought over roughly the same ground, a century later. Both campaigns ended with the British Armies, and their Allies, triumphant over a large Continental power. And both campaigns, to borrow another phrase from the Iron Duke, were "damn near run thing[s]."[2]

The feat of British arms during the 100 Days campaign of the Great War, from Amiens, 8 August 1918, to the triumphant return to Mons, 11 November 1918, is a remarkable event in military history. Battered and nearly forced off the Continent by the German *Kaiserschlact* of spring and summer 1918, the army that Kaiser Whilhelm had once ridiculed as "contemptible" rebounded in only a few short months to drive the vaunted German military machine to destruction and defeat. Spearheading this turn of the tide were men from nations that had been but sparsely populated colonies during Napoleon's 100 Days. Now, as part of the largest British Army ever, units from far-flung parts of the British Empire rose to play a crucial role in the defeat of the German Army on the Western Front.

One of these formations was the Canadian Corps, under its commander, Lieutenant General Sir Arthur Currie. From Amiens to Mons, the Canadian Corps acted as a spearhead for the armies of the BEF and its Allies, playing a direct and significant part in the Allied advance to victory in World War One. Unfortunately, the story of the 100 Days has been obscured in both British and Canadian military history. In Britain, this was because of a nearly morbid fixation on the costly and controversial battles of 1914-1916, especially the Somme and Ypres.[3] In Canada, the victories of the 100 Days have languished unappreciated in the shadow of the Canadian Corps' earlier and more publicized victory at Vimy Ridge in April 1917.

This work seeks to redress that historical oversight by providing not only a narrative history of the Canadian Corps' battles, but also an examination of the campaign's more significant effects on the eventual strategic outcome of the Great War. This study will reveal that during the late summer and autumn of 1918, the Canadian Corps played a significant role in breaking the back of the German Army on the Western Front, thereby helping to bring the Great War to a close that year. Further, it examines the operational, tactical, and organizational innovations adopted and developed by the Canadian Corps during this campaign, and the subsequent effect on military thought in general, and on Canadian military doctrine in particular.

Specifically, this work will address a number of topics crucial to a wider understanding of the Great War in modern military history. One of the issues examined will be whether the Canadian Corps was actually more successful than other corps formations, and the factors in its success. Also investigated is Field Marshall Sir Douglas Haig's seemingly deliberate use of the Canadian Corps, along with other "elite" formations in the BEF, as spearheads for offensive operations during the 100 Days campaign. The lessons learned by the Canadians during the 100 Days, and the subsequent effect of these experiences on the Canadian "way of war," will also be considered.

No less staunch an English patriot than Sir Arthur Conan Doyle conceded that "there are no better soldiers in the world than those of the Dominions."[4] Yet the superior operational achievements of the Canadian Corps stemmed not from a particular genius for battle on Currie's part, but rather through the collective efforts of a number of pragmatic men finding functional, and at times unconventional, solutions to difficult and pressing problems.[5] Currie's practical approach to war meant that the tactical advances made by the Canadian Corps were *evolutionary*, not *revolutionary*, and are therefore more difficult for casual students of military history to discern. The result, as Dennis Winter has pointed out, is that, "Currie remains the most successful Allied general and one of the least well-known.... But he had a great capacity for war.... His capture of the Drocourt-Queant Switch in autumn 1918 *remains the British Army's single greatest achievment on the Western Front* (author's emphasis)."[6]

Winter may have overstated the brilliance of the breaking of the Drocourt-Queant defenses in terms of generalship; as will be seen, the breaching of the Canal du Nord is probably a better example of Currie's true "capacity for war." Nonetheless, Winter is correct in his claim that Currie's achievments, and those of the corps he commanded, have for the most part been overlooked by serious military historians.

Recently there has been a renaissance in scholarship on the 100 Days, led primarily by Tim Travers' 1992 book *How the War Was Won: Command and Technology in the British Army on the Western Front, 1917-1918*. Subsequent research has focused on the success of the Canadian Corps "set-piece battle" operations, and the adoption of new technology.[7] It is the intention of this work to investigate not only why the Canadian Corps' operational and tactical doctrine proved so successful, but also to examine the less obvious aspects of this style of warfare. Furthermore, it will show that the Corps' success was due not to the slavish application of a tactical doctrine, but rather to a pragmatic, and at times innovative approach to the unique problems operations posed during the battles of the 100 Days. Lastly, but perhaps most importantly, the Canadian Corps' experiences during the battles of the 100 Days may point to problems faced by many land formations engaged in modern, "high-intensity" operations, especially offensive operations.

Insights culled from the specific Canadian experience may prove to have a broader, more universal application, for both soldiers and scholars alike, about not just the unique nature and history of the Great War, but about war in general. The lessons learned by Canadian soldiers so many years ago in the fields of Artois and Picardy may prove enlightening to future generals faced with situations that demand "hard pounding." In the words of Clausewitz, "historical examples clarify everything and also provide the best kind of proof in the empirical sciences. This is particularly true of the art of war."[8]

THE MUSICAL METAPHOR

The grand successes enjoyed by the Canadian Corps during the 100 Days campaign were not just a function of its capability to pound harder than its foe, any more than the repeated mindless banging on a drum or the keys of a piano creates a musical score. There was a deliberateness to the efforts of Sir Arthur Currie that resembles the work of a maestro. The creation of great music, like the creation of a successful battle, requires the genius to bring an abstract concept in one man's head to life through the synchronization of a large number of instruments, each with its own characteristics, into a single real whole that is greater than the sum of its parts. The general, like the maestro, must keep in mind the characteristics of each instrument, carefully putting them in order that they may compliment and not detract from or mask the qualities of another. Like sheet music for a symphony, an army requires some means with which to guide each instrument to its task, and a conductor to lead the disparate groups to the final, melodious, harmonic result. Without this guidance, the orchestra does not make music; it creates simple cacophony. Armies, without the same kind of guidance and control, do not win battles, but rather generate simple violence and mayhem. It is only through experience, coordination, and hard work that the abstract ideas of a composer can be brought to living sound by a symphony orchestra, or a general's plan for battle can be executed successfully. As Lieutenant General Sir John Monash, Currie's friend, and Commander of the Australian Corps, once stated, "a perfected modern battle plan is like nothing so much as a score for an orchestrated composition, where the various arms and units are the instruments, and the tasks they perform are their respective musical phases.[9]"

Call it what one will -- synchronization, orchestration -- the goal remains the same: to create a physical effect on the receiver that is far greater than the sum of its individual parts, and that eventually proves overwhelming. This is as true for battle as it is for music, and this may be why consistently successful martial nations --

Germany, Russia, and Israel, for instance -- have also produced great symphonies.

Noticeably lacking from this list is, of course, Canada. It is this author's contention, however, that if Canada has not produced a musical legacy on par with those of the aforementioned nations, then it has at least produced a military force of world-class stature: the Canadian Corps of the Great War. Throughout this work, it will become clear that the Corps' success during the battles of the 100 Days was due in great part to the same kinds of things that make great symphonies: masterful and innovative leaders, close, harmonious working relationships between all of its various "instruments", and an ability to orchestrate its workings to create the synergistic effects that make both great battles and great music.

There remains a third element to the Canadian Corps' success: the ability to consistently produce tactical victories over a *sustained* campaign. In short, this called for the Canadian Corps to develop an ability to think at the *operational* level of war. Some purists may object to the use of the terms "operations" and "operational" throughout this work, because it implies that Currie and his corps were thinking beyond the tactical level of battle. The term "operational level" is, however, if anything, a contentious and amorphous concept. It has been described as the "grey area between strategy and tactics, in which strategic ends are achieved through tactical means." More practically, it has been described as the way in which a military force turns *one* victory into a continuous *string* of successes, thereby acheiving a higher aim. If this second definition is used, then it may be said that Currie and the Canadian Corps, before and throughout the 100 Days campaign, grappled with *operational* questions; in other words, not just how to win *once*, but how to win *ultimately*. Lastly, American historian Richard Swain has noted that the labels of "strategic, tactical, and operational levels" in war are merely artificial intellectual constructs created by academics in order to fashion neat boundaries that actual practitioners of war cannot be concerned with and may not percieve. It is in keeping with Dr. Swain's caveat that the efforts of Currie and the Canadian Corps are viewed; in short, this work will show that their role in the 100 Days straddled the imaginary and amorphous boundary between tactical and operational levels of war.[10]

General Sir Henry Horne, commander of the First British Army, under which the Canadian Corps served for most of the 100 Days, once complained that "the Canadian Corps is perhaps rather apt to take all the credit it can for everything and to consider that the BEF consists of the Canadian Corps and some other troops."[11] Indubitably, some readers will make the same criticism of the perspective of this work. They should also note, however, that this work has been purposefully kept narrow in its historical focus, being limited to an examination of the Canadian Corps' participation and performance during the 100 Days campaign. The parallel developments and efforts of the myriad of formations on the Western Front, Allied and German alike, have been left deliberately untreated, except where absolutely necessary. The object, of course, was not to skew the historical record, but rather to leave the investigation of the exploits of other formations to other historians. Excellent books with a wider scrutiny of Western Front operations have already been written by numerous historians, including Tim Travers, Paddy Griffith, Bruce Gudmundsson, and

Hubert Johnson.[12] As these writers have shown, there can be no doubt that there was a tremendous amount of technological and tactical innovation spurred by the cross-pollination of ideas in the hot-house environment of the Western Front. The purpose of this work, however, is to *specifically* examine the Canadian Corps' adoption and generation of new ideas in this brutally fertile climate.

This work has adopted a "criminal law" approach in its search for answers. Long quotes are often included so that "witnesses," as much as practicably possible, are allowed to testify in their own words. Where the reliability of one's testimony has been called into question, the focus will be not on what that actor *said*, but instead on what he *did*. This will especially be the case when dealing with the motives of Field Marshal Sir Douglas Haig, whose actions and statements continue to stir up a maelstrom of academic controversy.[13]

The reader must also be cautioned that this is a work of *analytical* history. It must be constantly kept in mind that the Canadian Corps *was* successful throughout the 100 Days, often spectacularly so for the Great War. Nonetheless, this is a critical analysis of the Corps' operations, and not a laudatory narrative. As a result, this work will often spend more time examining those operations that did not unfold exactly as planned in order to better comprehend the reasons behind those that did. In short, this study is a work of historical pathology, focusing on the diseased in order to better understand the healthy.

This last consideration points to another dilemma: the problem of perspective to history. That the Canadian Corps was victorious in its battles during the 100 Days remains undisputed. Yet clearly, though the Corps as a whole was successful, to a private soldier in an infantry battalion, the 100 Days must have been one of the most harrowing, bewildering, and exhausting periods of the war. As will be seen, repeated assaults over numerous days against desperate defenders led to the highest Canadian casualty rates in history.[14] It is for future infanteers, in hopes that they may never have to pay the terrible price extracted by the "hard pounding" of battles like the Drocourt-Queant Line, or Cambrai, that this work is written.

NOTES

1. Wellington, at Waterloo, speaking to a group of German soldiers; quoted by Elizabeth Longford, *Wellington: The Years of the Sword* (New York: Harper and Row, 1969), p. 474.

2. Quoted in ibid., p. 489.

3. John Terraine makes the same assertion that the "100 days" has been overlooked by historians in his book *To Win a War: 1918, The Year of Victory* (London: Sidgwick and Jackson, 1978), p. 13. See also Shelford Bidwell and Dominick Graham, *Firepower: British Army Weapons and Theories of War 1904-1945* (London: George Allen and Unwin, 1982) pp. 131-132, 145-146.

4. Sir Arthur Conan Doyle, *The British Campaign in France and Flanders, July to November, 1918* (London: Hodder and Stoughton, 1920), p. 261.

5. Historian Sandra Gwyn has succinctly put it,"There was nothing flashy or original

about their tactics. Their defining style was the application of common sense. Currie won his battles by combining all availible armaments...and by launching under conditions...as near as possible to complete surprise." *Tapestry of War* (Toronto: Harper Collins, 1992), p. 473.

6. Dennis Winter, *Haig's Command: A Reassessment* (London: Viking, 1991), p. 270.

7. See, for instance, Ian Brown, "Not Glamorous, But Effective: The Canadian Corps and the Set-piece Attack, 1917-1918," *Journal of Military History*, Vol. 58 (July 1994), pp. 421-444. Another excellent work that looks at the technological and tactical changes adopted by the Canadian Corps is Bill Rawling's, *Surviving Trench Warfare: Technology and the Canadian Corps, 1914-1918* (Toronto: University of Toronto Press, 1992).

8. Carl von Clausewitz, *On War*, ed. and trans. Michael Howard and Peter Paret (Princeton, NJ: Princeton University Press, 1984), Book 2, Chapter 6, p. 170. For ease of reference for those who do not have this version, the book and chapter will be cited, rather than the page number.

9. Lieutenant General Sir John Monash, *The Australian Victories in France* (Sydney: Angus and Robertson, 1936), p. 56.

10. Most of these ideas on the "operational" level of warfare were generated by the 1995 Royal Military College of Canada Military History Symposium entitled "The Operational Art." Dr. William McAndrew, from the Directorate of History at the Canadian Department of National Defence, claimed in his paper on "The Canadian Way of War" that Canadians had never worked at the operational level of war, an assertion that this work cannot wholly agree with. The "continuous string" definition was forwarded by Dr. Jacob Kipp, of the U.S. Army Combined Arms Command. Dr. Swain's point was made in a foreword to his presentation. Proceedings from this symposium are to be published in a collection of papers entitled *The Operational Art,* to be released by RMC sometime in 1997.

11. Lord Horne to Arthur Currie, in a letter dated 27 March 1919, quoted by Tim Travers in *The Great War, 1914-18,* ed. R.J.Q Adams (London: Macmillan, 1990), p. 186.

12. See, for instance, Tim Travers, *How the War Was Won: Command and Technology in the British Army on the Western Front, 1917-1918* (London: Routledge, 1992); Paddy Griffith, *Battle Tactics of the Western Front: The British Army's Art of the Attack, 1916-1918* (New Haven: Yale University Press, 1994); Bruce Gudmundsson, *Stormtroop Tactics: Innovation in the German Army, 1914-1918* (New York: Praeger, 1989); and Hubert Johnson, *Breakthrough! Tactics, Technology, and the Search for Victory on the Western Front in World War 1* (Novato, CA: Presidio, 1994).

13. Haig remains a landmine for historians because of the number of diverse opinions held about the motives, ability, and honesty of the man. Biographies range from sycophantic to scurrilous, and there is not yet a truly objective look at him. To get a general idea of where the two sides stand, compare Duff Cooper, *Haig.* 2 vols. (London: Faber, 1935-36), or John Terraine, *Douglas Haig: The Educated Soldier* (London: Hutchinson, 1963), with Winter, *Haig's Command: A Reassessment,* or John Laffin, *British Butchers and Bunglers of World War One* (Gloucester: Alan Sutton, 1988). Other recent biographies include Gerard De Groot, *Douglas Haig, 1861-1928* (London: Unwin Hyman, 1988); and Philip Warner, *Field Marshal Earl Haig* (London: Bodley Head, 1991).

14. See Chapter 9 for casualty rate comparisons.

1

"PRELUDE": BACKGROUND

To teach the art of war entirely by historical examples...would be an achievement of the utmost value.... Anyone who feels the urge to undertake such a task must dedicate himself for his labours as he would prepare for a pilgrimage to distant lands.

Clausewitz, *On War*
Book 2, Chapter 6

The Allied advance to victory that the Canadian Corps played such an instrumental role in during the autumn of 1918 was by no means guaranteed or even expected by the various Allies in the late summer of that year. The British and French had managed to hold on through 1917, the *annus horribilis* that saw their great Eastern ally, Russia, collapse and capitulate, the French Army mutiny, and the German adoption of unrestricted submarine warfare, bringing shortages and the prospect of starvation to the isolated island kingdom of Britain. At the political level, the one shining ray of hope in 1917 was the entry into the conflict on the Allied side of the sole power capable of tipping the scales in its favor: the United States. Yet, despite America's entry into the war, Britain and France would continue to shoulder the weight of the contest on the Western Front.

By summer 1918, America had two armies totalling over 1 million men in Europe under General John Pershing. The American armies were, however, suffering from the inevitable growing pains experienced by any armed force that rapidly balloons in size and finds itself thrust into a high-intensity conflict of which it has little direct experience. The need to gain experience in what had by 1918 become a very modern and complex war marginalized the effect Pershing's men could have. The commander of the British Expeditionary Force, Field Marshal Sir Douglas Haig, reported to his superiors as late as October 1918 that "the American Army is disorganized, ill-equipped and ill-trained. It must be at least a year before it becomes a serious fighting force."[1] Haig's dreary assessment continued: "In 1920, the real crushing of Germany will be possible, always provided that the British Army is kept up to its present strength. It is well to remember that the American Army, being fresher, will be the decisive factor."[2] Haig's bleak forecast merely reflected what politicians in Britain, France, and the Dominions had anticipated and had been planning for: the continuation of the agonizing stalemate on the Western Front until 1919, or even 1920.[3]

Manpower was the chief problem for the Allies. The French armies remained intact, although bordering perpetually on the verge of mutiny should their generals demand another blood sacrifice in the name of the offensive.[4] The British were only marginally better off. Prime Minister David Lloyd-George and others in his government were quite aware of the brutal cost in life and limb the Western Front was exacting, a cost that threatened to undermine the economic and social foundations of British society permanently. Throughout 1917 and 1918, Haig had come under increasing pressure from his political superiors to find a way to achieve victory cheaply, at least in terms of lives. The other side of Haig's manpower problem was the need to replace casualties from British divisions that had grievously suffered, first by Haig's own Passchendaele offensive in late 1917, and then later in stopping the German Spring and Summer Offensives in 1918. The Americans seemed to hold the solution to the Allied manpower dilemma. Canadian Prime Minister Robert Borden remarked that "the [Allied] victories [of July 1918] would have been impossible but for the Americans. One million have arrived since I left Ottawa on 24 May."[5]

It was against this burgeoning tide of American manpower that chief of the German General Staff, and "de facto" German commander of the Western Front, General Erich Ludendorff had gambled with his Spring and Summer Offensives, commencing on 21 March 1918. Termed the *Kaiserschlacht* (the king of battles) or the "Peace Offensive," these attacks were aimed at forcing the British and French to seek a negotiated settlement with the Germans before American forces could be decisively employed in battle, and before the Royal Navy's counterblockade of Germany could weaken it further. Ludendorff's strategic concept was to drive a wedge between the British and French armies, hoping to collapse one of them, thereby forcing the other, or both, to sue for peace on Germany's terms. In Ludendorff's words, "we hack a hole. The rest comes on its own."[6]

The German Army transferred nearly 50 divisions from the Eastern to the Western Front, giving it more than 200 divisions in France and Belgium. Ludendorff hoped that his increased mass of forces, coupled with the "stormtroop" tactics adopted by General Oskar von Hutier in the German Eighteenth Army, would create the strategic breakthrough the Germans so desperately needed. Ludendorff's first main blow fell on the BEF, which was sorely pressed, especially on the front of the Fifth and Third British armies, but the breakthrough achieved by Hutier's tactical innovations and the General Staff's detailed planning could not be followed up by a strategic blow capable of splitting and collapsing the Allies. The second German stab, this to the south on the French front, managed to bring the Germans within 50 miles of Paris, but the Franco-British front did not collapse. Ludendorff's gamble had

been a shining tactical success, but it ultimately resulted in a strategic failure.[7]
The ramifications of Ludendorff's venture were significant to the armies of both sides. In the German Army, the collapse of the "Peace Offensive" had two critically deleterious effects, one quantitative, the other qualitative. The quantitative effect was the loss of nearly *1 million men* during the six months of attacks, casualties that could simply not be replaced in the near future.[8] Qualitatively, the heavy fighting and high casualty rates, coupled with its failure to decisively break the French and British armies, left the German Army, especially the infantry battalions, the artillery, and the High Command, exhausted and demoralized.[9] For the Allies, the desperate fighting of the spring and summer had led to the appointment of French Marshal Ferdinand Foch as the commander-in-chief of all Allied forces on the Western Front, a development which was probably long overdue, and which finally allowed a more closely coordinated effort not only between the BEF and French armies, but also the steadily swelling American Expeditionary Force (AEF). In a brilliant counterattack on 18 July , along the Marne River in Champagne, a combined Franco-American force under General Mangin ground the German advance to a halt, and then turned the tide. Foch, Haig, and the Allies were now poised for the counterstroke.[10]

Despite their exhaustion and skidding morale, the German armies remained like a good boxer who, having failed to knock out his opponent with a desperate flurry of punches, faced the necessity of going on the defensive in order to weather the opponent's inevitable counterpunches. The Germans during 1916 and 1917 had already developed a defensive doctrine that should have allowed them to do this. Described as "elastic defense," the doctrine's underlying tenet was simple and successful: use firepower and space in order to blunt an adversary's attack, then counterattack when the enemy's own assault had stalled due to casualties and confusion (see Figure 1.1). This doctrine was originally conceived to cut down on casualties incurred in defending against the massive assaults seen earlier in the Great War, and had proven highly effective for the Germans throughout 1916-17, as Allied casualty lists could well attest. Elastic defense doctrine had the added benefit of "stealing" the initiative from the attacking side by incorporating strong counterattack elements, thereby regaining any ground lost to an attacker. At the operational level, railroads gave the German armies the operational and strategic mobility necessary to move these counterattack forces wherever they were needed before the attacker had the opportunity to reorganize his forces, consolidate his gains, or exploit a gap.

Elastic defense doctrine requires a closer examination because in order to understand the Canadian Corps' operational solution to it, one must first understand the operational and tactical problems posed by it. Elastic defense doctrine of this period divided the battlefield into three (and later four) zones.[11] The first zone was called the "outpost" or "forward battle zone" *[Kampffeld]*. This was usually constituted of small outposts armed with machine guns in mutually supporting positions who would fight tenaciously in order to inflict casualties and confusion on the enemy, thus absorbing the initial impetus of the attack. The outpost zone was usually held by troops of the "trench" divisions, generally those men who were older, previously wounded, or found otherwise less fit for battle than those in the more elite

Figure 1.1
Elastic Defense 1918

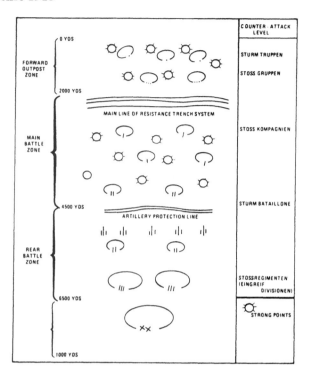

Source: J.A. English, *On Infantry* (New York: Praeger, 1984), p. 16.

"stormtroop" divisions.[12] If an attack forced itself through the forward battle zone, the enemy then faced the main battle zone [*Hauptkampffeld*], consisting of the main forward defensive positions of continuous trenches, sited to provide flank and rear protection, as well as an ability to withstand repeated attacks until reinforcements could arrive. Here, the main garrison of troops from the forward trench units were expected to use firepower -- mostly machine guns and light artillery -- in order to destroy the main elements of an Allied attack, and perform local counterattacks. The depth of the main battle zone varied according to terrain, but it could be anywhere from 1,500 to 3,000 meters deep, and in some cases, like at the Drocourt-Queant (D-Q) Line, even deeper. The third zone was termed the "rearward zone," which was later broken down into further positions [*Ruckwatigge Grosskampffeld*]. This area formed both a backstop for forward divisions retiring from the main battle zone, and also positions into which counter attacking/reinforcing [*eingreif*] divisions could move in order to complete the destruction of the enemy attack. The role of the *eingreif* divisions is best illuminated by a literal translation of their name, which means "cooperating," or "locking into gear". In essence, their role was to come forward and "lock" into the defense at the correct time, crushing by firepower and mass whatever remained of the Allied attack; they were the rocks upon which the waves of the attack were to ultimately break. More important, by the summer of 1918, many of these *eingreif* divisions were made up of the better class of German soldier, better equipped, and therefore supposedly more effective in combat. The role they should have played was that of the glue that held the German defenses together.[13]

Behind the battle zones were the rear zones, the area where most of the heavy artillery was positioned, and the assembly areas for the *eingreif* divisions and operational reserves were located. Throughout 1917 and 1918, as the Allies began to use the tank in their attacks, the depth of the forward zones got deeper, allowing for more space and firepower to deal with the shock value and attack impetus generated by the tanks. Therefore increasing the depth, in concert with the diminution of German manpower due to the heavy casualties incurred in the *Kaiserschlacht*, meant that the outpost zone was more lightly held, and that *eingreif* divisions were more scarcely allocated. Nevertheless, employed properly, the elastic defense doctrine was an effective tactical solution which substituted firepower for manpower, and made any attack a seemingly costly adventure in terms of Allied lives. Interestingly enough, the basic tenets that underlaid much of elastic defense doctrine in 1918 have worked themselves forward in history, and continue to form the basis of some modern tactical defensive doctrines to this day. The terms have changed, but the basic concept -- absorbing the impetus of the attack by using space and firepower, and then counterattacking when the enemy is spent -- remains the same.[14]

The Allies were not unaware of the doctrine of elastic defense, and had in fact been attempting to incorporate its concepts into their own defensive doctrine. Historians Tim Travers and Martin Samuels have claimed that it was the improper application of elastic defense doctrine by units of the BEF that aided in the confusion caused by, and the success of the German attacks in spring 1918.[15] Yet more important than helping to form the basis for British (and therefore Canadian) defensive doctrine, knowledge of the principles of elastic defense helped Allied generals arrive at tactical and operational solutions to it. Arthur Currie had been developing his particular solution since being dispatched by General Julian Byng, then commander of the Canadian Corps, in early 1917 to study and report on the French operations at Verdun.[16] Throughout 1917, Currie had successfully overcome German positions considered impregnable by using carefully orchestrated set-piece attacks that relied heavily upon firepower, specifically artillery, to obliterate the outpost and main battle zone. This was done primarily with a "creeping" bombardment that moved slowly forward, followed closely by the infantry who were taught to "lean into" the barrage. Currie stated that the infantry should follow this barrage "as closely as a horse follows its filled nosebag." Coupled with a proper counterbattery (a term used to describe artillery fire directed against an enemy's artillery resources) program to supress enemy artillery, the cooperation of the close support artillery and assaulting infantry meant that the Canadians dominated German defenses with firepower, allowing the Dominion soldiers to overcome successive forward trench lines before the Germans could react with enough coordinated force to blunt the assault. The momentum of the attack was thus maintained, despite the "energy absorbing" aspect of elastic defense.[17]

The success of the initial assault was not unusual for most attacks on the Western Front, but often these assaults were rendered futile by the inevitable counter-attack that pushed an attacking force back to its start line, with nothing more to show for its efforts than a fist full of dogtags. The unique element of Currie's attack doctrine was how the *eingreif*, or counterattack divisions were dealt with. Either by prepositioning some artillery well forward, or by pushing his artillery forward as quickly as possible, Currie sought to catch the counterattack forces either forming up for the attack, or during their assault, thus enabling his artillery and machine gunners to inflict heavy damage and casualties upon the German *eingreif* divisions. Currie had turned German defensive doctrine against itself; as historian Ian Brown has put it, "the use of artillery as an operational tool, combined with better infantry tactics than were used at Vimy,[18] turned the Germans' propensity to counterattack against them by creating a deliberate killing ground in front of the Allied positions, ensuring that counterattacks would be very costly."[19]

One of the ramifications of this style of attack meant that by necessity, the objectives had to be limited in order to allow the infantry time to consolidate its gains and prepare for the counterattack, and in order to allow the artillery to keep the counterattack forces within range. Basically, Currie had, by the end of 1917, developed an effective, if largely unwritten, tactical and operational doctrine based on "bite and hold" tactics, and, in terms of time and space, limited set-piece attacks.[20]

Currie's tactical concepts meshed well with what Sir Douglas Haig claimed to be the overall strategy of "attrition" on the Western Front.[21] If, in fact, the Allied strategic aim was to "bleed the enemy white" by destroying Germany's manpower, and thus its material ability to wage war effectively, then an operational attack doctrine that focused *not* on gaining huge pieces of territory, or in ripping and exploiting gaps in the enemy's line for wild thrusts at command centers, but rather on chewing up as many German divisions as possible (preferably the best divisions) can be seen as both appropriate and effective. Currie's doctrine had the added benefit of economy of effort and security; objectives were limited, and assaulting troops could, once their objectives were taken, rely on the German defensive positions for protection, while counterattacking German troops were forced to effect a highly hazardous assault, necessarily high in casualties. Moreover, the highly coordinated nature of the set-piece attack reduced the "friction" of war and confusion caused when attacking by keeping such operations short in terms of time, simple in terms of conception, and limited in terms of objectives. Simply put, Currie had developed an economical way to destroy Germans efficiently, efficiency always being a prime consideration in an age of "industrial" warfare. Thus, the Canadian Corps' operational doctrine of limited objective set-piece attacks, developed primarily by Currie throughout 1917, provided the operational means to successfully achieve Haig's unstated strategic goal of attrition.[22]

Faced with the same challenges, the Australian Corps came up with a slightly different solution. The Australians, in the summer of 1918, found it simply easier to take the trench raid, a common feature of the Western Front by that time, one step further. Paying close attention to which parts of the outpost zone were being held by German detachments, and which were only being occupied at certain intervals, the Australians soon became adept at slipping into the outpost zone at night, and then consolidating their gains by fighting off the German detachments sent to retrieve their outpost. This was not only frustrating for the Germans; it was also unnerving. These stealth tactics denied the Germans the opportunity to absorb and destroy the impetus of the attack because there was no real attack -- only a constant picking at the periphery that eased the Germans out of territory at the slightest slip of vigilance on their part. The Australian official historian, Dr. C.E.W. Bean, coyly termed this approach "peaceful penetration," for it involved no large battles or artillery duels.

At Villers-Brettoneux, from 5 July to 30 July 1918, the Second Australian Division managed to gain all the objectives assigned to it by the Fourth Army without having to make lengthy preparations for a costly deliberate attack. The Germans, befuddled by the melting away of their outpost zone to "ghosts," were forced to withdraw their main elements even further, thus surrendering the jumping off points for the upcoming battle of Amiens.[23] Thus, two different corps, confronted with similar conditions, devised two different tactical solutions, one relying on stealth and initiative that yielded territorial advantages, the other relying on firepower and coordination, yielding material (i.e., manpower) advantages.

The Australians had also been at the cutting edge of developments in another area of attack doctrine: the use of the tank. On 4 July 1918, the Fourth Australian Division, reinforced with 60 of the newly available Mark V tanks from the Royal Tank Corps, attacked the German positions around the village of Hamel. This operation had been planned by General Sir Henry Rawlinson, Commander of the British Fourth Army, and incorporated a number of innovative changes. First, American squads had been attached to the Australian infantry in order to gain experience at set-piece attacks. More important, Rawlinson wanted to experiment with the new technology of war. He had expected that a combined tank-infantry assault, coupled with new artillery barrage techniques practiced by both the French Army and the Canadian Corps, would prove more successful and less costly in terms of casualties than simple artillery-infantry attacks. Furthermore, strong air support, in the form of bombing runs, contact patrols, and low-level ground attacks by aircraft were also incorporated. Finally, Rawlinson limited the depth of the attack to 2500 yards, ensuring that his assaulting elements would not outrun their fire support, and would therefore not expose themselves to the danger of a German counterattack.

Rawlinson's intention had been to "test not only the strength of the German positions, but also the state of German morale." The Fourth Army history also claims that Rawlinson saw Hamel as "a good trial run" for a larger offensive being considered in the area of Amiens. Interestingly enough, the limited objective concept, coupled with the artillery barrage techniques, and the proposed destruction of the counterattack force appear surprisingly similar to the Canadian Corps' attack doctrine developed in the previous year's fighting.[24] The tanks and air support, however, were new technological twists that gave added impetus to the attack's weight.[25]

The attack at Hamel on 4 July 1918 was, in the words of the Fourth Army history, "a complete success." It seemed to show that when tanks were used *en masse* in an attack, the infantry suffered fewer casualties, and German troops surrendered more easily. Bean noted that most on the Australian side felt as if the victory had been, "too easy." In his words, "Hamel was a lesson in how to use the Mark V tank with aggressive infantry in breaking through the German trench lines on the Western Front....[I]t show[ed] an effective method of using with infantry those tanks with which the B.E.F. was likely to be furnished with for the remainder of the war."[26]

The outcome of the battle of Hamel led Rawlinson to continue planning for a similar, but much larger attack in the area of Amiens, where the German advances of the summer had created a dangerous salient threatening a vital railway hub for the Allies. Haig had received a request from Foch on 12 July to begin an offensive somewhere on the BEF front. Haig had already been contemplating an attack near Arras, spearheaded by the Canadian Corps. When Rawlinson approached Haig on 16 July with the proposal for the Amiens operation, Haig agreed, and passed the plan along to Foch. It also appears that Rawlinson, at the urging of Lieutenant General Sir John Monash, commander of the Australian Corps, asked specifically for the Canadian Corps to make up the right flank of the assault. To this request Haig also agreed, for it was for just such an attack that he had been waiting to unleash the Canadians.[27]

NOTES

1. The best recent look at the problems of the AEF is David Trask, *The AEF and Coalition Warmaking, 1917-1918*, (Lawrence: University Press of Kansas, 1993).

2. Letter from Field Marshall Sir Douglas Haig, dated 19 Oct 1918, to British Cabinet, quoted in Winter, *Haig's Command*, pp. 214-215.

3. For a good, concise review of the conditions faced by all the combatant nations in 1917, see Brian Bond, *War and Society in Europe, 1870-1970* (London: Fontana, 1984), pp. 121-130. The politicians' bleak forecast is reflected well by Sir Winston Churchill's personal asides in his The World Crisis, 1916-1918, Part II (London: Thornton Butterworth, 1927). General J.F.C. Fuller's "Plan 1919," which called for an overwhelming tank attack to paralyze the German High Command also reflects the belief generally held in early 1918 that the war was going to drag on at least another 18 months. C.P. Stacey shows how this belief impacted on Canadian participation in the Imperial War cabinet in *Canada and the Age of Conflict: A History of Canadian External Policies, Vol. 1: 1867-1921* (Toronto: Macmillan, 1977), pp. 200-240.

4. See Bond, *War and Society*, pp. 123-124.

5. For an excellent discussion of the manpower question, see D. R. Woodward, "Did Lloyd-George Starve the British Armies of Men Prior to the German Offensive of 21 March 1918?" *Historical Journal*, Vol. 27 (1984); see also Churchill, *The World Crisis*, pp. 375-390; Borden is quoted in Winter, *Haig's Command*, p. 207.

6. The best book in English on this topic may be Martin Middlebrook's *The Kaiser's Battle* (London: Penguin, 1978). The quote is from Ludendorff in Correlli Barnett, *The Swordbearers: Studies in Supreme Command* (London: Eyre and Spottiswoode, 1963), p. 282.

7. Terraine, *To Win A War*, pp. 31-71. For the German innovations, see Bruce Gudmundsson, *Stormtroop Tactics*, pp. 155-171; Martin Samuels, *Doctrine and Dogma: German and British Infantry Tactics in the First World War* (Westport, CT: Greenwood, 1992), pp. 1-110; Hubert Johnson, *Breakthrough!*; and John English, *On Infantry* (New York: Praeger, 1984), pp. 18-22.

8. Figures are from the German Official History for the months of March to mid-July 1918, and quoted in Travers, *How the War was Won*, p. 108.

9. For the effect on German infantry units, see Gudmundsson, *Stormtroop Tactics*, *p. 171*, for its effect on artillery, see Herbert Sulzbach, *With the German Guns* (London: Leo Cooper, 1973); for the reversal's effect on the German High Command, especially Ludendorff, see Roger Parkinson, *Tormented Warrior: Ludendorff and the Supreme Command* (London: Hodder and Stoughton, 1978), pp. 162-171.

10. The Battle of the Marne is considered by most historians to be the beginning of the end for the Germans on the Western Front; see, for instance, Terraine, *To Win a War*, pp. 79-101; Barrie Pitt, *1918, The Last Act* (London: Cassell, 1962); and C.E.W Bean, *The Official History of Australia in the War, 1914-1918, Vol. 6, The Australian Imperial Force in France During the Allied Offensive, 1918* (St. Lucia: Universtity of Queensland, 1983), pp. 441-462.

11. The basic tenets for elastic defense were originally laid out by Ludendorff in 1916, and later updated as necessary, in his *Manual of Position Warfare For All Arms - Part 8: The Principles of Command in the Defensive Battle in Position Warfare*. There is an English translation of this document held in the Canadian Corps files in the National Archives of Canada (NAC) in Ottawa: NAC Record Group (RG) 9, Part III D, Vol. 4792, File 30, see especially pp. 28-30.(hereafter referred to as Ludendorff, *Defense Principles*).

12. Gudmundsson, *Stormtroop Tactics*, pp. 157-158; Samuels, *Doctrine and Dogma*, pp. 72-82.

13. Brigadier-General Sir James Edmonds, *Official History of the Great War: Military Operations in France and Belgium, 1918, Volume 5 - The Advance to Victory* (London: H.M. Stationery Office, 1947), pp. 12-13. (hereafter Edmonds, *BOH*, Vol. 5.); also Major Timothy Wray, *Standing Fast: German Defensive Doctrine on the Russian Front During World War II* (Fort Leavenworth, KS: U.S. Army Combat Studies Institute, 1986), pp. 1-9.

14. The author was struck by the similarity between the elastic defense doctrine as laid out by Ludendorff, and the doctrine currently taught by the Canadian Land Forces at its Combat Training Centers based on Canadian Forces Publication B-GL-301-001/FP-001 *Land Formations in Battle* (Ottawa: Queen's Printer, n.d.), especially Chapter 4, and B-GL-301-002/FP-001 *The Battle Group in Operations* (Ottawa: Queen's Printer, n.d.), Chapter 4.

15. Travers, *How the War Was Won*, pp. 50-108; Samuels, *Doctrine and Dogma*, pp. 125-135, 175; see also Gudmundsson, *Stormtroop Tactics*, p. 157.

16. The report Currie wrote on his examination of Verdun was critical in changing the Canadian Corps approach to warfare, and was instrumental in making the Corps offensive doctrine and tactics as effective and innovative as they were. Currie's report may be the single most influential report in Canadian military history. See, for example, A.M.J. Hyatt, *General Sir Arthur Currie: A Military Biography* (Toronto: University of Toronto Press, 1987) pp. 63-66; Hugh Urquhart, *Arthur Currie: Biography of a Great Canadian* (Toronto: Dent, 1950), pp. 141-145; Daniel Dancocks, *Sir Arthur Currie: A Biography* (Toronto: Methuen, 1985), pp. 82-94; the actual 11 foolscap page notes Currie made on this trip are availible in his papers, *"Notes on French Attacks North-East of Verdun in October and December, 1916,"* NAC,

Manuscript Group (MG) 30, E 100.

17. Currie is quoted in Daniel G. Dancocks, *Spearhead to Victory: Canada and the Great War* (Edmonton: Hurtig, 1987), p. 85; the importance and effectiveness of the creeping barrage was one of Currie's recommendations from his trip to Verdun; see Hyatt, *Currie*, pp. 64-65.

18. For a study of the evolution of these tactics, see Bill Rawling, *Surviving Trench Warfare*, Chaps. 4-5.

19. Ian Brown, "Not Glamorous, But Effective," p. 427.

20. For a more detailed look at the development of Canadian Corps methods, see William Stewart, *Attack Doctrine in the Canadian Corps, 1916-1918*. (Unpublished Thesis, University of New Brunswick, 1980). Stewart focuses on the first stages of the attacks, the preparation and actual assault, which he characterizes as "soft spot" doctrine borrowing heavily from German infiltration doctrine, among others (pp. 196-200).

21. Of course, some historians claim that Haig had no real strategic conceptions of how to win the war, and used the "attrition" excuse only to justify his mistakes and the high casualty rates accrued thereby; see Travers, *How the War Was Won*, pp. 1-31, or Winter, *Haig's Command*, pp. 41-257.

22. Ian Brown, in his excellent article, "Not Glamorous but Effective," criticizes Bill Rawling's book *Surviving Trench Warfare* for failing to place the efficiency of the Corps' doctrine "in the broader context of operational art," (p. 441); however, in an extension of his own argument, Brown has failed to point out how the Corps' "operational" efficiency contributed to the achievement of Haig's overall strategic aim. It is this vacuum that the present work hopes to fill.

23. Bean, *AOH*, Vol. 6, pp. 336-440.

24. This was no doubt because of GHQ's dissemination of the new attack techniques in instructional pamphlets to all formations; Robin Prior and Trevor Wilson do not attribute Rawlinson creating the plan for Hamel so much as "co-ordinating": "Rawlinson was becoming less and less the creator of great operations. Rather, his role was diminishing to that of a manager drawing forth and co-ordinating the endeavours of others,"; see Robin Prior and Trevor Wilson, *Command on the Western Front: The Military Career of Sir Henry Rawlinson, 1914 - 1918* (Oxford: Blackwell, 1992), pp. 289-300.

25. Major General Sir Archibald Montgomery, *The Story of the Fourth Army in the Battles of the Hundred Days August 8th to November 11th 1918* (London: Hodder and Stoughton, 1919), pp. 6-10; Bean, *AOH*, Vol. 6, pp. 242-335; and Travers, *How the War Was Won*, pp. 112-113.

26. Bean, *AOH*, Vol. 6, p. 328.

27. Winter, *Haig's Command*, pp. 194-195; Travers, *How the War Was Won*, pp. 114-115; Bean, *AOH*, Vol. 6, pp. 463-489.

2

THE ORCHESTRA
AND ITS CONDUCTOR

According to Greek mythology, the goddess Athena sprang forth into the world from the head of Zeus, fully armed and girded for battle. The same, however, could not be said of the Canadian Corps. At its conception in the summer of 1914, it was but a motley collection of veterans of the Boer War, a small number of full-time "Permanent Force" members, part-time militiamen, and patriotic neophytes gathered on the plains of Camp Valcartier, desperate for both equipment and training, and lacking everything except the short-lived enthusiasm that unblooded soldiers have for the adventure that is war. The Corps that was destined to play such a prominent role in the battles of the 100 Days had taken a long and painful path to maturity, through the fields of mud and blood in France and Flanders. Yet by 1918, it could rightly be considered one of the BEF's elite organizations, led by a General who, though considered an amateur at the start of the war, had since seen more combat than his "professional" peers had seen in many of their long and uneventful careers before the Great War.[1] To understand why the Canadian Corps was so successful during the 100 Days, one must first examine how it differed, in both organization and outlook, from its British counterpart. In short, this chapter will examine how the conductor, Sir Arthur Currie, prepared his orchestra for its upcoming performances.[2]

An examination of the transformation of Sir Arthur Currie from a colonial militiaman into a highly respected corps commander provides a fascinating study of generalship. A modest real estate broker and part-time artilleryman before the war, Currie received command of an infantry brigade in 1914 mostly due to his political connections, being a close friend (and later bitter enemy) of Garnet Hughes, son of the infamous Canadian Minister of Militia Sir Sam Hughes. Currie was a mediocre, if uninspiring, brigade commander, but he was a keen student of war, and he eagerly devoured every tract on military science and war he could get his hands on, according to Brigadier General N.W. Webber, Currie's Brigadier-General, General Staff (BGGS).[3]

By September 1915, Currie's self-education had made him the equal of many of his formally Staff College-trained British counterparts, and he was awarded command of the First Canadian Division, distinguishing himself during the battles of 1916. By 1917, Currie's earnest, hardworking approach had been recognized by the British general commanding the Canadian Corps, Sir Julian Byng. It was Byng who recommended Currie be sent along with the British delegation to study the French tactics at Verdun. Currie's report from this trip formed the basis for the innovative tactical changes that brought about the now almost mythological victory at Vimy Ridge in April 1917. When Byng was promoted and given command of the Third British Army, due in large part to the triumph at Vimy, he recommended Currie as his replacement. Unfettered by the burden of "Regular Army" prejudices, Currie approached the problem of war with the only skills he had, that of a studious, pragmatic man. Analytical and open-minded, Currie took a practical approach to the solution of tactical problems, seeking the advice of the best minds with which he could surround himself. By the time of his appointment to Corps command in summer 1917, Currie was a true professional, having recieved his military education in that most efficiently brutal school of all, the actual battlefield. Like another general with a similiar background, Ulysses S. Grant, Currie had learned about war *from* war. Unlike some of his British peers, he had had the advantage of receiving the bulk of his education and experience not in "colonial" wars, but in the industrial meatgrinder of the Western Front. More than any one person, Currie was responsible for the Canadian Corps' success in 1917-18.[4]

Rawlinson's request to have the Canadian Corps for the Amiens operation in July 1918, and Haig's willingness to put it into action, were based on two fundamental considerations. Foremost was the reputation the Canadian Corps had built for itself since its attack on Vimy Ridge in April 1917. Since then, the Corps had successfully taken objectives at both Lens (Hill 70) and Passchendaele, which other Allied corps, including the vaunted Australian, had failed to take.[5] Currie's ability to produce victories under even the worst conditions, exemplified by Passchendaele, earned the Corps the respect of most of the BEF, and the gratitude of Douglas Haig for saving his reputation from falling victim to the same muddy ooze that had claimed the lives of so many soldiers in late 1917.[6] The esteem in which Haig held the Canadian Corps is indicated by an anecdote from the spring of 1918, recorded in one of Currie's letters:

I had never seen the Chief [Haig] so visibly moved.... With tears showing plainly in his eyes he said something like this: "In all the dark days of this spring -- and God knows they were dark enough – one comforting thought came to me, that I still had the Canadian Corps unused and fresh; and I felt that I could not be defeated until the Corps had been in action."[7]

Haig's selection of the Canadian Corps for the Amiens attack was based not solely on its reputation, but also on the second consideration: its sheer combat power. As will be seen, Currie and his subordinates had created a formation superior in organization and training to most other corps on the Western Front at this time.

The operational superiority of the Canadian Corps stemmed to a large degree from the freedom Currie had to manipulate its doctrine and organization. First, the Canadian Corps was much more than just another formation in the order of battle of the BEF. The Canadian Corps was distinct from most other formations in that it ultimately answered not to the British government under which it fought, but rather to the government of the Dominion of Canada, by which it was created and sustained. In effect, the Canadian Corps was a small "national army" consisting of four Canadian Divisions, a Corps Headquarters, and numerous ancillary troops. Although under the operational control of the BEF, it also reported to, and was represented by, the Canadian Ministry of Overseas Military Forces of Canada, headquartered in London, under a Canadian Cabinet Minister, Colonel A. E. (Edward) Kemp. There was also a special Canadian Section at British General Headquarters (GHQ) in France, through which the Corps effected liaison with the Overseas Ministry, and for dealing with matters pertaining specifically to the administration of the Canadian Corps. This difference, though often overlooked by earlier "Imperial" historians, is critical to note because unlike other British corps commanders, Currie had both the right and the duty to exercise a *de facto* veto over what Haig and British Army commanders could or could not ask the Canadian Corps to do. Currie had used this power on more than one occassion to forestall potentially disastrous decisions on Haig's part, and would so so again during the 100 Days.[8] As Canadian military historian Desmond Morton has rightly put it, the Canadian Corps was the military extension of "a junior but sovereign ally."[9]

While Haig and some of his British Army commanders may have occasionally resented the Canadian Corps' autonomous status, it also provided both them and Currie with some distinct advantages, chiefly in manpower. The Canadian government had introduced conscription after the December 1917 national election, and the Canadian Corps could therefore draw from a relatively much deeper manpower pool than was left in Britain. The Canadian Corps also controlled its own training schools and reinforcements. This allowed the rapid and universal adoption of even the most basic tactical innovations into the Canadian Corps, a control over doctrine and tactics that British corps commanders could never gain.[10] More important from Haig's perspective, Canadian manpower was less of a political liability to him than British. Put bluntly, Canadian casualties did not represent the same political threat to Haig's future as commander of the BEF as did British casualties, because Haig answered to British voters through David Lloyd-George, and not to Canadian voters through Robert Borden. In the stark terms of political capital, Canadian lives were, for Haig, cheaper than British lives. The reality was that with each British casualty, domestic political pressure mounted in Britain for Haig's removal.[11]

The semiautonomous nature of the Canadian formations meant that they did not have to be organized the same as their British counterparts. It was at the divisional level that the most significant difference manifested itself, in the size and number of infantry battalions per division. Unlike their Canadian counterparts, British were slowly being strangled by a lack of infantry replacements, a condition caused primarily by the unwillingness of British politicians to offer up any more "lambs for the slaughter," and as a consequence of casualties incurred in the Ypres offensive of late 1917.[12] The result was a change in British divisions from four infantry battalions per brigade, for a total of 12 per division, to the triangular organization of three infantry battalions per brigade, for a total of nine battalions per division. The British High Command had expected its dominion Corps to follow suit, thus dangling the prospect of an Army command appointment in front of Arthur Currie. Despite considerable pressure from both British and some Canadian quarters, Currie refused to dilute the Canadian Corps, claiming that, "the Canadian Corps in the existing formation had proved itself a smooth-running machine of tremendous striking power, and any radical alteration in its constitution might have resulted in a reduction of such power without any compensating advantages."[13]

Canadian divisions did not just have more infantry battalions; they also had bigger infantry battalions. The breaking up of the Fifth Canadian Division in early 1918[14] had given Currie the opportunity to transfer many of its soldiers as reinforcements into units that were already tempered by the heat of battle. As a result of this and other organizational changes, which will be discussed later, Currie did not just bring his battalions up to strength, but in fact overposted each one by 100 men, thus giving the unit Commanding Officers (CO) the manpower necessary for immediate replacements, work parties, and all the other various tasks that often drained off the effective strength of an infantry battalion. More important, these reinforcements were available to train with the units and men they would fight with, learning their drills and idiosyncracies, and developing the elusive bond of *esprit de corps* that was vital in getting men to risk their lives under fire.[15] Thus, while British formations had their capacity to undertake sustained offensive operations downgraded by manpower shortages and a resultant organizational change, the Canadian divisions were, by the summer of 1918, more than ever prepared to become the spearhead to victory.

In many respects a Canadian division in fact resembled a British *corps*. This was especially true in the area of combat support organizations, where Canadian divisions held a rough advantage of 3:1 in firepower support in comparison to their British cousins (see Figure 2.1). A British division possessed only three Engineer Field Companies totalling 657 men, and a Pioneer Battalion of 900 men, whereas a Canadian division maintained a full brigade of engineers -- roughly *nine* Field Companies, totalling over 3000 men -- plus a pontoon bridging unit of another 66 specialists.[16] Each British division contained an integral Machine Gun Battalion of roughly three companies, for a total of about 450 men, whereas a Canadian division fielded a Machine Gun Battalion more than three times as large, with 1,500 men. The Supreme War Council produced a report in May 1918 comparing the firepower available from automatic weapons in divisions of various nations. According to historian Dennis Winter, this report found that in a Canadian division there was one automatic weapon for every 13 men, but in a British division there was only one per every 61 soldiers.[17] This discrepancy is surprising considering that automatic weapons accounted for so much of the firepower of a division, especially its infantry units. In terms of total strength, the average British division mustered approximately

Figure 2.1

Comparison of Canadian and British Divisions, Summer 1918

CANADIAN DIVISION

Div HQ

3 Infantry Brigades	2 Artillery Brigades	MG Battalion	Engineer Brigade
of	T.M. Battalion	Service Support elements (incl Ammunition	comprised of
4 Infantry Battalions	3 T.M. Batteries	Medical Supply, etc.)	3 Engineer Battalions
	Heavy T.M. Battery		Pioneer Battalion

BRITISH DIVISION

Div HQ

3 Infantry Brigades	2 Artillery Brigades	MG Battalion	Engineer Battalion
of	T.M. Battalion	Service Support elements	Pioneer Battalion
3 Infantry Battalions	2 T. M. Batteries		

Source: Sir James Edmonds, *Official History of the Great War: Military Operations in France and Belgium, 1918 -- Volume 5 -- The Advance to Victory* (London: H.M. Stationery Office, 1947).

15,000 men to a Canadian division's 21,000. This comparison is even more telling when measuring actual infantry strength -- the arm which bore the majority of the fighting, and, therefore the majority of the casualties. British divisions, after the "triangularization" of their brigades in January 1918, fielded only 8,100 infantry, whereas the Canadian divisions had nearly 50 percent more, at just under 12,000.[18] In many respects, then, a Canadian division could be seen as the combat equivalent of a small British *corps*, with less infantry, but with the equivalent amount of firepower, combat support, and combat service support elements.

The organization of the Canadian Corps headquarters was similarly larger than its British counterpart. Two additional Mechanical Transport Companies gave it approximately 100 more trucks than a British corps, thereby facilitating greater inherent mobility for both logistics and the tactical movement of its headquarters. In addition, the Corps headquarters had a highly developed signals service with the additional personnel and equipment necessary to maintain command and control capabilities in a nonstatic environment; whereas most British Corps included only two signals cables sections, the Canadian Corps held four.

The Corps maintainance organization was similarly much larger than anything other Imperial Corps had to work with, with the exception of the Australian Corps. A British Corps possessed only one Medium Ordnance Mobile Workshop (essentially a semimoveable repair shop for trucks, howitzers, and heavy equipment), while the Canadian Corps had two, and the Australian Corps three. In place of the single Light Ordnance Mobile Workshop (a repair depot for machine guns, personal weapons, and light transport) found in most British Corps, the Canadian version had *four* -- essentially one per division. In service support "ancillary" troops, then, the Canadian Corps had a distinct quantitative advantage over its British counterpart.[19]

It was in indirect firepower -- artillery and mortars -- that the Canadian Corps most distinctly outweighed its British peer. Currie, an ex-gunner himself, has been credited with being the driving force behind the Canadian Corps' superiority in this area. Recognizing early in 1917 that this would be chiefly an "artillery war," Currie took every opportunity to improve the Canadian artillery in terms of organization, equipment, and tactics.[20] At Corps level, Currie had gained two extra field artillery brigades by retaining the Fifth Canadian Divisions' field artillery brigade intact, and adding an extra Corps field artillery brigade. According to a report on artillery organizations:

The former [Fifth Canadian Divisions' artillery brigade] is peculiar in that it is an independent formation without the remainder of the division. For supply purposes it is permanently provided with a divisional artillery's proportion of train and mechanical transport. Its tactical value is comparable to that of two army field artillery brigades but the possession of a C.R.A. [Commander, Royal Artillery] and staff is an advantage in warfare where field artillery is often divided into numerous temporary groups, in that it decreases the possibility of having to use...an improvised staff to command one of the groups.[21]

The same report went on to point out that there was a critical difference in the way the artillery was commanded between British and Canadian Corps. The General Officer Commanding Royal Artillery (GOCRA) in a British Corps performed much more of an advisory role, leaving the actual orders to the various artillery units to be issued by the Corps General Staff, and thereby abrogating his role as unified commander of Corps artillery. In the Canadian model, the GOCRA, Major General E. Morrison, was in fact, as well as in name, a "commanding officer," exercising direct tactical control over *all* artillery in the Corps during some phases of operations. This highly centralized control was used, as will be seen, during the opening phases of set-piece attacks, "in order that he [the GOCRA] may co-ordinate barrages, bombardments and counterbattery work on the whole Corps front."[22] Unlike its British counterpart, the Canadian Corps did not have a Heavy Trench Mortar (TM) battery. This shortcoming was more than compensated for, however, because each

Canadian *division* had a heavy TM battery, resulting in a total of four in the Canadian Corps, versus one in a British Corps.[23] Last, but certainly not least, the Canadian Corps also boasted a counterbattery organization that became the envy of the BEF.[24]

The Corps' counterbattery organization merits further description because it was another area in which the Canadian formation held an advantage, at least qualitatively, over both its British peer and German foe. The brain of the counterbattery effort was the Corps Counterbattery Staff Office (CBSO), headed first by Colonel A.G.L. McNaughton, and later, when McNaughton was promoted, by Colonel H.D.G Crerar. It is interesting to note that both these men later went on to command of the First Canadian Army in World War Two, while a third officer that had worked with them in the CBSO, Alan Brooke, became Chief of the Imperial General Staff (CIGS) under Winston Churchill. The CBSO acted as an information nexus, processing data from a wide variety of intelligence sources, including sound-ranging equipment, air photographs, artillery and infantry patrol debriefs, and hostile battery and shell reports. With this information, the disposition and location of enemy artillery assets in the Corps' area of interest were plotted on a 1:20,000 scale map, and kept constantly updated. If there was a "hole" or area in which the CBSO was uncertain about the number and kinds of artillery batteries, intelligence assets could then be focused on this area in order to fill in the picture. In particular, the Canadian Corps CBSO benefitted greatly not only from McNaughton's ability as an administrator, but also from his personal interest in the new science of sound-ranging and artillery locating. McNaughton's own innovations in this field, stemming from even earlier British experiments, were to put the Canadian Corps on the leading edge of counterbattery technical expertise.[25]

By 1918, the CBSO had become highly adept at sifting through a large amount of information in order to create an extremely accurate picture not only of the enemy's guns, but of also its ammunition dumps and supply facilities. These could then be targeted, in order of priority, by the CBSO, and engaged with the Corps' heavy artillery assets. Crerar put it thusly: "the primary object of all Counter Battery work is the reduction of enemy fire at critical periods....[This] is obtained by previous destruction of guns and prepared positions, by previous destruction of personnel and lowering morale, or by surprise effect."[26]

The preferred method of engagement for the CBSO was heavy artillery shoots using air or ground observers to adjust the fire and report the damage. When this was not possible, or not practical given the tactical situation, "NF," or unobserved shoots based on the CBSO's updated activity maps, and often using gas shells to improve the nuetralizing effect of the counterbattery fire, were used. Perhaps most important in explaining the success of the Canadian Corps CBSO was the close working relationship between it and the actual executioners of its plans, the Corps heavy artillery. By mid-1918, McNaughton had become the *de facto* commander of the Corps heavy artillery, working in place of its ailing chief, Brigadier-General R.H. Massie. This arrangement would be formalized during the 100 Days by McNaughton's promotion and appointment to GOCRA Heavy Artillery.

For all the *quantitative* differences between Canadian and British formations, there was also one crucial *qualitative* difference. Through the continued efforts of

Arthur Currie and Edward Kemp, the four Canadian Divisions had been kept together under the Canadian Corps as a single operational entity. Because the division, and not the corps, was the basic operational formation in the BEF, British corps tended to be "task-oriented," ad hoc groupings of between two and five divisions, depending on the threat and forces availible. British General Sir Ivor Maxse, commanding the XVIII British Corps at Cambrai in 1917, had had *30* different divisions pass through his corps in a matter of a few *weeks*.[27] In reality, therefore, a corps actually only permanently consisted of a headquarters element with a smattering of ancillary support arms; its sub-formations could (and did) change regularly. Moreover, as one Canadian report stated:

[British] Corps were not very mobile -- the move of a Corps headquarters requires a large number of lorries [etc.]... There is also a marked tendency to inertia in any formation. Theatres and parade grounds are built...comfortable messes are furnished, and the whole formation gets so settled that it is difficult to move.... *The Canadian Corps, however, developed along different lines, and became a real fighting formation* (emphasis added).[28]

Throughout 1917 and most of 1918, the Canadian Corps was regularly comprised of the four Canadian divisions overseas, but could, and did, easily accept "outside" divisions into its operations.[29] The aforementioned report continued:

It [the Canadian Corps] controlled its own reinforcements, and thus could be sure of having enough men.... The units...were accustomed to living and fighting together, the Corps and Divisional staffs accustomed to working together, and the Canadian Corps thus became a homogeneous, self-contained and mobile force.

Thus, by 1917, the Canadian Corps had become a "fighting formation" more highly adept at operations at the corps level than its British counterparts.

As seen, Canadian divisions could be viewed as the rough equivalent of a small British corps formation. By extension, the Canadian Corps could be described as a "mini" British Army, encompassing all of the necessary logistical and firepower resources of the larger formation, without the addition of another level of headquarters (see Figure 2.2). This may have been exactly what Currie was hoping for when he rejected the opportunity to dilute the Corps into an Army-size formation. As Currie had pointed out:

Instead of one Corps staff and four divisional staffs and twelve brigade staffs and 48 battalion staffs, we would have under the new organization 2 Corps staffs, six divisional staffs, 18 brigade staffs, and 54 battalion staffs....It would have been impossible to double our staff without reducing our efficency.[30]

Currie went on to point out that for an actual increase of about 3,600 fighting soldiers, (approximately one brigade,) a Canadian Army would require an additional *10* large headquarters: an Army headquarters, another Corps headquarters, two additional Divisional headquarters, and six brigade headquarters. The Army proposal had the added disadvantage of requiring a near doubling of the necessary number of staff- trained officers, already in short supply in the Canadian Corps. Currie preferred

Figure 2.2
Canadian Corps Organization and Key Command Appointments, Summer 1918

CANADIAN CORPS

General Officer Commanding (GOC)
Lt. Gen. Sir Arthur CURRIE

Corps HQ

Brigadier General, General Staff (BGGS) - Brig. Gen. N.W.S. (OX) WEBBER [1]
Corps GOCRA - Maj. Gen. E.W.B. MORRISON
Corps Engineer - Maj. Gen. W.B. LINDSAY
DA & QMG - Brig. Gen. J.G. FARMAR
GOC, CMGC - Brig. Gen. R. BRUTINEL
GOC, Heavy Artillery - Brig. Gen. R.H. MASSIE [2]

FIRST CAN DIVISION	SECOND CAN DIVISION	THIRD CAN DIVISION	FOURTH CAN DIVISION
Maj. Gen. A. MACDONNEL	Maj. Gen. H. BURSTALL	Maj. Gen. L.J. LIPSETT (change on 12 Sept 1918 to) Maj. Gen. F.O.W. LOOMIS	Maj. Gen. D.W. WATSON
1st CIB Griesbach[3]	4th CIB McCuaig	7th CIB Clark	10th CIB Hayter / J. Ross as of 12 Oct 1918
2nd CIB Loomis / Clarke as of 6 Oct 1918	5th CIB Tremblay	8th CIB Draper	11th CIB Odlum
3rd CIB Tuxford	6th CIB A. Ross	9th CIB Ormond	12th CIB MacBrien

---

[1] Replaced by Brig Gen R. Hayter on 28 Oct 1918.

[2] Replaced by Brig Gen A.G.L. McNaughton on 21 October 1918.

[3] All Brigade Commanders held the rank of Brig Gen.

Source: G.W.L. Nicholson, *The Official History of the Canadian Army in the First World War: Canadian Expeditionary Force 1914-1918* (Ottawa: Queen's Printer, 1962).

to focus his manpower at the cutting edge, keeping the infantry battalions and engineer units effective, rather than saddling his organization with another level of unnecessary headquarters. Thus, in its 1918 configuration, the Canadian Corps represented a completely effective compromise between the punching power of a British Army-size formation, with the flexibilty and economy of a British corps-size organization.[31]

Many of the changes to the structure of the Canadian Corps did not actually come about until just before the period of the 100 Days, during summer 1918. During the tumultuous spring, the Canadian Corps had been manning the sector of the Western Front near Vimy. The Germans chose not to attack this area during their repeated offensives of the *Kaiserschlacht*, and therefore the Canadian Corps had not been as hard pressed as those formations to the south and north, especially in the Third and Fifth British Armies.[32] Except for a short period during the spring offensive, the Canadian Corps had remained intact near Vimy Ridge, defending what Haig considered to be "the backbone and centre of our [the BEF] defensive system." Yet it was political more than military considerations which had kept the Canadian Corps united near Vimy Ridge.

When the Canadian divisions under Currie's control had been taken away from him in the first weeks of the onslaught, Currie had complained, suggesting instead that the Canadian Corps would be more effective if kept together rather than if its divisions were simply meted out piecemeal to reinforce crumbling British corps. Currie's argument, backed by Sir Edward Kemp in London, made sense from both a military and political standpoint: the divisions had grown accustomed to fighting under Currie and the Canadian Corps staff, and, politically, the Canadian public expected the Corps to be kept as one.[33]

British Secretary of State for War Lord Derby was sympathetic to the Canadian request, and therefore ordered his subordinate, Field Marshal Haig, to reunite the Canadian formations. Haig resented this political interference into what he considered a purely military matter, claiming that "some in Canada regard themselves rather as `Allies' than as fellow citizens of the Empire." Nonetheless, Haig acquiesced in Derby's decision, recognizing the truth in Lord Derby's words: "We must look upon them in the light in which they wish to be looked upon rather than in the light we would wish to do so."[34] Reunited, except for the Second Canadian Division, which would remain with VI Corps until the end of June, the Canadian Corps could now prepare for its crucial role in the final 100 Days. From the beginning of May to 1 July 1918, the Canadian Corps was placed in First Army reserve, giving Currie an opportunity to fine-tune his orchestra.

Training in the Canadian Corps during the summer of 1918 focused on what had heretofore been a rarity in the Great War: "open warfare."[35] Currie leapt at the opportunity to refresh his men on the conduct of the offensive, mostly because he felt that the highly experienced Corps was at its best in the attack. Using translations of captured German documents, and GHQ's *Notes on Recent Fighting*, Currie and his staff at Corps HQ concentrated on "combined training...so [as] to give the different Arms and Services an opportunity of practising co-operation and mutual support."[36] Each arm, however, continued to train on its own in preparation for "open warfare offensive tactics."

Infantry units continued to incorporate the innovative platoon level tactics into their training, borrowing much from German "stormtroop tactics" and from innovations made by others in the British and French armies, such as Ivor Maxse. This tactical system focused on small, independent groups of about 40 soldiers fighting their way to a specific objective using dispersed formations, the terrain, support fire, and movement to their advantage. Fire support came in the form of Lewis light machine guns and other light support weapons, such as grenades and light mortars.[37] Gone were the days when waves of infantry charged into a hail of machine gun fire, replaced instead with carefully planned, short, sharp dashes under the cover of vicious, close-range supporting fire.

Less glamorous and more annoying for the infantry was Currie's personal penchant for gruelling route marches. As part of his military self-study, Currie had read and was highly influenced by a biography of Civil War general Stonewall Jackson, and Currie had hoped to emulate the terror caused by Jackson's rapid marches and unexpected attacks. So keen was Currie on the necessity of march discipline that in August of 1918, just prior to the opening of the battle of Amiens, he wrote this note to himself:

March discipline is:
1. The ceremonial of war
2. A battalion which is slack in march discipline is slack in war.
3. Make section commanders feel that when a man falls out in the line of marchers, his unit is disgraced. A fit man can march 50 minutes [per hour].
4. The more tired men are the stricter must be the march discipline
5. Inspect feet immediately after each march.
6. Officers must march in rear of the platoons, companies, battalions etc.
7. Once more, march discipline is the discipline of battle.[38]

Lastly, the Canadian Corps continued to preach the necessity of "leaning into the barrage," or of having the infantry follow so close behind their supporting artillery barrage that German defenders could not recover from the bombardment in time to put up an organized defense before the Canadian infantry were upon them. This, however, required great faith by the infantry in the artillery's ability to deliver their rounds on time and on target.

In order to keep their end of this bargain, the artillery had to undergo its own reformation. Long accustomed to firing from the same positions for days on end, the artillery now had to relearn how to keep up with the attack. Key to past Canadian successes had been the ability to dominate German artillery in the main battle zone, and win the counter battery duel. To do this under the more fluid conditions of "open" warfare meant that artillery would have to move quickly into new forward positions in order to cover longer advances. Lieutenant Colonel (later Brigadier General) Andrew McNaughton, Corps counterbattery officer recognized this:

The transition to open warfare has to be mighty carefully planned. You have to be able to develop your artillery immediately in the close support of your infantry far forward. The deliberate techniques of seige warfare must give way to others even at the cost of some efficiency....I wanted everything on wheels....[39]

The artillery also came up with other inventive solutions to problems created by the nature of operations they were about to undertake. One such predicament was created by the necessity to open barrages without prior live registration in order to ensure surprise; this meant that there was no way to be positive that the opening rounds would be exactly on target. In response, the gunners perfected ways to ensure their opening rounds were accurate and effective by calibrating muzzle velocity changes due to barrel wear by firing at specially designed static screens, and then developing standardized tables for the data collected.[40] Some gunners were also selected and trained in the use of German artillery, thus enabling them during battle to turn captured German guns on their previous owners. Survey and counter battery techniques, such as sound ranging,[41] were also perfected during 1918. All these advances helped to insure that by the summer of 1918, Canadian Corps gunners were ready to fire the "ultimate round."[42]

The most significant changes came about in the organization of the Engineer Corps within the formation. Previous to 1918, the Canadian Engineers had been allocated the same way as in British divisions: three Engineer companies per division. This, however, meant that the bulk of the manual labor for any major project fell on the already stooped shoulders of the infantry. Currie disliked this, thinking it unreasonable "to ask the infantry to fight a battle one day and perform engineering work the next." It also meant that the Engineers' primary workforce was not subject to their control, a situation which often created unnecessary inefficiency. Corps Chief Engineer Major General W. B. Lindsay proposed a solution that would triple the size of a division's engineer force, thereby providing it the integral manpower and expertise to accomplish its tasks without having to drain men away from the fighting battalions, while simultaneously making the engineers more efficient. By July 1918, the expanded engineer organization was in place. The resulting change brought an Engineer brigade, nearly 3,000 strong, to each division, plus a pontoon bridging unit of 66 specialists. Currie knew well the value of engineers, especially in operations that might call for stretched and shattered supply lines to be repaired quickly. "I would rather go without infantry than without Engineers," he told Kemp when explaining his organizational change. Currie's foresight would pay dividends throughout the tough fighting of August to November.[43]

The climax of the Canadian Corps summer training was the preparation for a contemplated large scale attack in the Lys salient. Code-named "Operation Delta," this Army-level attack proved to be a nonstarter, for it would have left the British First Army without any reserves, and its flank dangerously exposed. Nonetheless, the planning exercise had proved to be an excellent final exam for the Corps, divisional, and brigade staffs. Currie himself said "the preparations for the projected "Delta" attack exercised a most vivifying influence on the training of the Canadian Corps; it familiarised all Arms and Services with the difficulties, both administrative and tactical, inherent to a surprise attack intended to penetrate suddenly to a great depth."[44] Although "Delta" was cancelled, the staff work had not been an exercise in futility; the Corps would soon enough find itself taking part in just such an attack for real.

The result of all these aforementioned organizational changes and of the concerted effort put forth during the summer training, had been to forge a formidable fighting formation out of what had already been a veteran Corps. The Corps' combat readiness did not go unnoticed by outsiders. Both Haig and Foch spoke in glowing terms of the Canadian Corps after inspecting it, the latter declaring it an "Army second to none, deriving its immense strength from the solid organization of each of its component parts, welded together in battle conditions."[45] Prime Minister Borden was also impressed, and his comments were both more profound and more enlightening than Foch's when it comes to modern students understanding the way in which the Corps was to be employed, and its success in the upcoming battles of the 100 Days. In a letter to cabinet, Borden stated:

You would be greatly inspired by the wonderful prestige of the Canadian Army Corps. It is admitted that it is the most effective and reliable fighting unit of its size in the British forces. *In reality, it is almost as strong numerically, and certainly is as effective for either offence or defense as any other of the British Armies*, although each Army is supposed to comprise two [or more] army corps (emphasis added).[46]

There are periods in history when fate seems to dictate that one person, or innovation, or organization can have an effect on global events out of all proportion with their individual size or import. By the end of July 1918, the conditions seemed ready for the emergence of just such an organization, a military formation capable of helping to break the deadlock arrived at after four years of bitter fighting. The Canadian Corps, forged by Currie, hardened by four years of battle, and honed to a razor's edge by a summer of intensive training, stood waiting. At Monash's suggestion, Rawlinson had asked for it, and Haig would allow him to use it to strike the first blow -- at Amiens.

The audience had gathered. The Corps had finished its rehearsals and fine tuning under its able conductor, Sir Arthur Currie, who had made the necessary modifications with a fine ear trained by four years of war. Its stage would be the battered fields of Amiens and Picardy, its instruments the rumbling percussion of its artillery, the stacatto rapping of its small arms, and a chorus of voices gathered from across a cold land thousands of miles away. The curtain was about to rise for the Canadian Corps.

NOTES

1. Currie said as much in his diary on 3 May 1918; Currie diary, 1918, Currie papers, NAC MG 30 E 100, Vol. 43. For a good explanation of how the Corps overcame their "amatuerism," see W. F. Stewart, *Attack Doctrine in the Canadian Corps*, pp. 227-258.
2. It is beyond the scope of this work to give either an in-depth history of the development of the Canadian Corps from 1914-1918, or a biography and analysis of the development of the "orchestra's conductor," Sir Arthur Currie. Both these subjects have been very well investigated by other historians, and the interested reader is encouraged to consult these works. On the Canadian Corps' development, see G.W.L. Nicholson's brief but excellent official history, *The Official History of the Canadian Army in the First World War: Canadian Expeditionary Force, 1914-1918* (Ottawa: Queen's Printer, 1962) (hereafter Nicholson ,*CEF)*; Bill Rawling, *Surviving Trench Warfare*; William Stewart, *Attack Doctrine*; or John Sweetenham, *To Seize the Victory: The Canadian Corps in World War I* (Toronto: Ryerson

Press, 1965). On Sir Arthur Currie, see Urquhart, *Arthur Currie*, Chapters 3 - 23; Dancocks, *Sir Arthur Currie*, Chapters 3 - 25; or Hyatt, *Currie*.

3. Webber is quoted by Winter, *Haig's Command*, p. 263.

4. For more about Currie's career rise, see Urquhart, *Arthur Currie*; Dancocks, *Sir Arthur Currie*; and Hyatt, *Currie*.

5. Ian Brown, "Not Glamorous But Effective," pp. 426-428.

6. John Swettenham, *To Seize the Victory*, pp. 165-189.

7. Currie, in a letter to Canadian Prime Minister Robert Borden, quoted in Hyatt, *Currie*, p. 107, and Urquhart, *Arthur Currie*, p. 225.

8. Currie had also done this in the past, most notably at Passchendaele in October 1917, when Currie told both First Army Commander General Horne and Haig that the Canadian Corps would not fight under General Gough in the Fifth Army because of Gough's incompetence; see Dancocks, *Sir Arthur Currie*, pp. 110-117, and Hyatt, *Currie*, pp. 79-81.

9. On the Overseas Ministry, see *Report of the Ministry of Overseas Military Forces of Canada, 1918* (London: Government Press, 1919) pp. xii-xv; Stacey, *Canada and the Age of Conflict*, pp. 172-239; Desmond Morton, *A Military History of Canada*, 3rd ed. (Toronto: McClelland and Stewart, 1992), p. 161.

10. Sir Ivor Maxse, one of the more brilliant British corps commanders of the Great War, repeatedly railed about the inconsistency of training within the British Army. See Paddy Griffith, *Battle Tactics*, pp. 95-100, 184-186. Hyatt makes this same point; *Currie*, p. 88.

11. See Winston Churchill, *The World Crisis*, pp. 375-393.

12. See B. H. Liddell - Hart, *A History of the World War, 1914-1918.* (Boston: Little, Brown, 1935), pp. 383-481.

13. "Proposed Re-Organisation of the Canadian Corps," *Report of the Ministry of Overseas Military Forces*, pp. 333-335.

14. The breaking up of the Fifth Canadian Division was ostensibly done because it would have been difficult to sustain five large divisions in France given Canada's manpower situation. It also created a great deal of resentment against Currie by its commander, Garnet Hughes, and his father, ex-Minister of Militia Sir Sam Hughes; see Nicholson, *CEF*, pp. 230-232; Hyatt, *Currie*, pp. 72-73, 95-105; and Dancocks, *Sir Arthur Currie*, pp. 101-104.

15. Unsigned Manuscript, "The Canadian Corps -- Principle Differences Between Canadian Corps and British Corps," NAC RG 9, III, D2, Vol.4809, File 196 (hereafter referred to as "Principle Differences").

16. "Principle Differences," p. 1.

17. This report is quoted in Winter, *Haig's Command*, p. 148.

18. For these figures, see "Principle Differences," p. 1.

19. Edmonds, *BOH*, Vol. 5, Appendices III and IV, pp. 623-624; see also "Principle Differences."

20. Andrew McNaughton commented after the war:

[A]nd so it came about that by 1917 the organization of the Canadian Corps Artillery and its ancillary intelligence and other services had reached an advanced state, and that our lead over similar organizations was maintained until the end of the war. The credit for this is largely due to our Corps Commander, who, in developing his policy of giving his infantry the maximum of support, was invariably sympathetic in his attitude towards the Canadian gunners...and put into practice a very thorough system of co-operation between the artillery and the infantry; it was always the object of the Canadian Corps to exploit gun power to the limit for the purposes of saving the lives of our infantry.

Major-General A.G.L. McNaughton, "The Development of Artillery in the Great War," *Canadian Defence Quarterly*, Vol. 6, No. 2 (January, 1929) pp. 162-163.

21. Brutinel papers, "Draft Report on the Canadian Corps -- Artillery," NAC, Manuscript Group (MG) 30, Vol. E414 (hereafter referred to as "Artillery Doctrine"), p. 1.

22. "Artillery Doctrine," p. 2.

23. See Edmonds, *BOH*, Vol. 6, p. 624, and "Artillery Doctrine," p. 1.

24. Sir James Edmonds, *BOH*, Vol. 5, Appendices III and IV, pp. 623-624; "Principle Differences," p. 3; Army commanders tried to "hire" some of Currie's best counter battery officers away; see Swettenham, *McNaughton: Volume1, 1887-1939* (Toronto: Ryerson Press, 1968), pp. 131-132; on the counter battery office itself, see "Organization of the Corps Counter-Battery Staff Office," n.d, n.a. NAC RG9, III, D2 Vol. 4793, File 40.

25. Colonel H.D.G. Crerar, "Organization of Corps Counterbattery Staff Office," RG 9, III, D2, Vol. 4793, File 40; see also Swettenham, *McNaughton*.

26. Crerar, "Organization of CBSO," p. 16.

27. Maxse went on to become the Britsh Army's Inspector General of Training. He rated the 30 divisions that had served under him as follows: "two had been well trained. Twelve were trying. Sixteen were without training of any sort. It was a remarkable state of affairs in an army which had been at war for three years." Winter, *Haig's Command*, p. 147.

28. "Principle Differences," p. 2.

29. A list of some of the Britsh divisions that operated under control of the Canadian Corps during the 100 Days includes: 4th British, 51st Highland, 32nd British, 11th British, 1st British, 56th London, 49th West Riding, 63rd Royal Naval, 8th British, 52nd Lowland (total = 10). This list does not include tank or other support units, such as artillery. For further information on the activity of these formations, see the reports on each held in NAC, RG 9, III, Vol. 4809, files 190-191, and NAC, RG 9, III, Vol. 4798, files 95-106.

30. Dancocks, *Sir Arthur Currie*, p.128.

31. Bean quite rightly makes the same argument for the Australian Corps, *AOH*, Vol. 6, pp. 1074-1096.

32. This did not mean that the Canadians were not active, or that they did not play a key role in stopping the Germans; some Canadian historians have speculated that it was precisely because the Canadian Corps held Vimy Ridge that the Germans left it one of the few places they did not attack during the summer. The Corps also held an inordinantly long front for a Corps formation during this period, thereby freeing up many British units to fight elsewhere; see Nicholson, *CEF*, pp. 362-385; Dancocks, *Sir Arthur Currie*, pp. 135-141; and Sir Arthur Currie's own report *Canadian Corps Operations During the Year 1918* (Ottawa: Dept. of Militia and Defence, 1919), pp. 2-20.

33. Nicholson, *CEF*, pp. 378-382.

34. Sweetenham, *To Seize the Victory*, pp. 203-206; Morton, *A Military History of Canada*, p. 161.

35. "Open Warfare" is a term used to describe a type of warfare that incorporates movement and mobility, where "lines" tend to be more fluid than in "static" or "positional" warfare characterized by the trench stalemate of the Great War from late 1914 to early 1918.

36. Daniel Dancocks, *Spearhead to Victory*, pp. 20-26; Currie, *Corps Operations in 1918*, pp. 20-26.

37. For an examination of the development of these tactics, see Gudmundsson, *Stormtroop Tactics*, John English, *On Infantry*, pp. 1-29; and for the Canadian adoption, Rawling, *Surviving Trench Warfare*, Chapters 5-7. Dr. Ron Haycock, an expert on small arms of this period, noted during a discussion with the author that the British and Canadian platoons were equipped with Lewis machine guns, which were substantially lighter than the Maxims

their German counterparts used; the point being that the German machine gun was more suitable for the static defence, where mobility of the gun was less of a factor, whereas the British light machine gun was easier to carry forward on the assault. The machine gun comparison points once more to the fact that even at this very low level, tactics and technology had a close symbiotic relationship.

38. Currie, quoted in Daniel Dancocks, *Spearhed to Victory*, p.32.

39. McNaughton, quoted in Swettenham, *McNaughton*, p. 130.

40. For a closer look at these developments, see C.N.F. Broad, "The Development of Artillery Tactics, 1914-1918," *Canadian Defense Quarterly*, three parts; Vol.1, No. 1 (June-July 1922); see also Swettenham, *McNaughton*, pp. 139-140.

41. Sound ranging uses the shock wave of a gun's firing, recorded by microphones and triangulated using trigonometry, in order to discover and plot the gun's location.

42. For a discussion of these developments, see G.W.L. Nicholson *The Gunners of Canada: The History of the Royal Regiment of Canadian Artillery, Volume 1: 1534-1919* (Toronto: McClelland and Stewart, 1967), pp. 258-335; Major General A.G.L. McNaughton, "The Development of Artillery", pp. 161-171.

43. Hyatt, *Currie*, pp. 110-111; Dancocks, *Spearhead*, p. 25.

44. Currie, *Corps Operations, 1918*, p. 24.

45. Foch, quoted in Dancocks, *Spearhead*, p. 26.

46. Canadian Prime Minister Robert Borden, quoted in Dancocks, *Spearhead*, p. 27.

3

THE OVERTURE: AMIENS, 8 AUGUST 1918

It was chiefly a Canadian battle.
> *The Times*, London, 27 August 1918, on the battle
> of Amiens.

August 8 was the Black Day [*der Schwarze Tag*] of the German Army in the history of this war.... Everything I had feared... had here, in one place, become a reality.
> General Erich Ludendorff, *My War Memories*, II, p. 679

When a battle is lost, the strength of the army is broken -- its moral even more than its physical strength.
> Clausewitz, *On War*, Book 4, Chapter 13.

The battle of Amiens, which commenced on 8 August 1918, is often viewed as the starting point for the Allied advance to victory during the final 100 Days of World War One. Upon deeper investigation, however, one finds that Amiens holds a much more complex place in military history than just as the first battle of a bloody, but ultimately successful, campaign. The battle of Amiens was not only the beginning of the end for the German Army on the Western Front, but also the culmination of technological and tactical changes that foreshadowed the development of modern mechanized warfare. It was for precisely this reason that military writer J.F.C. Fuller declared the battle of Amiens, 1918, to be one of the "decisive battles of the Western World."[1] Coming together from opposite sides of the globe, the Canadian and Australian Corps provided the spearhead of the BEF thrust at Amiens. The British, Australian, and Canadian triumph at Amiens was in fact a story of technological innovation, tactical metamorphosis, and careful, detailed planning and orchestration that acted as a harbinger of the sea change that had taken place in modern European land warfare during 1917 and 1918.

Amiens remains an anomaly in the Canadian Corps' history of the 100 Days. Planned predominantly by an outside agency, Sir Henry Rawlinson and his staff at the British Fourth Army, Currie had less room to use his personal initiative and developing operational and tactical doctrine. Instead, he was called upon to carry out the plans and visions of others. Nonetheless, the Canadian Corps' impact was made both by its sterling execution of Rawlinson's plan and also by Currie's role in ensuring that defeat was not snatched from the jaws of victory.

From the outset, it must be reiterated that it is impossible to tell the full story of the Canadian Corps' role in the battle of Amiens without giving due consideration to the efforts and achievements of all the other forces present, including the German defenders. History does not, and cannot, take place in a vacuum. These stories, however, fall outside the scope of this work, and have already been adeptly handled by other historians; any reader who is seeking a wider account of the battle of Amiens is urged to consult these works.[2] This investigation addresses only one piece of the puzzle, in hopes that by making this one fragment as enlightening as possible, it may help both to place it more easily into the context of the greater whole and, conversely, to allow the whole to have greater definition.

BACKGROUND

The set-back suffered by the German Army at the Marne, and the subsequent termination of its large-scale offensives in July 1918 did not signal the end of German hopes for a military victory on the Western Front, at least not to Ludendorff. His armies had been stopped, but only at a huge cost to the Allies, and the Germans still held large pieces of French territory wrested from the Allies in the hard fighting of the spring and summer. Ludendorff, and his superior Field Marshal Hindenburg, still held out hopes that their armies could stabilize the military situation enough to allow a favorable peace agreement from the Allies. On 2 Aug 1918, Ludendorff outlined his conception of a "strategic defensive," combined with a limited tactical offensive:

The situation demands that on the one hand we prepare ourselves for defense, but on the other hand that we go over to the attack as soon as possible . . . with these attacks . . . it is less important that we should gain more territory than we should inflict defeat on enemy forces and secure more favourable positions.[3]

Despite this optimistic outlook, Ludendorff's mental condition reflected the state of his battered armies, staggering from confidence to despair, seemingly teetering on the brink of collapse if pushed hard enough. Nevertheless, it remained the Allies' task to find the means to force the issue, and they had yet to prove they were equal to the test. The tide may have turned on the Western Front, but it still remained to be seen whether or not Haig and Foch could now take advantage of the punched out state of their foe. Ludendorff doubted his adversaries' ability to capitalize on this opportunity, claiming in a further directive on 4 August: "I have a feeling that there is much concern felt by many people over enemy attacks. This is not justified.... As I have already explained, we should be pleased if the enemy does attack, since he will expend his strength all the quicker by doing so."[4]

In retrospect, it appears that Ludendorff made the critical error of underestimating his enemy's capacity to counterpunch. Even as Ludendorff's own offensive was being ground to a halt on the Marne, the Allied High Command was devising a scheme to bring about the defeat of the German Armies. The first blow having been struck by the French and Americans in July, Foch now turned to Haig for the British contribution. Haig had the weapon. He had saved the Canadian Corps, and the nascent Royal Tank Corps, for just such an opening. With the help of Rawlinson and the staff of the British Fourth Army, he had the plan.

PLANNING AND PREPARATIONS

Sir Arthur Currie first heard of the plans for the Amiens operation on 20 July. By this time, the planning process in the Fourth Army had given form to the basic outline of the scheme, and it had already been approved by Haig. Rawlinson had envisioned an attack much like the one at Hamel, only on a wider front, with the limited objective being the old Amiens defense line approximately 6-10 miles behind the present German positions. The attack was also to have a clearly defined start and endpoint in terms of time; in essence, it was to be a one-day attack that allowed for subsequent set-piece operations during following days. The outline conception of the attack was uncomplicated. The Australian and Canadian Corps would launch the main assault supported by a large number of tanks, while the flanks of the thrust would be covered on the left by the British Third Corps, and on the right by the French First Army under French General Debeney. Cavalry divisions of horsemen and a force of the light "Whippet" tanks would be kept in reserve during the initial breakthrough phase. Once the heavy tanks and the infantry had breached the German forward defensive line, the cavalry and light tank forces would be sent forward to exploit and seize further ground.[5]

Currie attended a conference at Rawlinson's HQ on 21 July 1918, along with his fellow Corps commanders Lieutenant-General Sir John Monash (Australian Corps), Lieutenant-General Sir Richard Butler (III British Corps), and Lieutenant-General Sir Charles Kavanagh (Cavalry Corps). Also in attendance was the General Staff Officer (GSO) 1 of the nascent Royal Tank Corps, Lieutenant Colonel J.F.C. Fuller (who would later gain renown as an armoured warfare theorist and military pundit), and a representative from the Royal Air Force, newly-created out of the old Royal Flying Corps on 1 April 1918.[6]

For the Canadians, there were three crucial decisions made at this conference. Rawlinson stressed the need for utmost secrecy to be maintained if the attack were to achieve surprise. The Germans would be sure to be tipped off to an oncoming onslaught if the most feared attack formations in the BEF, the Canadians and the Australians, were to be brought together; in historian B.H. Liddell-Hart's words, "regarding them as storm troops, the Germans tended to greet their appearance as an omen of a coming attack."[7] Currie went Rawlinson one better -- he would continue to plan and issue orders for an attack by the Canadian Corps in the area of Arras, further to the north.[8] The second key decision was to increase the size of the tank force from 8 battalions to 12. In addition to this sudden jump in tank numbers, Canadian officers were to be sent to the Australian training school at Flixecourt in order to learn the latest in tank-infantry cooperation from the Australian experience at Hamel. The Australians had been working with tanks for some months, and Currie felt it essential to take advantage of their seasoning. The third decision made was to enlarge the operation, and to include the opportunity for the cavalry to act as an exploitation force should the combined infantry-tank assault be successful in ripping a gap in the German defense.[9]

Currie further added to Rawlinson's plan by organizing his own mechanized force under Brigadier General Raymond Brutinel. Designated as the "Canadian Independent Force," its task was to provide flank security and liaison with the French First Army on the Canadians' right.[10] Brutinel was the obvious choice for this crucial job. Born in France, Brutinel had been in Canada when the war started. Unable to return to France because of the hostilities, Brutinel had joined the Canadian Expeditionary Force (CEF) to fight. Early in the war he had been a strong advocate of both the machine gun, and of mechanization. As a result, Brutinel had been allowed to experiment with a "motor machine gun" company, essentially made up of Vickers machine guns mounted in trucks. He had also been instrumental in developing the innovative and effective machine gun (MG) tactics used by the Corps and throughout the BEF as a whole.[11] At Amiens, his Canadian Independent Force, also known as Brutinel's Brigade, consisted of the Corps' First and Second Canadian Motor Machine Gun units (1 and 2 CMMG), the Canadian Corps Cyclist Battalion, and a section of 6-inch Newton Mortars mounted in trucks. Currie and Brutinel envisioned the Independent Force as a highly mobile unit capable of seizing and holding key terrain features in advance of the infantry, or as a means of dominating terrain with firepower until some means could be worked out to actually take and hold it.[12] Their experiments put the Canadian Corps on the leading edge of developing a doctrine of "mechanized" warfare, albeit a primitive one. Currie's use of such an eclectic, ad hoc organization showed not only a flair for the innovative, but also a faith in his subordinates, (in this case Brutinel) that would be well rewarded at battle's end.

Despite the plan's simplicity, much of its chance for success depended heavily on secrecy and surprise. Rawlinson and Currie knew that arrival of the Canadian Corps would be considered as a portent of impending attack by the Germans, and therefore devised an elaborate deception plan to convince the Germans that the attack would come not at Amiens, but north, in Flanders.[13] Currie agreed to mislead not only the Germans, but even his own staff by continuing preparations for an assault on Orange Hill in the British Second Army's area. Two Canadian units, one each from the Second and Third Canadian Divisions, were moved into the Second Army's area, where they carried out small raiding actions, conspicuously losing some of their distinctive equipment and insignia to the Germans. False orders were promulgated by Fourth Army HQ that the Canadian Corps would be transferred to the British Second Army front. To complete the ruse, Currie dispatched wireless sections from his Corps' HQ north into Second Army's area to transmit false messages -- thus devising what might be called the first electronic deception plan. Also dispatched were casualty collection stations, easily the most difficult elements to move and a most valuable resource, and therefore the surest sign of a Canadian Corps concentration in Flanders.[14]

Finally, on 29 July 1918, Currie informed his divisional commanders as to the real objective of the attack, but swore them to secrecy; they could not discuss the operation with any of their subordinate commanders until Currie gave permission. The secrecy was pushed down to the lowest level, with each man having a notice admonishing "Keep Your Mouth Shut!!" pasted in his paybook.[15] Plans continued for the attack on Orange Hill, and, once completed, were wisely shelved for later use.[16]

Headquarters at all levels now engaged in a flurry of activity. Throughout the first week of August, the Canadian Corps, less elements of those units involved in the ruse, completed a difficult road move into their assembly areas in the rear of the Fourth Army area. Given the conditions of secrecy, and the congested and shattered transportation network in this sector, the work of the Division, Corps, and Army staffs in moving the mass of men and material may have proven to be the real key to the success of the Amiens operation. Often the most difficult part of any attack in modern war is massing the necessary forces. In a high-intensity conflict, this means much more than simply getting the soldiers and guns into position. It also means getting the infrastructure in place in order to support those troops, especially in prolonged offensive operations where ammunition expenditure and logistical requirements can be much heavier than in other phases of war. This kind of "behind the scenes" action is sometimes the most desperate, most thankless, and least glorious task of all, falling on those invisible and overlooked minions of military history, the staff officers and logistics personnel.[17] The story of the logistical triumph which preceded the tactical victory at Amiens has seldom been told, and then only in a precursory manner; but, as with any military endeavor, it is what happened in the days *before* the attack that truly had a critical impact on the issue.[18]

Of all the formations, the Canadian Corps had by far the hardest task in the days leading up to 8 August. It had to move from under command of the British First Army, under which it had fought for almost the entire previous two years, to the command of the Fourth Army. This not only entailed a physical move of some 60 kilometers, but also a mental reorientation in order to become acquainted with the personalities and operational procedures of a new army headquarters. The move of a corps-size formation was difficult at best, but even more so under the conditions of strict secrecy. First, the movements of all the units were to take place at night.[19] Currie noted that this restriction was "a severe handicap, as the nights were very short this time of year."[20] Units had to deploy under the cover of darkness, and through unfamiliar territory into their "laying up" positions in order to await either further orders or for another deployment. Moreover, most of the sector the Canadians were to operate in had been until quite recently under the control of the French Army, and therefore none of the logistical facilities -- ammo dumps, railheads, fuel points -- necessary to support a British formation had yet been developed. Compounding all these difficulties was Rawlinson's demand that only the senior commanders be apprised of the attack; in the Canadian Corps case, this meant that until 29 July, only Currie, his chief staff officer in Corps HQ, BGGS N.W. "Ox" Webber, and seven other officers at Corps headquarters knew of the objective of all the commotion in the Corps.

The logistical problem these preparations posed was nothing short of a nightmare. First, Corps Deputy Adjutant and Quartermaster General (DA & QMG) Brigadier General G.J. Farmar -- the Corps' senior logistics authority -- was not informed of the objective of the attack until 29 July. This gave him and his subordinate staffs at Corps and divisional HQs precisely one day to actually plan and begin implementing the rail and road move that was to bring the bulk of the Corps' manpower south. On the night of 30 July, most of the infantry units entrained and moved into the wooded areas around Amiens, followed by the artillery. Having brought the personnel there, the Canadian Army Service Corps (CASC), the Corps' logistics branch, now had to get ammunition to them. This proved to be the biggest logistical challenge. First, in the interest of secrecy, the logistics staff (or "Q" staff, to use contemporary parlance), at Fourth Army HQ had not been told that the Canadian Corps was coming under their command. As a result, the Corps found that "the first request to the Army for 10,000,000 S.A.A. [small arms ammunition] was apparently not taken seriously and S.A.A. came up in small quantities, and could not be supplied to divisions as quickly as they required it."[21] More importantly, artillery ammunition was difficult to bring forward. Even in war in the 1990's, the majority of a formations' heavy tactical lift may be devoted to the resupply of artillery ammunition, and the same was true for the Canadian formations in 1918. In the case of the Amiens operation, the closest artillery ammunition dumps were, "so far in the rear that lorries [trucks] could only make one trip from Army dumps daily."

Two other factors added to this problem. The first was the congested state of the only two available roads leading to the concentration areas of the Corps. Only the Amiens-Roye and the Amiens-Villers Bretonneux roads were allocated to the Canadian Corps, which also had to share use of the latter with the Australian Corps. The second factor was that because of the nature of the tactical move, and its short notice, the heavy artillery brigades arrived only 72-48 hours before the attack, so that their integral transport capabilities were unavailable to augment Corps logistical movement capacity during the buildup. One logistical problem then created another. When the heavy artillery brigades' trucks did arrive, the Fourth Army was unprepared for the large number of them, and so "was unable to supply sufficient petroleum and lubricating oils (P.O.L.)." As a result, at one point, the entire Army reserve of fuel had been used up, and many trucks sat idle waiting for fuel instead of hauling artillery ammunition. Given the attack's dependence upon a large fleet of fuel-burning tanks, the fuel shortage could have proven disastrous had it not been for the transportation of fuel from "ABBEVILLE, an absurdly long and extravagant journey."[22]

The Canadian Corps, unlike some other Imperial formations, was fortunate enough to have had nearly all of its logistical transport companies motorized by 1918. It must be remembered, however, that horses remained the prime mover for artillery units until long after the end of the Great War, and they created another logistical nightmare. Luckily enough, there were large woods near Amiens in which the horses could be concealed, but the animals still choked up the available roadways on their thrice daily trips to the water points, creating a "continual stream of horses, both ways, between BOVES Wood and the River." More grisly was the need for extra labor units to follow close behind the battle, both to assist with battlefield salvage, and to bury dead horses.[23]

It was the secrecy involved in all these preparations that caused the "Q" staff the most problems, and they resented not being taken into confidence sooner. The Canadian Corps "Q" report read:

While it is recognised that the whole success of the operations was due to the secrecy under which the operations were arranged, it is considered that the responsible Staff Officers could have been taken into confidence, with considerable benefit to all concerned...and without any danger of information reaching [the enemy].... It was only by chance and good luck that trench munitions were obtained and issued to the 3rd Canadian Division.... There is much less chance of information reaching the enemy through a Staff Officer than there is from the enemy observing the preparations from the air. In this case, although such precautions were taken to prevent the staff knowing what they were to do, all horses were taken out three times a day to water in the open.[24]

Fortunately for the Canadian Corps, the weather conditions proved favorable to the Allies. The sky remained too overcast to permit enemy reconnaissance flights during the preparations, yet it did not rain. Had the weather been wet, the two main supply routes (MSRs) could have become impassable mires, further compounding the logistical problems faced by the Canadian Corps.[25]

Despite all these challenges, the Canadian Corps "Q" staffs and the Canadian Army Service Corps had effectively laid the logistical foundations for the tactical victory of 8 August. In a period of one week, they had successfully moved all four Canadian divisions, plus the Corps' ancillary troops, into their concentration areas, and, furthermore, had been able to scrounge enough ammunition, trench mortar bombs, flares, grenades, and other necessities, such as food, to outfit each soldier. Even those commonly disposed to derision of the higher headquarters, such as the common infantry soldier, had gained a new respect for the red-tabbed staff officers. G.S. Rutherford, a member of the 52nd (New Ontario) Battalion, reported, "you had the feeling that everything was well-planned, well-organized. People knew what they were about, the staff was on the job. Everything seemed to go like clockwork, and for the first time you could hear the troops singing."[26]

The transport personnel of the CASC had overcome a tremendously overburdened transport system in order to provide the artillery with ample ammunition: 291,000 rounds of all calibers, with a total weight of 7,065 tons, had been trucked into position in a period of just over three days, the last delivery being made only five hours before the attack was scheduled to begin.[27] At least at the logistical level, the Canadian Corps had lived up to its reputation for creating small miracles.

While Farmar and his "Q" organization were working feverishly to achieve the "massing of forces" required, the operational plan had undergone a significant metamorphosis. The "limited objective" offensive Rawlinson had been devising had inexorably grown. Haig, perhaps under pressure from Foch, now stressed the need to go deeper with the attack and exploit far beyond the initial objectives of the old Amiens defense line. A conference between Haig, Foch, and Rawlinson on 5 August changed the operation from a limited objective attack by the Fourth Army to a general offensive involving the First and Third French Armies to the south. Rawlinson was

told that his new objective was "to push forward in the general direction of the line
Roye-Chaulnes with the least possible delay, thrusting the enemy back in the general
direction of Hamm -- 15 miles south-east of Chaulnes."[28] In essence, the attack at
Amiens had evolved from a "limited" to an "unlimited" offensive.[29]   As Fuller has
pointed out,

> to double the depth of penetration three days before the attack was due meant that corps
> commanders would not have the time to change the intricate administrative detail which all
> offensive plans in this war demanded. It followed that the plans as they stood would have to be
> fitted to a situation for which they had never been contemplated.[30]

Even though Haig and GHQ now expected much more from the attack than
was originally envisioned, Rawlinson's plans for the Amiens operation changed little.
The orders from GHQ were passed by Rawlinson onto the corps commanders, but he
made no major modifications.[31] The true intention of expanding the limits of the attack
was diluted and filtered through the Fourth Army staff, who still conceptualized a
limited objective attack. As a result, Fourth Army HQ downplayed the new
"unlimited" nature of the Army's intended operation, perhaps because its Chief of Staff
Major General A. A. Montgomery was afraid that such a significant change in the
operational aim may have thrown the already well-advanced preparations and planning
into complete disarray, jeopardizing the potential success of the attack. In any event,
Rawlinson's adjustments were characterized by Montgomery as nothing more than a
"minor modification."[32]

In order to achieve the depth of penetration envisioned in the new plan, the
Canadian and Australian Corps were each to receive an additional British division
under their command on the day of the attack, thus giving them the fresh forces
necessary to carry out additional attacks on Z plus 1 day.* Simultaneous to these
changes, the date of the attack was also moved up, from 10 August to 8 August,
allowing Currie even less time to prepare. Canadian military historian Brereton
Greenhous has argued that the imperious attitude evinced by these relatively late
changes by Fourth Army HQ "doomed" the battle of Amiens "to failure at the
operational level while, ironically, its strategic effect was to be far greater than anyone
dreamed of."[33] While this may be too strong an indictment against Rawlinson's HQ,
Greenhous is nonetheless correct in his assumption that last-minute changes were to
dramatically affect the plans for fighting on days following the initial attack.

If the nature of the operation at Amiens was beginning to blur in the minds
of the Fourth Army staff, it did not affect Currie's tactical approach to the upcoming
battle. Currie's plan reflected the Canadian Corps attack doctrine he had been so
instrumental in developing during the previous year. First, Currie divided the
battlefield into three distinct and subsequent objectives, denoted in the operational
orders as the Green, Red, and Blue dotted lines. For the Canadian Corps, solid
marked lines were used to represent intermediate or final objectives, while dotted lines

---

* In military parlance of the times, "Z" or "zero" was the date and time of the attack, so "Z
plus 1 day" is the day after the initial assault.

denoted the limits of exploitation expected to be reached by "follow on" forces after the conclusion of the set-piece assault by lead divisions.[34] At Amiens, these lines also divided the battlefield into three separate, successive objectives. The Green line denoted the intermediate goal, the capture of the forward or "outpost" zone. The Red line symbolized the end of the static reserve defense and the artillery positions in the Main Battle zone, and the Blue dotted line the "rearward " zone of scattered enemy strong points and counterattack positions.[35] In reality, and as will be seen, the German positions in this area were poor reflections of the doctrine of elastic defense, and therefore it was difficult to plot exactly where one zone began and another ended.

The plan called for no halt by the attackers at the Green line, but rather a short pause, with the line acting primarily as a control measure indicating the end of the first phase of the assault and its supporting barrage. Attacking divisions would then be allowed to pass fresh brigades through, if necessary, in order to carry on the assault to the Red line. This pause served to maintain the momentum of the attack by keeping it united and coordinated, thereby minimizing energy dissipated by the "friction" of war. The depth of the attack's projected objectives made it difficult to get artillery support deep enough to cover the infantry's advance to the Red line, and therefore Currie and his GOCRA, Major General E.W.B. Morrison, requested and were allotted extra heavy artillery from the Fourth Army capable of reaching out the extra distance to the Red line. The Blue dotted line was the limit of exploitation for the infantry divisions only. In keeping with Haig's hope for a decisive breakthrough, Currie pointed out that "the cavalry was to exploit beyond it should the opportunity occur."[36] (Map 3.1 shows the Amiens operations.)

Currie's plan of attack for the Corps was simple: three infantry divisions forward, one in depth, the latter to be pushed forward as necessary to overcome tough resistance or to exploit where the German defenses were weakest. In Currie's words:

The general scheme of the attack was to overrun rapidly sections of the enemy's forward area...under the cover of a dense artillery barrage; then, without halting, to seize the Red Line, relying on the help of the Tanks to overcome the machine gun defense. At that moment the Cavalry was to pass through the infantry and seize the area as far as the Blue dotted line.... The Calvalry [sic] was to be followed as quickly as possible by the 4th Canadian Division passing through the 3rd Canadian Division on the right, and by Reserve Brigades of the 1st and 2nd Canadian Divisions in the centre and on the left. Every effort was to be made to exploit success wherever it occurred.... Sections of Field Artillery were detailed to advance in close support of attacking Infantry.
The attack had been synchronised with the Australians, who were to jump off at the same hour as the Canadian Corps....
    The Canadian Corps being, as it were, the spearhead of the attack, the movements of other formations were to be synchronised with ours.[37]

The enemy against which this tide of destruction was to crash was not nearly as formidable as the one fought by the Canadians at Vimy, Hill 70, or Passchendaele. The Fourth Army operation would fall primarily on the Second German Army of General von der Marwitz, which had suffered grievously, first from the *Kaiserschlacht*, and more recently from an outbreak of influenza. This formation was well below strength in many of its infantry battalions, with the weakest divisions, the

Map 3.1
Amiens Operations

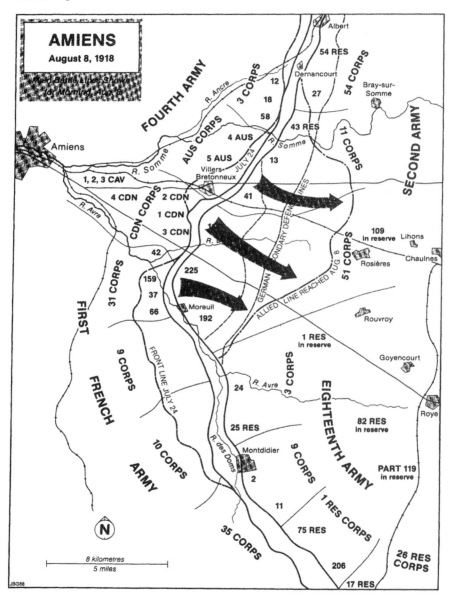

AMIENS
August 8, 1918

Main Battle Lines Shown
for Morning Aug. 8

41st and 13th, facing the Australian front east of Villers Bretonneux.[38]

The Canadian Corps, relying on excellent intelligence from the Fourth Army and the Australian Corps, believed that they would initially be faced with less than three divisions, comprising a total of less than 30 understrength battalions, with another four divisions in reserve. The German defensive positions were poorly prepared, a reflection of both the eroding morale and manpower of the German Army, and of Ludendorff's hope to go over to the offensive again in the near future. Frontages were also much wider than should have been held by infantry battalions in such desperate shape, and only a feeble attempt was made by most units to create wire and other obstacles. Currie succinctly reported that the German defense consisted "chiefly of unconnected elements of trenches and a vast number of machine gun posts scattered here and there, forming a very loose but very deep pattern."[39]

If the German defense placed a heavy reliance upon the direct firepower of the machine gun to compensate for its other disadvantages, then the Canadian offense placed an equal reliance on the indirect firepower of the artillery to dominate and destroy the Germans' ability to defend. As with virtually all attacks on the Western Front, the most crucial element of the Amiens operation was the artillery. Morrison had at his disposal 17 field artillery brigades (using lighter, more mobile horse drawn guns), 9 heavy artillery brigades, and 4 long-range "seige" batteries, totalling 646 guns.

The fireplan for the battle of Amiens reflected the simplicity of the maneuver plan. After having subjected the Germans to weeks of only sporadic harassing fire, the heavy creeping barrage behind which the infantry and tanks would advance would be opened as a complete surprise. This barrage would be fired by 14 of the 17 field artillery brigades, and was designed to move slowly forward at a rate of 200 yards per minute, the rate of advance calculated from the Canadian Corps and BEF experiences of 1917. The barrage would dwell at the Green line to cover the "leapfrogging" through of fresh assault brigades, and then continue to the limit of field gun range (approximately 9,000 - 12,000 yards). Once this limit was reached, roughly the area of the Red line, the three remaining field artillery brigades that had begun moving forward at "Z" hour, attached one per assault division, would begin firing on targets designated by divisional staffs. The Infantry divisions were further allocated one brigade of heavy artillery to bombard selected targets in advance of the field artillery barrage. When the majority of the field artillery brigades had completed their part in the creeping barrage, they were to revert to their "mobile" role, moving forward as quickly as possible in order to cover further advances.

The majority of the ammunition to be fired was shrapnel, with the newly developed timed fuse. Smoke rounds would also be used to cover the advance of the infantry, but only once they reached the Green line so as to guard against confusion caused by obfuscated visibility during the assault. High explosive (HE) ammunition was sparingly used in order to minimize potential mobility problems due to its cratering effects. Despite the plan's seeming simplicity, the coordination involved in order to insure that such a large number of guns could deliver their rounds on time and on target, especially when considering that many batteries had no opportunity for live registration, was very complex, and virtually took the entire period allotted for preparation.[40]

The opening barrage was made doubly effective by the excellent counterbattery work done by the British and Canadian gunners under the direction of Colonel A.G.L. (Andy) McNaughton and his Corps Counter Battery Staff Office. The artillery duel, which so often became a battle within a battle, was quickly and decisively won at Amiens through superior tactical intelligence gathering and resource allocation. Each known German battery was carefully plotted and monitored, but was not engaged unless absolutely necessary until the initial barrage. Then, in a veritable "storm of steel," each of these carefully plotted batteries received 200 rounds of gunfire, often including gas shells, fired by the heavy artillery batteries under the CBSO's control. Thus silenced or preoccupied at the exact moment they were most needed, the German artillery batteries were to be for all intents and purposes wiped from the face of battle for the initial assaults on 8 August.[41]

McNaughton's efforts in the counterbattery field were crucial to the evolving Canadian Corps' "way of war." Victory in the artillery duel meant that, at least initially, the assaulting Canadian infantry could cross no-man's land and begin their assault unhindered by the prospect of "death from above." It reduced a multidimensional space problem into one plane: that of the direct fire systems and terrain. To use modern technical parlance, the Canadians had "won the firefight," establishing the firepower superiority that thence allowed them greater freedom to maneuver on the battlefield. By robbing the enemy of the ability to retaliate in kind, the Canadian counterbattery effort, in essence, created space and time for the assault elements to manoeuvre on the battlefield to destroy the more difficult to silence direct fire systems (i.e., machine guns). Artillery, in short, was used to create "artificial" cover from direct fire.

Even the most thorough and intense bombardment, however, inevitably left some wire obstacles, machine guns, and carefully concealed artillery positions intact. It was in order to deal with these threats that the "land cruiser," or tank, was developed. The most prevalent of the tanks used at Amiens were the British Mark V version, with lighter "Whippet" tanks being assigned to the cavalry formations for use in the exploitation role. (See Figure 3.1 for technical characteristics). The Canadian Corps was allocated the 4th Tank Brigade, with each of the assaulting infantry divisions receiving under command a tank battalion. A tank battalion had approximately 36 Mark V's, and 6 replacement Mark V's, for a total in the Canadian Corps of 168 tanks. Added to this total were a number of supply tanks, approximately one per battalion, to assist in carrying forward ammunition, water, food, and other combat supplies. Each supply tank could carry 40,000 rds S.A.A., 150 two gallon water tins, 150 shovels, 75 picks, 500 Stokes shells, and 250 Lewis Gun ammunition drums, thus relieving the infantry soldier of some of his steadily growing burden.

The trip to the Australian Tank Cooperation School at Flixecourt by Canadian officers had proven beneficial, but there was simply not enough time to familiarize every infantry soldier with the problems of operating with the tanks. The

Figure 3.1
Tank Characteristics -- Technical Data for British Tanks Used at Amiens

	Mark V Male	Mark V Female	Mark V * Male	Mark V * Female	Whippet
Weight (tons)	29	28	33	32	14
Crew	8	8	8	8	3
Armament	2 x 6 pdr 4 x HMG	6 x HMG	2 x 6 pdr 4 x HMG	6 x HMG	4 x HMG
Max Speed (mph)	4.6	4.6	4.0	4.0	8.3
Avg Speed (mph)	3.0	3.0	2.5	2.5	5.0
Approx. Range (on one fuel tank, in miles)	25	25	18	18	40

Note: Mark V* could carry 16-20 men in addtion to its crew. HMG = Heavy Machine Gun.

Source: J.F.C. Fuller, *The Decisive Battles of the Western World, Volume3.* (London: Eyre and Spottiswoode, 1956) p. 282.

tentative solution to the problem of tank-infantry coordination and communication was surprisingly simple, however:

The commander of every Infantry detachment to which a detachment of tanks is allotted, will detail one infantryman to ride in each Tank. This man will be responsible for watching the infantry advance and the [i]nfantry [s]ignals, and keeping the Tank Commander informed as to the progress and requirements. He will also operate signals from the Tank to the Infantry.[42]

Despite the simple solution to communications problems at the lowest tactical levels, Canadian commanders were still grappling with the problems of combined arms tactics at higher levels, and Amiens would prove to be a vital learning experience.

Like the discovery of the Canadian or the Australian Corps, the arrival of a large number of tanks in any vicinity would have tipped Rawlinson's hand to the Germans. In order to conceal the concentration of tanks from the Germans, additional measures were incorporated to the already elaborate deception plan. The noise of the tanks moving forward into their assembly areas just east of Amiens was covered by low-flying RAF bombers buzzing incessantly over the German lines. The effectiveness of this ruse was debatable, however, as German troops did report hearing sounds of tanks approaching, only to have these reports derided by the German High Command as being "nervousness or imagination."[43] Thus, with the unknowing complicity of the German High Command, the British were able to mass their tanks at Amiens without the Germans taking effective notice or countermeasures.

The noisemaking RAF bombers (crewed predominantly by Canadians, incidentally) were not the sole representatives of the air arm. As at Hamel, the RAF played a large role in both the preparations for and the execution of Rawlinson's plan. The RAF's primary mission during the week leading up to 8 August was to gain air superiority over the battlefield, and, by denying the enemy reconnaissance flights, provide security for the massing of forces. While the weather greatly assisted the RAF in this task by keeping German planes grounded due to overcast skies, the meteorological conditions proved to be a double-edged sword, preventing the RAF from reconnoitering German defenses. Nonetheless, on the few available flying days, the RAF ruled the sky over Amiens, mustering in co-operation with their French counterparts a decisive superiority in numbers of aircraft: 1,904 Allied to 365 German.[44]

For the ground battle, each corps had been allocated a "close support" squadron, whose role was to report on the progress of forward assaulting elements through the use of "contact patrols." These planes could also, if necessary, act as ground attack craft against enemy strong points, such as machine gun nests or artillery positions. The Canadian Corps had under its command Number 5 Squadron RAF for these tasks. Beyond these forces, the RAF employed "day bomber" squadrons in what proved to be an unsuccessful attempt to isolate the battlefield and interdict German reinforcements by bombing railway centers, and the bridges over the Luce, Somme, and Ancre Rivers.[45] Though primitive in execution, the incorporation of airpower into the Fourth Army's battle plan was revolutionary, and paved the way for future use of airpower as a tactical tool on the battlefield.[46]

The concentration of so many forces in such a confined space as the area around Amiens created great concern for the commanders. The Canadians had the greatest problems, with four full divisions jammed in the small triangle formed by the German lines to the east, the Amiens-Villers Bretonneux road to the north, and the Amiens-Roye road to the south. The night of 7 August would find the Allies at their most vulnerable, because the forces would be extremely concentrated while moving into their jumping off points. Commanders were especially afraid that the Germans might employ "yellow cross" (phosgene) gas shells against such a concentrated target, creating a confused and suffocating mob out of what had been a highly organized attack force.

The Canadian Corps contingency plan should any such German spoiling attack occur was to forego any attempt at the surprise bombardment scheduled for zero hour, which would have been rendered pointless anyhow, and to begin the counterbattery effort immediately in order to silence the German guns. In effect, this left McNaughton, as head of the CBSO, in charge of initiating the battle early. This was no small responsibility, and it says something of both Currie and McNaughton that the former would have the confidence to place such an important task in the hands of the latter. Although McNaughton spent a sleepless night, fortunately for both him and all the Canadian and Australian soldiers, the night of 7-8 August saw little activity from the Germans opposite.[47]

At literally the last minute, the assaulting divisions of the Canadian Corps moved into their attack positions just south of Villers-Bretonneux.[48] The Fourth

Australian Division turned this area over to the Canadian Corps on the nights of 4-7 August, and Currie had taken command on 5 August, allowing the Australians to slip northward to take over part of their Corps' frontage. Canadian units continued to arrive right up to the very final instant, with the last of the Third Division troops, under Major General L.J. Lipsett, getting into position just 20 minutes before zero hour, the time the attack was supposed to commence. Side by side, the fighting men of the two Dominions waited to go into battle together. Security, secrecy, deception, and diligent staffwork had set the stage for what would be a culmination of the technological and tactical advances of four years of bloody struggle. Major General Sir Archibald Macdonell, commander of the "Old Redpatch," the First Canadian Division, wrote in his diary on the night of 7-8 August, "everything is arranged that can be arranged -- men in splendid fettle -- I never was more confident in my life of victory."[49] Like the tense silence that befalls an orchestra just before the maestro picks up the baton, the Canadian Corps sat ready. The overture was about to begin.

THE BATTLE JOINED

The battle of Amiens began with a percussion crescendo at precisely 4:20 a.m., 8 August 1918, with over 2,000 artillery pieces roaring out death to the defenders of the German front line. In the Canadian Corps area, the barrage obliterated the outpost and forward defensive positions. The counterbattery fire was so deadly and accurate that German batteries were cut down en masse while trying to limber up their guns, or were destroyed before they could fire a shell.[50] In McNaughton's own words, "it appears that I have swamped his [the German] batteries." McNaughton added, in a letter to his wife, "4:20 -- They are off, well together and on time, all along the front. A terrific racket. The Boche is getting his now. Long live Canada!"[51]

The attack was further aided in its initial stages by a thick mist that enveloped the battlefield and hid the advancing waves of infantry from German observers and machine gunners. The attack formations for all of the assaulting divisions were roughly the same, and reflected the tactical innovations that had taken shape during the war. The lead wave was an extended line of infantry "skirmishers," whose job it was to act as scouts, and to help guide the tanks, which followed in an extended line in the second wave approximately 100 meters behind. Behind the tanks came infantry sections, in single file, in three successive waves. Following the lead battalions were usually elements of carrying parties, and then follow-up battalions or brigades behind them. Sections, platoons, and companies were to push ahead relentlessly, overcoming resistance with a combination of speedy flanking movements and violence created by grenades, Mills bombs, and Lewis gun fire. Strong points that could not be taken would be reduced to rubble by the tanks, and isolated and left for the depth battalions to finish off.[52]

On the right of the Canadian Corps, Major General Lipsett's Third Canadian Division had probably the toughest job, having to secure the Amiens- Roye road and the crossings over the River Luce, and to keep these open for the exploitation forces, while simultaneously maintaining contact with the French attack scheduled to start 30 minutes after the Canadian Corps' initial assault. Lipsett decided to advance with two brigades forward, the 9th Canadian Infantry Brigade (CIB) on the right, and the 5th Canadian Infantry Brigade on the left. The supporting tanks found the going difficult, as they were blinded by the thick mist and moving across swampy ground, but by 7:30 a.m., the 9th CIB had reached its first objective, and paused there to reorganize. The 7th CIB then took over the assault, reaching its objective, the Red line, by 10:30 a.m. after facing only minor opposition. Brutinel's Independent Force and the Fourth Division then passed through to continue the advance. Contact with the 31st French Corps immediately to the south was maintained through the use of a combined Franco-Canadian International Platoon, under the command of the 43rd Canadian Infantry Battalion. This force of 30 French and 30 Canadian soldiers provided "excellent results."[53] Currie noted: "The very complete arrangements made by the 3rd Canadian Division to keep the bridge [over the Luce] open, and to repair the road quickly allowed the reserves to go forward without delay. The heavy task of the Engineers was remarkably well carried out."[54] The rest of the advance in this sector would be conducted by the Fourth Canadian Division.

In the center, Major General Archibald Macdonnel's First Canadian Division pushed forward, led by Brigadier General G.S. Tuxford's 3rd CIB. Again, the mist acted as a double-edged sword, protecting the attackers from observation by German machine gunners, but leading to navigational difficulties and confusion among the tanks. Once the mist lifted, at about 10:00 a.m., troops in the German front line discovered they had been overrun, and depth elements of the Canadian attack found it necessary to deal with surprised yet stubborn machine gunners who refused to surrender. Tuxford reported:

CROATES [a nickname] trench was attacked, offering heavy resistance, but finally an enfilade fire was brought to bear, and the Hun raised a white flag. Upon our men advancing they were met with heavy fire again, and the fight recommenced. Two white flags were soon displayed by the HUN, but this time our men took no notice and practically exterminated the garrison.[55]

Despite a few such isolated pockets of fierce resistance, Macdonell's division easily fought its way to the Blue dotted line by the early afternoon of August 8.[56]

The Second Canadian Division, under Major-General Henry Burstall, also scored easy success over the German defenders. In this sector, the Canadians were opposed mainly by scattered machine gun posts. Burstall commented:

The enemy's positions gave the earliest indication of the lack of morale and discipline in his troops.... Although there was an abundance of tools and material, very little work had been done on the defense which consisted mainly of unconnected sections of trench with a little local wire entanglement. There was, however, one fairly continuous defensive line, well wired...[57]

This single line of trenches, and the outposts, were quickly overcome, in some cases through excellent cooperation with the Australian battalions on the left flank of the Division.[58] By early afternoon on 8 August, the Second Division had reached the outer Amiens defense line, and were consolidating along the Blue dotted line.

The initial and subsequent objectives for the Canadian Corps had been seized incredibly quickly, despite the stout defense put up by some of the German machine gun outposts and positions. The Australians had kept pace, and so, by the early afternoon of 8 August, the exploitation phase involving the cavalry and reserve infantry divisions was taking place, with the hope of putting the Germans to abject flight. In the Canadian Corps area, this exploitation task fell to the horsemen (and Whippets) of the Third Cavalry Division, led by the Canadian Cavalry Brigade. They began their "charge" for the Blue dotted line from just behind the forward positions of the Third Division in the early afternoon. The tired infantry were now treated to the glorious spectacle of a cavalry charge, described by Lieutenant Ronald Holmes of the 49th (South Saskatchewan) Infantry Battalion as "a sight for the gods."[59] The German defenders were probably equally inspired, but for different reasons: they were fighting for survival.

The shattered ground, the stubborn resistance of German machine gunners, and the devastating effects of what little German artillery was left wreaked havoc on the mounted horsemen. As thrilling as cavalry charges may have appeared, they spelled almost certain death for those who attempted them against the more modern yet less romantic methods of carnage manned by desperate troops. The experience of a Royal Canadian Dragoon officer near Beaucourt Wood on 8 August 1918 is typical of what awaited many of his fellow cavalrymen:

Pennons fluttering, the regiment rode into a regular storm of fire.... The squadron was riding hell bent for election...swords drawn and yelling like mad. We were losing heavily on that ride...and the gunners had a field day for 130 odd men and horses are a great temptation...only about 50 all ranks survived -- almost every horse was killed.[60]

All that remained for the now dismounted cavalry was to hang bravely onto the ground they had been thrown onto, and await the infantry to arrive and save them, a role reversal that would surely have made a mockery of any Hollywood cowboy-indians movie.

Coming to the cavalry's rescue, at least on the right-hand flank of the Corps, was the Fourth Canadian Division, commanded by Major General C. D. Watson. This formation passed through the Third Canadian Division at about noon on 8 August, and had recieved orders to clear to the Blue dotted line in the southern sector. Unfortunately, the German artillery and machine gunners had survived in better condition in this area, and were therefore better prepared to repulse the tank-infantry onslaught that had been planned. An experiment with the new Mark V* tank, which, in addition to its guns, could carry a section of infantry internally, failed when half of the infantry detachments were forced to dismount before reaching the battle area due to heat exhaustion and asphyxiation caused by engine fumes.[61] Half the remainder of these pioneering armoured personnel carriers were knocked out by a single German field battery that had been well hidden, thereby escaping McNaughton's "steel rain." Eleven of the original 37 Mark V*'s reached their objective, but were forced to pick up their infantry and retire due to fierce German fire coming from Le Quesnel. The flat terrain in front of Le Quesnel provided excellent fields of fire for German machine gunners, and repeated attempts by numerous battalions failed to take the position.

Wisely, General Watson dug in and planned an attack for the next morning. By nightfall, the small pocket around Le Quesnel was the only objective the Canadian Corps had failed to take.[62]

Brutinel's Independent Force had demonstrated remarkable success at securing the Corps' right-hand flank with the French. Though not used in an exploitation role like the cavalry forces, the armored cars and truck-mounted machine guns had proven adept at working around to the flank of lightly defended positions, and forcing some of the less stubborn German pockets to retire. Brutinel's real success lay not in the ground he took, but in his ability to cooperate with the French 31st Corps, helping them to keep pace with the momentous advance of the two Dominion corps to the north, and thereby ensuring that the Canadian Corps' flank was protected. If Brutinel's achievements went largely unnoticed inside the Canadian Corps, they certainly were not overlooked by the French. The commanders of the two northernmost French divisions had high praise for Brutinel's force, referring to it as "elite" troops. Included in their letters of appreciation to Brutinel were 16 *Croix de Guerre* to be awarded to members of the Independent Force for their distinguished combat at Amiens.[63] Currie's and Brutinel's innovative experiment at "motorized" warfare had been a success.

The effect of the Fourth Army's combined arms attack on the opposing German forces was utterly devastating. In the Canadian sector, the German lines were hammered back as much as eight miles, and the forward German divisions had been completely annihilated. Heinz Guderian, Germany's famed "father of Blitzkrieg," described the battle from a German perspective:

The Canadian Corps, which also had a reputation for aggressiveness, was on the attack to the south of the Australians.... Canadian 1st Division was...led by a battalion of tanks, and it hit 117th Jager Division. This was an excellent formation which was fully up to combat strength, and it had a fine leader in Major General Hoefer. All the same, two of the infantry regimental commanders of the division were taken prisoner, and the third died a hero's death.... Every attempt at resistance was broken by the way the Canadians mounted a turning movement to the north, and only when the Canadians halted...were the Germans able to form a new front.[64]

Official German figures give the total losses for the one day, 8 August, at nearly 30,000, two-thirds of which were prisoners. The Canadian Corps alone accounted for having taken over 5,000 prisoners, and 161 guns.[65] While the material losses were significant for a German Army already overburdened with supply problems, the mental effect of 8 August was catastrophic; the attack administered the *coup de grace* to an already eroding German army morale. Troops in the front lines who had been told by the High Command that the sounds of tanks moving to their front were merely "figments of their nervous imagination," awoke that morning to find those "figments" grinding through their shattered defense.[66]

The mental paralysis that comes with such complete surprise was transmitted upward to the highest levels of the German Army. General Erich Ludendorff was later to write: "August 8 was the black day [*der Schwarze Tag*] of the German Army in the history of this war.... Everything I had feared...had here, in one place become a reality."[67] When Ludendorff informed Kaiser Wilhelm of this disaster, the Kaiser became sick with depression, and could only interject, "the war must be terminated." The blow had been dealt not just to the body of the German Army, but to its very nervous system; as the Fourth Army historian puts it, "the Germans were swept off their feet, and never really recovered from the overwhelming nature of the disaster."[68]

By being able to mount such a overwhelming attack in such a unexpected sector, Rawlinson and the Fourth Army had clearly achieved operational and tactical surprise. Operationally, the Germans had expected the offensive to come in the area of Flanders, as they had been completely deceived by Rawlinson's and Currie's masterful deception plan. German prisoners expressed disbelief when they saw the Canadians; one skeptical German prisoner declared, "the Canadians are in Belgium!"[69] Tactically, the Germans were unprepared for the timing of the attack, and for the tanks that gave the assault its extra impetus. German generals were captured at their breakfast tables, and confused troops were happy to surrender so as to avoid being crushed by the tanks or shot by the steadily advancing infantry.[70] Surprise turned to panic, and so insured the rout that the German official history refers to as *Die Katastrophe des 8. August 1918*.[71]

Yet it seemed that the German Army was not the only one surprised by the relatively stunning success of operations on 8 August. Both Currie and Monash were given the impression that Haig and General Headquarters were almost as equally unprepared as their foe for the rapid advance of the Canadians and Australians. Now the confusion over the "limited" versus "unlimited" nature of the attack's objective began to play itself out. In reality, Haig had already directed Rawlinson to push on to the line Chaulnes-Roye, but confirmation of these orders to the corps commanders was not passed to Currie until late the night of 8 August.[72]

According to Rawlinson's earlier instructions, Currie had expected to receive under command the 32nd British Division to help him continue the advance on 9 August.[73] This intention was first formally communicated to Currie in orders from the First Army dated 31 July 1918, and was reconfirmed at Rawlinson's coordination conference on 5 August. Based on this information, Currie outlined his plan for operations on 9 August in "L.C. Instruction Number 6," entitled "Policy After Reaching Objectives." Currie's outline plan called for a renewed assault on 9 August with three divisions forward and two in depth. The 32nd British Division was supposed to be the right forward assault division, relieving the Fourth Canadian Division, with the Third Canadian Division in the center, and the First or Second Canadian Division, depending on which one was in the best condition to continue, on the left flank.[74] At 9:55 p.m., 8 August, however, the Canadian Corps was informed that although it would continue the attack the next day as anticipated, it would not receive the 32nd Division under command.

This dilatory arrival of counterorders put Currie in a difficult position, for Rawlinson had made amendments to the original plan which now affected both the Canadian Corps strength and the projected starting time for operations on 9 August. To add to the problem, Corps HQ was in the process of moving so as to maintain contact with its now far forward divisions, and therefore confirmation that the new orders had reached the Divisional HQs was not obtained until 3:00 a.m. 9 August. What was now to happen was that the advance would continue with the Fourth

Division finishing its assault on the German holdouts in Le Quesnel, the First Division in the center, and the Second Division on the left flank, attacking in conjunction with the Australian Corps.[75]

Compounding these difficulties were the rudimentary and sometimes unreliable means of communications. Orders had to be drafted, coordination effected, plans amended, and orders passed, all on tenuous wireless communications, or miles of highly vulnerable wire strung for field telephone links, or along roads choked with guns, troops and prisoners. Despite the Canadian Corps' larger signals organization, the depth and speed of the advance caused a communications breakdown both inside the Corps and at Fourth Army HQ. Despite repeated attempts to call them off, 2nd CIB reported to First Division HQ that friendly planes "have been bombing and machine gunning our troops in [the] final objective all night...also guns of all calibres have been constantly firing short...serious casualties caused."

First Division HQ had repeatedly asked for the Corps signals organization to help run line to the forward Divisions, because, "personnel 1st Cdn. Div. Signals [are] not sufficient to maintain communication from...forward to adv[ance] HQ and Bdes [Brigades]."[76] Dispatch riders seemed the surest way of getting a message through, but the distance and unfamiliarity of the countryside made this method ponderous, often taking as much as three hours to deliver a message to another formation only a few kilometers away. It seemed that the Canadian Corps signals capabilities had failed their first test in conditions of "open warfare."[77]

The Canadian divisions received their new orders between 10 p.m. and 3 a.m. the night of 8-9 August.* These formations then had to make plans and co-ordinate efforts for what Currie had hoped would be an early morning, if not "first light" assault, agreeing originally to a zero hour of 5 a.m. The Canadian formations, therefore, had on average less than seven hours to complete "battle procedure" for at least brigade-size advances.** Upon receipt of the Corps' orders, the divisions subsequently had to produce orders and coordinate the efforts of their brigades, brigades had to issue orders and coordinate the efforts of their units, and so forth on down to the lowest level, the individual rifleman in an infantry section, or a single gun in an artillery battery. This task would have proven a daunting challenge even when communications were working well, let alone when the units were busy with consolidating from the longest and fastest advance they had ever achieved.

Currie's hope for a smooth transition into "open warfare" on day two of the Amiens offensive proved overly optimistic. The last-minute changes created coordination problems for all the elements of the Fourth Army, complicated by Fourth

---

* The "24-hour" clock method now widely adopted by militaries was not yet in universal use by the Canadian Corps, and therefore the times recorded in the original documents are in "a.m./p.m."; for accuracy's sake, the timings, as recorded, will be used.

** "Battle procedure," is the process by which a commander receives orders, prepares a plan, gives orders to subordinates, and effects preparations in order to undertake an operation. In short it encompasses all the activities necessary for the immediate preparation of a unit or formation for battle.

Army HQ's unusual abdication of the role of overall coordinator.[78] At 5 a.m., the tentative zero hour for 9 August, the Second Division wired in the following message to Corps HQ, showing that all was not well at the front: "Your [Canadian Corps HQ] G15 [operations order for 9 August] received [at] 2.5 [?] A.M. Are the Australians advancing on our left? Reply urgently requested please."[79]

The breakdown in communications caused Burstall's Second Division, whose 6th CIB was to lead off the attack, to be late. Yet everyone was suffering from seemingly identical problems in command, control, and communications, or what is today termed C3, and therefore no formation was ready to push off at the original zero hour. Frustrated, Currie was forced to amend zero hour to 10 a.m., 9 August -- broad daylight.[80] Even this long delay failed to finally surmount the confusion. Brigadier General J.M. Ross, commander of 5th CIB in the Second Division, claimed that on the morning of 9 August he received *four* different zero hours: 5:00 a.m., 10:00 a.m., 11:00 a.m., and 1:00 p.m. Regardless of which zero hour was correct, Ross had to jump off early because his flanking unit, 6th CIB, began its attack at 11:00 a.m. without any flank support.[81] The commander of 6th CIB, Brigadier General A. Bell, was operating under the assumption that zero hour had remained at 11:00 a.m. His report read:

Despite the postponement of ZERO hour, neither the 5th CIB nor the 15th AIB [Australian Infantry Battalion] were able to synchronize their advance and the Bde [6th CIB] attacked with both flanks in the air, under intense M.G. fire, entirely unsupported by tanks...and only by a very sketchy shrapnel barrage.[82]

With the lead battalions of 6th CIB suffering heavy losses, its flanking formations were rushed into action. 15th AIB was finally able to commence its advance at around noon, 9 August, and the First Division attacks began to ease the pressure on 6th CIB at around 2:00 p.m. Vicious fighting, mostly against machine gun outposts hastily established by the Germans during the previous night, finally left the Second Division in control of the fortified village of Meharicourt, and the First Division in possession of Rouvroy-en-Santerre. Yet this success, though dearly bought, would not end the suffering of the Second Division, especially 6th CIB.[83]

On the right flank of the Canadian Corps, the Fourth Canadian Division had successfully taken Le Quesnel, allowing the Third Canadian Division to push toward Roye. Here, too, the Germans had hammered in reinforcements, especially machine gunners. The 31st French Corps, on the Canadian Corps right-hand flank, was having an extremely difficult time with a heavily defended sugar beet factory on the outskirts of Arvillers. This held the advance up some time before elements of Brutinel's Brigade, crossing army boundaries, outflanked the position and took Arvillers from the north. By 5:00 p.m., the Third Division had taken Bouchior, and all three of the Canadian Corps' lead divisions -- the Third, First, and Second -- were now within sight of the old 1916 British defensive positions on the Somme.[84]

The Corps War Diary described the events of 9 August thusly: "Heavy fighting occurred during the day, but in spite of stubborn opposition and very difficult ground, our line was advanced approximately 2,500 yards.... Tank casualties were heavy from concealed anti-tank guns in the vicinity of LE QUESNEL."[85] This statement obviously misses the true nature of the problems encountered. Clearly, the Fourth Army attacks on 9 August were poorly coordinated and disjointed, lacking the impetus and surprise that had made the previous day's assault so effective. It was, in the words of the Australian official history, "a classic example of how *not* to follow up a great attack."[86] This was not, however, Currie's fault; he had made a contingency plan for continuing the advance, only to be thwarted by the vacillation of Fourth Army HQ when they unexpectedly countermanded the order that would have allowed Currie to use the fresh 32nd British Division. Last-minute counterorders, coupled with the unexpected and almost insurmountable C3 problems experienced at virtually every level, made a concerted effort similar to that of the previous day impossible. There simply had not been enough time allocated for proper battle procedure to be carried out at every level of the chain of command and, therefore, units were thrust into battle without proper preparations and with only ragged fire support. On top of all the command and control problems faced by the friendly forces, the Germans had managed to recover their composure, and had rushed in at least six divisions, with more coming.[87] Stubborn fighting against stiffening German resistance allowed the Canadians to take approximately three more miles of territory on 9 August, but it was becoming obvious not just to Currie, but also to his subordinates, that the attack was waning.[88]

By nightfall of 9 August, the fighting troops of the Canadian Corps were exhausted. The formation found itself facing the old Somme defensive works that it had once occupied, and would now have to clear. Currie planned to free these fortifications on 10 August, and then use them as the backbone upon which the Corps could consolidate, reorganize, and prepare for the inevitable German counterattack. At 7:30 p.m., 9 August, Fourth Army HQ finally placed the 32nd British Division at the disposal of the Canadian Corps, precisely one full day later than expected. Although Currie now had a fresh batch of troops, his tank forces were almost completely depleted, with his four tank battalions down to less than one-quarter of their original strength.[89] Nonetheless, pressure from Foch and Haig to continue the attacks mounted on both Rawlinson and Currie, and limited operations were planned for 10 August.[90]

Ominously, the confusion created by the communications breakdown had not yet righted itself. On the night of 9-10 August, the unfortunate Second Division was told to expect a dawn attack through its lines by the Fourth Division. When, by 7:30 a.m., this attack had failed to materialize, the 6th CIB from Second Division was once more forced to advance on short notice and with little support in order to cover the flank of the First Australian Division.[91] The Fourth Division's attack had been halted by the belated arrival of its tanks, but it was finally put in successfully. The Third Division was likewise successful in its attack on Le Quesnoy. The fresh troops of the 32nd Division managed to storm La Cambuse and the heavily contested Square Wood; however, they failed in their bid to take Parvillers and Damery. Here, the infantry had been left behind by their artillery barrage, and, afflicted brutally by the German machine gunners, suffered 1,500 casualties in a matter of minutes.[92] Currie, chastized by the quickly increasing casualty rates, had had enough.

To paraphrase the great poet T. S. Eliot, the battle of Amiens had ended "not with a bang, but a whimper." By nightfall of 10 August the advance had stalled. Currie and Rawlinson agreed not to press the offensive further if it entailed heavy losses. Neither Currie, Rawlinson, nor Monash could see the sense in continuing to grind forward in the face of increasing German resistance. In Andrew McNaughton's words, "it was obvious that the momentum had gone out of the attack...because we were trying to continue without the wherewithal to do so."[93] Currie had seen this happen before, at the Scarpe in May 1917, and at Hill 70 in August 1917. He knew that without thorough preparation, attacks on the days after 8 August would gain little and cost heavily. The increasing entropy of the Allied attacks was matched by the inevitable mass of defenders that the Germans could always, through the use of railways, hammer into the threatened sector in a matter of only 24-48 hours. The deadly law of diminishing returns then took effect, creating a stasis that could be termed the "three-day limit," because by the end of the third day of almost any operation, the attackers' increasing entropy had reached the same level as the defenders' incoming energy, thereby bringing a state of equilibrium to the battlefield.

Currie now played his part at the *operational* level of war. Despite the reality of increasing tactical friction, Foch was urging Haig to push on with the attack at Amiens. Both Haig and Rawlinson were vacillating on whether or not the attacks could continue, and were contemplating another full-scale operation for 11-12 August had it not been for Currie, who presented an alternate plan to Rawlinson. Using air photos and intelligence reports indicating that continued attacks around Amiens might work to snatch defeat from the jaws of victory, Currie persuaded Rawlinson to reject Haig's demand for a continued offensive around Amiens. Instead, Currie recommended that the Canadians be pulled out of the line at Amiens, and transported back northward to undertake yet another surprise attack in the area of Monchy.

Bolstered by Currie's firm opposition and lucid presentation, Rawlinson himself presented the alternate plan to Haig. Impressed by the excellent solution handed to him, and daunted by the unhappy prospect of increasing casualties, Haig became adamant in his opposition to Foch's urgings for the continuation of the assault at Amiens. He forwarded Currie's proposal to Foch, with this blunt reminder: "I am responsible to my government and fellow citizens for the handling of British Forces." Foch wisely acquiesced, and Currie's plan was accepted. As Tim Travers has pointed out, "thus the sequence of events in breaking off the Amiens offensive was from Currie to Rawlinson to Haig to Foch, showing that, as in 1916 and 1917, the further the commander was from the battlefield, the less grasp he had of reality."[94] Currie's role in defining and recommending an alternate operation to Rawlinson and Haig had an effect on the operations of the entire Western Front, and was out of all proportion to what other Corps commanders could achieve.[95]

On 11 August, Canadian Corps HQ issued the following order: "[Due to] enemy...increasing defensive strength...the Corps Commander has directed that the line gained yesterday is to be consolidated unless an advance can be made without *opposition or loss*."[96] The battle of Amiens, the BEF's most decisive battle of the Great War, had staggered to a close.[97]

Haig's blunt assertion to Foch of his responsibility no doubt reflected the stress he was under from Prime Minister David Lloyd-George and others back in

Britain not to squander Britain's manpower without decisive results. Intense public and political pressure was certainly on Haig, as it was on all of the Allied generals, to conserve manpower and to achieve results *cheaply*. Currie's recommendation to change the tactical thrust of BEF operations provided an excellent solution to Haig's problem for two important reasons. First, Canadian divisions would bear the brunt of the offensive operations, and therefore the brunt of the casualties. This was crucial because the Canadian Corps drew manpower from Canada and not from Britain, therefore its losses would not create the political turmoil for Haig that deaths from British divisions would. Second, and most important, the Canadian Corps was better prepared than any other Allied formation, save perhaps for the Australians, to undertake the gruelling offensive tasks awaiting Allied forces in France and Belgium because it had a greater number of men and resources at its disposal.

For Haig, the Canadian Corps was an ideal *tactical* tool with which to pursue *operational* plans without jeopradizing personal *political* considerations. It was a case of the right men being in the right place at the right time, and Haig, deliberately or not, took advantage of this propitious situation. It may rightly be said that the Canadian Corps was once again coming to the rescue of Haig's reputation.

AFTERMATH AND LESSONS LEARNED

Historian and armored warfare theorist Lieutenant Colonel J.F.C. Fuller had special insight into the battle of Amiens, having actually taken part in its planning and execution. Fuller claimed that Amiens was the first example of not just the efficacy of the tank, but the precursor of modern armored warfare. In particular, Fuller stressed the shock effect tanks had upon the enemy infantry, claiming that "the continuous forward movement of tanks created a feeling of irresistible power." Fuller also maintained that the victory of 8 August could have been even more complete had not the Royal Tank Corps' light Whippet tanks been burdened by operating with the ponderous and highly vulnerable cavalry. Fuller concluded that the tank's chief contribution in the Amiens battle was not its "killing power," but "the terror it instilled...without the tank, there would have been no surprise commensurate with the one achieved on the morning of the 8th, and it was the suddenness of the attack which detonated the panic."[98]

Testimony from the officers of the Canadian Corps would seem to support Fuller's contentions as to the efficacy of the tanks on the "Black Day." Major R.L.H. Ewing, CO of the 42nd Canadian Infantry Battalion, reported: "I cannot speak too highly of the work of the tanks. They never ceased patrolling the front, and whenever any resistance was encountered, they immediately came to our aid. They were largely responsible for the success of our operations."[99]

The 7th CIB report on Amiens echoed this sentiment, claiming that "the moral effect of the [t]anks, both upon the enemy and our own men justified their use in itself."[100] Brigadier General William Griesbach, GOC of the 1st CIB, also heartily endorsed the tanks, stating, "the tank is the answer to the Machine Gun."[101] Apart from the technological solution the tank provided to overcome the tactical dilemma of the direct firepower of German machine guns, it also provided a logistical solution for resupply at the unit level. The 7th CIB report concluded that "the two supply tanks allotted this Brigade were of the utmost use and solved the problem of supply for attacking troops";[102] in essence, they replaced infantry carrying parties as the units second line supply vehicles. Technology, in the form of tanks, had brought important changes to the battlefield on 8 August.

If the tank arm at Amiens sounded a clarion of things to come, then the cavalry's achievements sounded the last call for things that should have passed. Fuller's contempt for the use of cavalry at Amiens is easily borne out by the experience of the Canadian Corps. At the very least, the cavalry were largely ineffective; at their very worst, they were a serious impediment to operational effectiveness, taking and creating friendly casualties in a pathetic attempt to fulfil the atavistic hopes and beliefs of old cavalry officers, including Field Marshal Haig. Greisbach, Commander of the 1st CIB, bitterly criticized the cavalry action in his area:

A great many cavalry moved in the area [of 1st CIB]... There was no liaison between the cavalry and infantry, and I was unable to learn what they were doing or trying to do.... Cavalry galloping about...did destroy a great quantity of field telephone cable which had been laid at great trouble and risk[,] which seriously interfered with communications.

In fact, the same cavalry force Griesbach complained about entered Fresnoy-en-Chausse, captured 120 German prisoners, and then emerged from the village only to be mowed down, prisoners and all, by German machine gun fire.[103] If anything, the harrowing experience suffered by most of the cavalry confirmed in even the staunchest horseman's mind that the modern battlefield was a place fit for neither man nor beast unless they could take advantage of protection offered by terrain, superior firepower, or armor.[104]

Griesbach's comments on the battle of Amiens are revealing, for they show that while 8 August could be considered a great success, the days afterward pointed to some as yet unresolved problems. While the Mark V had proven a great success on 8 August, the relatively fragile nature of nascent tank technology could not guarantee battlefield superiority indefinitely. Griesbach's report continued:

It [the tank] is as yet mechanically imperfect, and the tactical handling of the tank is in the course of evolution.... As to the tactical handling of tanks, I am persuaded that we cannot sit down and allow the Tank people to dictate the tactical use of the Tank, except insofar as its mechanical capabilities are concerned.... [At] Parvillers, tank after tank went up against an impossible situation and [was] lost to the use of the attacking infantry. This was magnificent, but it was not war.[105]

Griesbach's comments lend credence to the arguments of other historians, such as Tim Travers and C. P. Stacey, who have claimed that the tanks were a "necessary, but not sufficient factor" in the victory at Amiens.[106] There had been many other ingredients as well, and to attribute the panic of the Germans solely to the tanks is to greatly oversimplify the complexity of the battle. First, not every German soldier ran before the tanks; as already seen, the tanks proved quite vulnerable to German artillerymen, who easily put nearly one-third of the tank force at Amiens out of action with their guns.[107]   Second, the presence of tanks was not the sole factor in the achievement of surprise on 8 August; the deception plan obviously had much more to do with this than the tanks.   The outstanding artillery support and near-perfect counterbattery fire plan also merit some mention.   Moreover, Allied Air Forces ruled the sky over the battlefield, mustering some 1,904 Allied aircraft over the front compared to 369 German.[108] Lastly, despite heavy attrition, there were still 145 tanks ready for the morning of 9 August, yet neither the Canadian nor the Australian Corps could effect another breakthrough of the dimensions that had occurred the previous day.   The German troops could not have become immune to the shock effect of armor overnight, so tanks alone cannot account for the rout of 8 August.

In direct contrast to Fuller's thesis, other historians have credited the breakthrough at Amiens to the common soldier, the infantryman.   Nicholson wrote that "far from constituting a 'massed tank' attack -- such a use of armour had not been planned -- the operation owed its success primarily to the work of the infantry and the machine-gunners, valuably supported by the artillery."[109]   Griesbach's comments support Nicholson's claim: "The Lewis gun...is the weapon par excellence and we may attribute our successes to it and to the men who handle it.   I am of the opinion that the Lewis gunners of this Brigade are more than a match for the best German Gunners."[110] Tim Travers echoed this sentiment: "The advance on 8 August of some 8 miles on the Canadian Corps front, although a dazzling success due to the 'elan' of the Canadian infantry, obscured the fact that neither the Canadian Corps nor the BEF generally had yet mastered the art of combined arms mobile warfare."[111]

Even if the Canadians had *not* mastered "combined arms" warfare, Currie and the Canadian Corps had, nevertheless, certainly displayed that they had become experts at what Travers refers to as the "traditional Infantry-Artillery" attack.[112] The high state of training and experience found in all levels of the Canadian Corps provided Currie with a potent, highly efficient, offensive weapon when properly used. Yet other equally good formations had been ground up in offensive operations in the past: what was the crucial element to the success of the Canadian and Australian Corps at Amiens on "the Black Day."

What did account for *die Katasrophe des 8. August 1918* was the *synergistic* effect of the many factors already discussed: surprise, new tactics, excellent artillery support, air superiority, superior morale, and tank support. Isolated, these factors are all *necessary*, but not sufficient to explain the Canadian Corps' and Fourth Army's success. The critical factor, the catalyst for the reaction that created conditions necessary for the breakthrough, was *coordination*. In this respect, the various levels of staffs, those invisible minions so often overlooked by military historians because of the dull nature of their tasks, must be given a good deal of the credit. Only through careful, detailed coordination and orders could all these advantages have been made to work so effectively. By synchronizing the effects of his "instruments," Currie, and likewise Monash of the Australian Corps, had become a master conductor, orchestrating a symphony of destruction on the bewildered Germans. When that detailed coordination broke down, such as on the morning of 9 August, the rhythm left the orchestra and the advance ground slowly to a halt.

THE NEXT STEP

While the higher commanders groped to find some way to follow up the success of the Amiens operation, the fighting troops of the Canadian Corps were engaged in the nasty business of consolidating their gains, and in securing their front from repeated and desperate German counterattacks. The days from 11-16 August saw the enemy counterattacks, "repulsed with sanguinary losses," while at night Canadian Corps units patrolled vigorosly in order to "peacefully penetrate" small pieces of vital ground, and to keep the Germans off balance.[113] More important, the respite from attack gave commanders at all levels an opportunity to critique their success and reflect on the lessons learned from the heady advance of 8-10 August in a more sober light.

As already seen, even the most seasoned units and formations had experienced difficulties, but one of the marks of the professionalization of the Canadian Army was a continuing effort to learn from its ordeals. In the German Army, this process of feedback and analysis was rigidly institutionalized as a function of the General Staff.[114] The Canadian Corps approach was less formal but no less effective. As with most formations in the BEF, it was standard procedure to produce reports on operations, including a section on "lessons learned." These reports were passed upward, with each level of staff and command having the opportunity to review the reports, integrate the comments, and add their own observations. These reports then helped to clarify and accentuate the operational and tactical predicaments encountered by the Corps, and allowed staffs to make changes in order to rectify these problems, or at least anticipate and minimize them in the future.

As a corps commander, Currie was highly receptive of criticism and suggestions, and open to new and innovative ideas, provided they were practical. Practicality, above all else, might best describe the Canadian Corps' approach to war. This semiformal feedback cycle helped to produce a steep learning curve in the Canadian Corps, a curve that Ian Brown has argued was steeper than most of its counterparts in the BEF, and even steeper than the vaunted German General Staff's.[115] Whether it was steeper or not remains a controversy; what is crucial to note is that the Canadian Corps had learned *how to learn* from their experiences during war, and now turned to examine their experiences at Amiens.

As with any organization, there were a few individuals who appeared to stand out in the effort to improve the Corps operational doctrine. One of the most prolific was the aforementioned Brigadier General W. Griesbach, commander of the 1st CIB. In his report dated 24 August 1918, Griesbach speculated that the Amiens battle, and future set-piece battles like it, could be broken down into *three* distinct but sometimes overlapping phases. The first phase was a "trench to trench attack...carried out under and to the limit of the Field Gun Barrage." The second phase was the "attack between the limit of the Field Gun Barrage and the limit of the Heavy Howitzers." The third and final phase was characterized only as "open warfare," where "there is no [planned] bombardment of any kind, and only such artillery assistance as can be secured."

The operation of 8 August had seen all three of these phases, whereas the attacks on 9-11 August were predominantly "open warfare" operations. Infantry formations and tactics could remain roughly the same for all three phases; the crucial difference lay, therefore, in the allocation and command of artillery, and its availability. Thus, Griesbach's conception of large-scale offensive operations reinforced the already prevalent heavy reliance upon the firepower of the artillery. His recommendations for the use of tanks in future attacks reflected the bitter lessons learned from the fighting around Amiens. During the first phase, tanks would necessarily lead the infantry as part of the "break-in" force, but during the second and third phases, the vulnerable tanks would follow the infantry, ready to deal with stubborn machine gun positions as necessary, but avoiding the trap of antitank guns at all costs. Griesbach also recommended that "in future attacks of this sort one gun or a section of guns be attached to each Battalion under an officer...and that an attempt be made to secure direct [artillery] fire upon enemy positions." In short, Griesbach was calling for increased mobile firepower to follow close on the heels of the infantry in order to effectively deal with the persistent threat of protected machine gun positions.[116]

While Griesbach was calling for a dispersion of lighter artillery resources during some stages of an attack, another powerful mind in the Canadian Corps was arguing for the consolidation of the longer range "heavies." McNaughton, coming forward during the morning of 8 August, had found that some of the heavy artillery resources that had been allocated under the command of divisions were sitting idle for lack of targets, when they could have been used by the CBSO for the destruction of retreating German forces. This inefficient use of artillery so enraged McNaughton that he "vowed then that never again would I not have guns under command, at all phases of an attack, that I could use."[117]

Griesbach's most telling comments, however, reflected the reality that the Canadian Corps' greatest difficulty lay not in finding the physical resources -- weapons, men, and firepower -- necessary to defeat their German adversary, but rather the intellectual dexterity to deal with the new conditions of longer term, deeper objective sustained attacks, and the command and control problems these engendered. While Griesbach stated that "it may be observed that as a first experience in open warfare, principles laid down in the training manuals are sound"[118] the application of these principles to real tactical problems often left much to be desired; hence, Griesbach's assertion:

All officers, and particularly young officers, must be required to forget many of the rules of trench warfare and rapidly master the principles of open warfare and thoroughly understand the different conditions which surround these two forms of warfare. In trenches, everything is cut and dried. In open warfare, everything is wide open, and anything may happen. Officers not trained in open warfare are often at sea [i.e lost]. They ask for a barrage, worry unduly about their flanks and think in terms of the continuous line. Officers cannot do better than study the manuals. They must think, read, and talk about open warfare. The men are all right, it is the officers who need the training. [119]

Griesbach's commentary points to the fact that those responsible for making tactical decisions in the Canadian Corps had recognized, but had not yet adapted to the dispersed, isolated, and fragmented style of warfare created by sustained, combined arms operations in a high-intensity environment. The lack of "order" to the battlefield was seemingly part and parcel of the breakdown of C3 caused by inadequate communications systems and coordination procedures. In all fairness, it would have been very difficult for leaders inside the Canadian Corps to anticipate these problems because of the speed of the tactical and technological revolution that was coming to the Western Front. In effect, the combined arms operations of 1917-18, culminating with the battle of Amiens, represented a very real break with past warfare. Until this point, a commander's efforts had been to neatly organize the battlefield in order to minimize the "friction" of war, and thereby maximize any given force's effectiveness.

By 1918, technology, in the form of advanced artillery procedures and munitions, the tank, and the aircraft, had created a situation of tactical advantage that the attacker was powerless to use to complete effect because the C3 doctrine and resources necessary were lacking. In short, what the Canadian Corps was faced with was not the problem of how to overcome the German defense -- they had already found that operational solution in 1917 -- rather, it was the problem of how to deal with and maintain their success. Thus, it was the dilemma of success engendering confusion that faced Currie and his Corps during the days of mid-August as they hurriedly prepared for their next engagement.

Currie summed up the Corps' impressive achievements at Amiens in stark numerical terms:

> Between August 8th and 22nd the Canadian Corps fought against 15 German Divisions: of these 10 were directly engaged and thoroughly defeated.... In the same period the Canadian Corps captured 9,131 prisoners, 191 guns of all calibres, and more than 1,000 machine guns and trench mortars. The greatest depth penetrated approximated to 14 miles, and an area of over 67 square miles containing 27 towns and villages had been liberated.[120]

What Currie did not report, and perhaps could not, at least not accurately, was the unquantifiable damaging psychological effect the Amiens operations had on the Germans. Yet the German Army was too highly trained, experienced, and organized to collapse from this single blow. Almost as if by an unconscious, instinctive reaction, the Germans responded by reinforcing their lines, plugging the gaps, and stabilizing the front, fighting what Currie characterized as a "stubborn rearguard action."[121] The German Army had been bent, but it remained unbroken.

The Corps' success at Amiens had come relatively cheaply in terms of casualties, yet it had been by no means free or bloodless. The Canadian Corps had sustained nearly 12,000 casualties during operations from 8 to 20 August 1918. A large part of these (nearly 4,000) had been inflicted on the "Black Day," 8 August. In comparative terms this meant that the advance the first day of the battle of Amiens had cost only 500 casualties per mile of advance -- slight in comparison to other Great War battles. The victory at Vimy Ridge, for instance, was bought at a price of about 3,300 casualties per mile of advance.[122] More than 5,000 more casualties were sustained in the next three days of fighting, 9-11 August, which yielded roughly another five miles of advance, or nearly double the casualties per mile of advance: 1,000 per mile. Thus, despite breaking through the main part of the German defense, and facing only hastily prepared defensive positions, the Corps' casualty rate per mile of advance doubled when moving from the carefully planned set-piece style of 8

August to the less well coordinated open warfare phase of the operation on 9-10 August. Nevertheless, Currie's assessment reflected the feelings of many of his peers: "considering the number of German Divisions engaged, and the results achieved, the casualties were very light."[123]

The battle of Amiens would be the first and last truly combined arms battle of the Great War. Tactical and technological innovations -- advanced artillery munitions and techniques, the use of various kinds of tanks, the use of aircraft in a ground attack and battlefield interdiction role, and the logistical "massing of forces" -- that began in 1916-17 found their culmination on the battlefield of Amiens. After this, and perhaps because of both the success and the loss rate of the tanks at Amiens, GHQ would allocate tanks out to Army formations in small "penny" packets for the remainder of the war, making another Army-level "mechanized," combined arms attack an impossibility.[124] But the lessons learned, and the experience gained at Amiens would not be lost for the balance of the conflict on the Canadian Corps. Although Currie would have to resort to a predominantly "traditional style" infantry-artillery attack for the rest of the 100 Days, many of the innovative ideas, including the use of tanks when available, the need for central control of heavy artillery in order to fight the "deep" battle, the importance of logistical routes and infrastructure, and the ad hoc grouping of a motorized Independent Brigade, remained as part of the largely unwritten attack doctrine of the Canadian Corps. More important, the Amiens operations had acted not only as a harbinger of what was to come in the future, but even hinted at the problems and advantages of modern "mechanized" warfare theory.[125]

The Canadian experience at Amiens is an excellent example of the effect of *synergy* on the battlefield, and what can happen when that synergy is lost. The Fourth Army's success on 8 August was due to more than just the presence of tanks; it was the result of careful planning and preparation, an imaginative and well-executed deception plan, close coordination of all arms by staffs at every level, and execution of that plan by a highly trained, innovative, and seasoned professional force. The problems encountered during operations on 9-10 August pointed to the need for proper battle procedure to take place in order to create the orchestration of weapons and tactical effects that begot synergy. Finally, the problems of the Canadian Corps on the days subsequent to 8 August pointed to the problems of C3 in high-intensity, sustained operations where communications and coordination methods remained primitive. These were problems that remained to be solved by Currie and his subordinates in the days that followed the battle of Amiens.

For historians, Amiens remains the best example of the BEF's tactical and technological superiority over the German Army by mid to late 1918. More significantly, the decisive victory at Amiens let Foch and Haig, as well as both the German and Allied political leadership, know that the war could in fact be won (or lost) in 1918, rather than 1919, as they had all expected. What this decision waited on was for the Allies to find the tools and doctrine necessary to keep pushing the German Army to collapse. The Australian and Canadian Corps had lived up to the reputations they had earned during 1917 as elite formations. Like other formations identified as "elite," their effectiveness would force them to bear more of the brunt of the assaults as the war closed.

Finally, the role played by Currie in the termination of the Amiens attack was indicative of the important position that the Canadian Corps held in the BEF. Currie, although nomininally only a corps commander, had the ability to influence theater-wide strategy, just as the success or failure of the Canadian Corps could influence the outcome of Allied military operations on the Western Front. As the curtain closed on the battle of Amiens, Currie now took his Corps, and its influence, north to rejoin the First Army under General Horne, for an attempt to break the "hinge" of Germany's strongest defense -- the Drocourt-Queant Line.

NOTES

1. J.F.C. Fuller, *The Decisive Battles of the Western World, Volume 3* (London: Eyre and Spottiswoode, 1956) pp. 276-299.

2. The best overall British account of Amiens is probably Edmonds, *BOH*, Vol. 4, pp. 1-177; another good general account is Gregory Blaxland, *Amiens: 1918* (London: Frederick Muller, 1968). For the Fourth Army's account, see Maj. Gen. Sir Archibald Montgomery, *The Story of the Fourth Army in the Battles of the 100 Days*, pp. 1-52. The Australian account is masterfully done by Bean, *AOH*, Vol. 6, pp. 463-713. The German side is told in their official history monograph entitled *Schlachten des Weltkreigs, Band 36: Die Katastrophe des 8. August 1918* (Berlin: Oldenberg, 1930); other good but shorter accounts are included in Terraine, *To Win a War*, pp. 103-123, and Fuller, *Decisive Battles*, pp. 276-299.

3. This is quoted from a directive issued 2 August from Ludendorff's HQ in Avesnes, in Parkinson, *Tormented Warrior*, p. 170.

4. See Gen. Erich Ludendorff, *My War Memories* (London: Hutchinson and Co, n.d.), pp. 673-679; Parkinson, *Tormented Warrior*, p. 170.

5. Montgomery, *Fourth Army*, pp. 11-26.

6. Currie mentioned only the members of the Canadian, Australian, and Royal Tank Corps' delegates in his *Corps Operations, 1918*, p. 28; see also J.F.C. Fuller, *Decisive Battles*, p. 281.

7. Liddell-Hart, *A History of the World War*, p. 547.

8. Currie, *Corps Operations, 1918*, p. 28; Nicholson, *CEF*, p. 389.

9. Fuller, *Decisive Battles*, p. 281; Currie, *Corps Operations, 1918*, p. 28.

10. The original orders for the Amiens operations can be found in a variety of files in the National Archives of Canada. The best ones to look at are the Corps Commanders' copies, NAC, RG 9, III, D2, Vol. 4789, File 7, "L.C. Instructions." The Canadian Corps' codename for the Amiens operation was "Llandovery Castle," after a Canadian hospital ship that had recently been sunk by a German U-boat; hence the abbreviated title "L.C."; hereafter, the operation orders will be cited as "L.C. Instruction, No.＿." There are also copies included in the Canadian Corps G.S. War Diaries, NAC RG 9, III, D2, Vol. 4789, File 1-3. For abbreviated versions and explanations of the concept of operations, see Currie, *Corps Operations, 1918*, pp. 28-29, and 36, and Montgomery, *Fourth Army*, pp. 11-40.

11. Brutinel shared the honour of leading the BEF in MG development with Captain G. M. Lindsay, a British Officer; see Griffith, *Battle Tactics*, pp. 120-129.

12. Papers of Brig. Gen. Raymond Brutinel, NAC, MG 30, E 414; Currie, *Corps Operations, 1918*, p. 36.; "L.C. Instruction No. 2," paragraph 4.

13. See Montgomery, *Fourth Army*, pp. 17-25; and Currie, *Corps Operations, 1918*, p. 29.

14. For details, see Currie, *Corps Operations, 1918*, pp. 28-29, and Dancocks, *Spearhead*, pp. 29-31. The "false" orders issued by the Corps can be found in NAC, RG 9, III, D2, Vol. 4789, File 1, "Canadian Corps General Staff War Diary," (hereafter "CCGS War Diary") "Warning Order," dated 28 July 1918.

15. Paybooks were each soldier's personal record of service, and were to be kept on their person at all times, so this warning would have been quite significant; see Dancocks, *Spearhead*, p. 118.

16. Currie, *Corps Operations, 1918*, p. 44.

17. Throughout its existence, the Canadian Corps had benefitted heavily from the generous number of excellent British senior staff officers attached to it. Three of them went on to be Chiefs of the Imperial General Staff: General "Tiny" Ironside, General John Dill, and General Alan Brooke. On this topic, see C.P. Stacey, "The Staff Officer: A Footnote to Canadian Military History," *Canadian Defense Quarterly*, Vol. 2, No. 1 (Summer 1973), p. 26. Ox Webber, Currie's BGGS for most of 1918, was also an outstanding British staff officer whom the British had generously posted to the Canadian Corps. He was thought of so highly by Currie that he was the only officer specifically thanked by name in Currie's report to the Canadian government; see Currie, *Corps Operations, 1918*, p. 85.

18. The story of the administrative victory is probably best told in Dancocks, *Spearhead*, pp. 34-35. Major General Sir Archibald Montgomery (-Massingberd), Chief of Staff, Fourth Army, in *Fourth Army* , mentions it only in passing, claiming that "the fact that the concentration was carried out...without a hitch...was not the least remarkable feature in the story of the 100 days." (p. 13). This omission is surprising given the critical importance the logistical success played in the ultimate victory.

19. "Canadian Corps Operations Order No. 214," dated 31 July 1918, "CCGS War Diary," was typical of the kind of instructions that had to be issued to all levels of command so as to move four divisions - more than 20,000 men, 400 guns, 2000 horses, and 1000 vehicles - into positions for the attack. It instructed the Third Canadian Divisional artillery to make a night march "not to commence before 10 p.m." from Villers Bocage to the area of Amiens.

20. Currie, *Corps Operations, 1918*, p. 31.

21. "Notes On Amiens Operations, Canadian Corps `Q', dated 14 September 1918," NAC, RG9, III, D2, Vol. 4789, File 9, p. 2. (Hereafter, this document will be cited as "Q Report-Amiens".)

22. "Q Report - Amiens," p. 3.

23. Ibid., pp. 3-4; Currie, *Corps Operations, 1918*, p. 32.

24. Ibid., p. 3.

25. Ibid., p. 4; Currie, *Corps Operations 1918*, p. 32.

26. Private G.S. Henderson, quoted in Dancocks, *Spearhead*, p. 32.

27. Nicholson, *Gunners of Canada* , pp. 336-338; Dancocks, *Spearhead*, pp. 34-35.

28. Fuller, *Decisive Battles*, p. 281.

29. There is much historical debate over whether Foch, Haig, or Rawlinson changed the nature of the attack at Amiens; for some of the better treatments, see Winter, *Haig's Command*, pp. 191-210; Terraine, *To Win A War*, pp. 102-106; and Prior and Wilson, *Rawlinson,* p.p. 301-308, and Travers, *How the War was Won*, p. 118.

30. Fuller, *Decisive Battles*, p. 281.

31. See Bean, *AOH* Vol. 6, pp. 505-506.

32. Montgomery, *Fourth Army*, p. 11; see also Edmonds, *BOH*, Vol. 4, pp. 574-575.

33. Brereton Greenhous, "... It Was Chiefly a Canadian Battle": The Decision at Amiens, 8-11 August 1918," *Canadian Defense Quarterly*, Vol. 18, No. 2 (Autumn 1988), p. 74. The "strategic effect" eluded to in Greenhous's quote was the psychological blow the attack had on German commanders.

34. Brown, "Not Glamorous," p. 433.

35. C.P. Stacey, "The Battle of Amiens," *Introduction To The Study of Military History for Canadian Students* (Ottawa: Directorate of Military Training, 1952) (hereafter cited as "Stacey, Amiens."), p. 35.

36. Currie, *Corps Operations 1918*, p. 35.

37. Ibid., pp. 36-37.

38. There is an intelligence report on all the German units engaged by the Canadian Corps during the battles of the 100 Days entitled "Narrative of the Employment of German Troops Engaged By the Canadian Corps, August 8 to November, 1918," in the CCGS War Diary, Vol. 38 (1-30 Sep 1918), NAC, RG9, III, D3, Vol. 4812. (Hereafter, the Intelligence Report will be referred to as "Int on German Divisions Engaged.") The German side of the tale is best told in English by "The German Catastrophe of the 8th of August 1918," *The Army Quarterly*, Vol. 25 (October 1932-January 1933); this is a review of the chapter of the same title on Amiens in the German Official Monograph on the War.

39. Currie, *Corps Operations 1918* , p. 36; see also Stewart, "Attack Doctrine," p. 203, and Blaxland, *1918*, p. 158.

40. "Artillery - Amiens," NAC, RG 9, III, D3, Vol. 4807, File 175; "L.C. Instruction Number 1," paragraph 6.; Nicholson, Gunners, p. 339; Stewart, "Attack Doctrine," p. 205; Brown, "Not Glamorous," pp. 433-434.

41. "Artillery-Amiens,"; Stewart, "Attack Doctrine," p. 206; and McNaughton, quoted in Swettenham, *McNaughton*, pp. 143-145.

42. "Tanks, L.C. Instruction No. 2," NAC, RG 9, III, D 2, Vol. 4789, File 2. The only question that remained was over who was being held hostage; had the infantryman commandeered the tank, or had the crew "shanghaied" the infantryman?

43. See "The Catastrophe of 8 August," *Army Quarterly*, pp. 66-67.

44. Stacey, "Amiens," p. 34.

45. Ibid., p. 38; Montgomery, *Fourth Army*, pp. 24-25; Travers, *How the War Was Won*, pp. 118-119; Nicholson, *CEF*, p. 393.

46. Much the same conclusion is reached by Bidwell and Graham in *Firepower*, p. 144.

47. Swettenham, *McNaughton*, pp. 140-145.

48. Nicholson, *CEF*, pp. 390-391.

49. Macdonell papers, entry on August 7 in "1918 Diary," NAC, MG 30 E 20, Vol. 1.

50. "Artillery-Amiens,"; Stewart, "Attack Doctrine," p. 206; Nicholson, *Gunners*, pp. 340-342.

51. Quoted in Swettenham, *McNaughton*, p.143.

52. For a discussion of tactical changes in the Canadian Corps, see Rawling, *Surviving Trench Warfare*, pp. 166-223; Nicholson, *CEF*, p. 398.

53. "3rd Canadian Division Corps Operations between 8 August - 16 August 1918," NAC RG 9, III, D2, Vol. 4795, File 63, (henceforth "3 Can Div Report-Amiens"); the International Platoon is mentioned specifically on p. 7. See also Nicholson, *CEF*, pp. 397-400.

54. Currie, *Corps Operations 1918*, p. 38.

55. Brigadier General Tuxford, 3rd Canadian Infantry Brigade, "Statements on Amiens Battle," Brutinel papers, NAC, MG 30, E414, p.18.

56. See "1st Canadian Division Report on Amiens Operations," NAC RG 9, III, D, Vol. 4809, File 194 (hereafter "1 Can Div Report - Amiens"); Nicholson, *CEF*, pp. 401-402; and J. D. Craig, *The 1st Canadian Division in the Battles of 1918* (London, Barrs and Co., 1919), pp. 9-13.

57. Major General Henry Burstall, " 2nd Canadian Division Narrative of Operations at Amiens," NAC RG 9, III, D, Vol. 4794, File 54, p. 7.

58. Nicholson, *CEF*, p. 403, and Bean, *AOH*, pp. 526-616.

59. Lt. Ronald Holmes, quoted by Dancocks, *Spearhead*, p. 52.

60. Major Roy Nordheimer, Royal Canadian Dragoons, quoted in Dancocks, *Spearhead*, p. 53. The British Cavalry did take the village of Cayeux; see Nicholson, *CEF*, p. 404. Unfortunately, most of the other units in the Cavalry Corps had similar experiences; see "Report on Cavalry Corps - Amiens - August 8 to 12, 1918," NAC RG 9, III, D, Vol. 4798, File 101.

61. This may be considered the first attempt at using an "armored personnel carrier," despite its rather inauspicious results; see "4th Canadian Division Report, L.C. Operations, 3rd Battle of the Somme, East of Amiens, 8-15 August 1918," RG 9, III, D, Vol. 4809, File 189. It is probably easier to find it in the secondary source material; see Nicholson, *CEF*, p. 405, and Dean Chappelle, "The Canadian Attack at Amiens, 8-11 August 1918," *Canadian Military History*, Volume 2, No.2 (April 1993) p. 94.

62. Nicholson, *CEF*, p.405; Montgomery, *Fourth Army*, pp. 31-58.

63. See "The Canadian Corps General Staff Machine Gun File," NAC, RG 9, III, d, Vol. 4787, File 86. The two letters are from French Generals Mathieu (Commander 126 Division) and Deville (Commander 42 French Division), copies of which are in this file.

64. Major General Heinz Guderian, *Achtung-Panzer!* trans. Christopher Duffy (London: Arms and Armour, n.d.), p. 118. It should be noted that Guderian based much of his chapter on Amiens on J.F.C. Fuller's work, although he seems to have personal knowledge of the fate of the 117th Jager Division. For the actions of other formations that faced the Fourth Army, see *Die Katastrophe des 8. August 1918*, pp. 47-191.

65. Nicholson, *CEF*, p. 407.

66. Liddell-Hart, *History of the World War*, p. 548.

67. Erich Ludendorff, *My War Memories* , quoted in Nicholson, *CEF*, p.408.

68. Montgomery, *Fourth Army*, pp. 7-8. Historians seem to be in general agreement that Amiens was the turning point in the war; see, for instance, Liddell-Hart, *History of the World War*, p. 543; Fuller, *Decisive Battles*, p. 276, and Dancocks, *Spearhead*, p. 58.

69. Liddell-Hart, *History of the World War*, p. 547; Dancocks, *Spearhead*, p.41; and Currie, *Corps Operations 1918*, p. 38.

70. Dancocks, *Spearhead*, pp. 41-43; and Fuller, *Decisive Battles*, pp. 278-297.

71. The German official monograph, *Die Katastrophe des 8. August 1918*, betrays the negative psychological impact best by its tone; see especially pp. 196-201, and the illustrations throughout.

72. See Bean, *AOH*, Vol. 6, pp. 617-619.

73. This intention was first communicated by the First Army Order dated 31 July 1918, and confirmed at the Army Commander's conference on 5 August; "CCGS War Diary," Vol. 36, Appendix 1.

74. "First Army Order," dated 31 July 1918, in the "CCGS War Diary," Appendix 1; Bean; *AOH*, Vol. 6, pp. 505-506; "L.C. Instruction No.6: Policy After Reaching Objectives," NAC, RG 9, III, D2, Vol.4789, File 2.

75. These timings are taken from the message log in "CCGS War Diary," Vol. 36, 1 August to 30 August 1918, Appendix 2.

76. These entries are from the "GSO II (I) Log" NAC RG 9, III, D2, Vol. 4790, File 18, (hereafter "GSO II (I) Log").

77. Bill Rawling has come to a similar, if more positive sounding conclusion in his article, "Communications in the Canadian Corps, 1915-1918: Wartime Technological Progress Revisited," *Canadian Military History*, Vol. 3, No. 2 (Autumn 1994).

78. This accusation is levelled by both Dancocks, *Spearhead*, p. 60, and to some degree, by Bean, *AOH*, Vol .6, pp. 621-624.

79. "GSO II (I) Log", p. 31.

80. "2nd Canadian Division Narrative of Operations, Mar 13 - Nov 11 1918," NAC RG 9, III, D2, Vol. 4794, File 52, (hereafter cited as "2 Can Div Ops, 1918".)

81. Statement of General Ross, 5 CIB, "Amiens Narrative," Brutinel papers, NAC, MG 30 E 414, pp. 69-70, (henceforth referred to as "Amiens Narrative-Brutinel papers").

82. Brig. General A. Bell, "Amiens Narrative, Brutinel papers," p. 73.

83. "2 Can Div Ops - Amiens," 9 Aug; see also Nicholson, *CEF*, pp. 408-413; Dancocks, *Spearhead*, pp. 60-68. The official Australian view seems a little rosier; see Bean, *AOH*, Vol. 6, pp. 621-638.

84. Nicholson, *CEF*, pp. 413-414.

85. "CCGS War Diary," Vol. 36, August 9 1918.

86. Bean, *AOH*, Vol. 6, p. 684.

87. This figure comes from Intelligence on German Divisions Engaged, "CCGS War Diary," Vol. 36.

88. Nicholson, *CEF*, pp. 408-414, Currie, *Corps Operations 1918*, p. 39.

89. The "GSO II (I) Log" gives the following figures for tank strength of the 4th Tank Brigade on the morning of 10 August:
1st Bn (attached to 4 Can Div) - 12 Mark Vs
2nd Bn (attached to 3 Can Div) - 9 Mark Vs
3rd Bn (attached to 1 Can Div) - 8 Mark Vs
4th Bn (attached to 2 Can Div) - 8 Mark Vs (?).
This from an original strength of 36 tanks plus 6 in reserve per battalion, not including supply tanks; see "GSO II (I) Log," p. 68.

90. See, for instance, Travers, *How the War Was Won*, p. 130; or Dancocks, *Spearhead*, pp. 68-69.

91. "2 Can Div Ops-Amiens," p. 16.

92. Nicholson, *CEF*, pp. 416-417. Currie was especially unhappy about the 32nd Division's mediocre showing because he had visited its commander, Maj. Gen. T.S. Lambert, the night before to inquire about the preparations for the assault, and was told that everything was in good shape; see Dancocks, *Spearhead*, pp. 72-73.

93. McNaughton, quoted in Swettenham, *McNaughton*, p. 146.

94. Travers, *How the War Was Won*, p. 131.

95. Currie, *Corps Operations 1918*, p. 40; Dancocks, *Spearhead*, p. 77; Travers, *How the War Was Won*, pp. 130-131; Prior and Wilson take an interesting look at these events from Rawlinson's point of view and arrive at the same conclusion, *Command on the Western*

Front, pp. 335 - 336.

96. "CCGS War Diary," 11 August 1918.

97. Nicholson, *CEF*, pp. 414-419.

98. Fuller, *Decisive Battles*, pp. 276-299.

99. Major R. L. Ewing, CO 42nd Infantry Bn, "Amiens Report-Brutinel Papers," p. 33.

100. "Amiens Narrative-Brutinel Papers".

101. Griesbach papers, "Lessons from Recent Fighting, 24 August 1918," NAC, MG 30, E15, File 14, p. 5.

102. "Amiens Report - Brutinel Papers"; reports from other divisions concur; see, for instance, "4th Canadian Division Report, L.C. Operations, 3rd Battle of the Somme, East of Amiens" (hereafter cited as "4 Can Div Report - Amiens"), NAC, RG 9, III, D3, Vol. 4861.

103. Brigadier General W. Griesbach, "Report on Amiens," dated 12 Aug 1918, Griesbach Papers, NAC MG 30 E 15, Vol. 5, File 35; "Amiens Narrative-Brutinel Papers," p. 5.

104. See "Narrative of Operations-Cavalry Corps - Amiens," NAC RG 9, III, D2, Vol. 4798, File 101.

105. Griesbach, "First Canadian Infantry Brigade - Lessons from Recent Fighting-Amiens," dated 24 August 1918, Griesbach papers, NAC MG 30, E 15, Vol.5, File 14, p. 5 (hereafter, this report will be referred to as "1st CIB Lessons - Amiens").

106. Tim Travers, *How the War Was Won*, p.114; C.P.Stacey, "Amiens," pp. 11-21.

107. See "Narrative of Ops-4th Tank Brigade-Amiens," NAC, RG 9, III, D2, Vol. 4798, File 102; also Fuller, *Decisive Battles*, p. 190.

108. Travers, *How the War Was Won*, p. 119.

109. Nicholson, *CEF*, p. 420.

110. Griesbach, "1st CIB Lessons - Amiens."

111. Travers, *How the War Was Won*, p. 122; Nicholson's opinion is nearly the same, in *CEF*, p. 420.

112. Travers, *How the War Was Won*, p. 110; see also Chappelle, "Amiens," p. 100.

113. See entries in "CCGS War Diary," Vol. 36, Aug 15 - 18.

114. See Timothy Lupfer, *The Dynamics of Doctrine* (Fort Leavenworth, KS: U. S. Army Combat Studies Institute), especially pp.55-58.

115.Brown, "Not Glamorous," p. 425. For a contrasting view, see Griffith, *Battle Tactics*.

116. Griesbach papers, MG 30, E15, Vol. 2, File 14, "G.454-8 Letter from 1st C.I.B. to 1 Can Div, dated 24 August 1918", (hereafter referred to as "G.454-8, 24 Aug 1918"), p. 4.

117. See Swettenham, *McNaughton*, p. 145.

118. Griesbach papers, NAC, MG 30, E 15, Vol. 5, File 35, "1 CIB Report on Amiens", dated 12 Aug 1918, p. 5.

119. Griesbach, "G.454-8, 24 Aug 1918," p. 4.

120. Currie, *Corps Operations 1918*, p. 41. Compare this with another great triumph for the Corps, the capture of Vimy Ridge, in which the Canadians captured 4000 prisoners, 54 guns, and 228 machine guns and trench mortars; Swettenham, *To Seize*, p. 161.

121. See Currie, *Corps Operations 1918*, p. 42.

122. Vimy totalled 10,000 casualties for roughly 3 miles of advance; see Nicholson, *CEF*, p. 264-265.

123. Currie, *Corps Operations 1918*, p. 41; also Nicholson *CEF*, p. 419.

124. See Travers, *How the War Was Won*, pp. 131 - 149.

125. The present author is not the only historian to believe that the seeds of even the most modern land warfare doctrine were sown on the battlefields of the Western Front in 1917-18; see, for instance, Griffith, *Battle Tactics*, pp. 153 - 175; and Bidwell and Graham, *Firepower*, pp. 131-146.

4

"CONCERTO GROSSO": BREAKING THE DROCOURT-QUEANT LINE

War does not consist of a single short blow.

Clausewitz, *On War*,
Book 1, Chapter 1

The Allies' first counterpunch, in the form of the spectacularly successful attack at Amiens, had landed a hard blow on the head and body of the German Army. Foch and Haig now searched for the magical combination of relentless, repeated strikes that they knew would be necessary to knock the veteran German Army out of the war in 1918. Foch's ebullient expression for this new strategy on the Western Front was as simple as it was descriptive: "*Tout le monde a la bataille!* (Everyone to battle!)" Haig's explanation was a little more precise; he described it as "a simple, straightforward advance by all troops on all fronts to keep the enemy on the move."[1]

The Canadian Corps' role in this strategy was crucial. Haig's plan, based on Currie's recommendations in the aftermath of Amiens, was for the Canadian Corps to break the "hinge" of the heavily fortified Hindenberg Line, and to assist in the seizure of the vital railway center of Cambrai. This heavily fortified city was vital to the Germans because it served as the hub of their railroad and communications network in the BEF sector. Its main approach, the Arras-Cambrai Road, was heavily defended, and Haig recognized that the Canadian Corps, because of its size and experience, was probably the formation most capable of withstanding the arduous and sustained combat necessary to take this critical point from the Germans. For his part, Foch agreed with Haig's selection of the Canadian Corps to spearhead the BEF attack towards the Hindenburg Line, commenting: "I think that the Canadians are the force on which I can rely to clean up between Arras and the Hindenburg Line.... [They are] the ram with which we will break up the last line of resistance of the German Army."[2]

In order to complete this assignment, the Canadian Corps would have to be

transferred back to the British First Army under General Horne. Denied the rest that
formations usually received after being involved in an action such as Amiens, the
Canadian Corps began moving northward to the area of Arras on 19 August 1918.
Before them stood an immense task: the breaking of the Drocourt-Queant (D-Q) Line.

An indication of the importance of this task was that Haig felt compelled to
give his orders personally to Currie, in the presence of Army Commander General
Horne:

> The C-in-C [Commander in Chief, Haig] indicated to the Corps Commander yesterday
> [that]...[t]he Corps, reinforced if necessary by other British Divisions, has the task of driving
> South of the SCARPE to break the QUEANT-DROCOURT Line and reach the line of the
> CANAL DU NORD. When this has been accomplished, the Corps is to swing Southward and
> sweep down behind the HINDENBURG Line.[3]

The significance of Haig's personal delivery of these instructions was that
Haig had in essence skipped a level in the chain of command, preferring to detail his
orders and expectations directly to Currie, instead of simply delegating the task to the
Army commander, and letting Horne decide how the operation should best be
conducted. Haig was explicit in how the Canadian Corps would be used in the
upcoming attacks. It was to be *the* leading edge of the First Army's operations. More
important, the tone of these instructions signified that Currie was to be given a freer
hand in planning his operations than would usually have been the case for a corps
commander. Tim Travers has noted that this was not an unusual state of affairs during
the latter part of 1918. As formations in the BEF developed their own doctrine, and
became considered "elite," Haig and GHQ became more and more willing to devolve
much of the responsibility for operational planning onto the shoulders of its better
generals, men like Currie and Monash.[4] If Haig himself was not brilliant, then at least
he was smart enough to recognize those commanders who were most effective, and to
let them get on with the job.

Haig's faith in the Canadian Corps commander, and the operational freedom
it afforded Currie, created the strange situation of an Army commander having to
surrender some of his authority to a subordinate, and an Army's operations supporting
those of a nominally subordinate formation. In essence, this meant that First Army's
task was to support the Canadian Corps attacks from the D-Q Line to Cambrai. This
left Horne in the difficult position of ostensibly commanding Currie, yet often forced
to acquiesce to his subordinates' demands because of Currie's unique position within
the BEF, and Haig's personal belief in the Canadians.

Haig hoped that if the D-Q Line, the northern hinge of the Hindenburg Line,
could be penetrated, it "would turn the whole of the enemy's organised positions on a
wide front southwards."[5] This was easier said, of course, than done. Before the
Canadians could even get to the D-Q Line proper, they would have to pound their way
down the heavily defended Arras-Cambrai road, through a bewildering array of
defenses that "the enemy had fortified with a skill that demonstrated his mastery in
military engineering."[6] Dominating these defensive positions were three heights of
land, all enemy-held: Orange Hill, Chapel Hill, and Monchy-le-Preaux. Only after the
Corps had fought through nearly six kilometers of heavily fortified enemy territory and

taken Monchy, would they then be able to actually see the D-Q Line, some three miles to the east. Behind this mass of thick wire and twisting trenches waited the daunting obstacle of the unfinished Canal du Nord, and the German defenses around Cambrai.

There would be no strategic surprise; the Germans had reinforced the area, and Ludendorff well knew the importance of the Hindenberg Line, the last complete defensive line before Germany. Nor were there to be the swarm of tanks that the Canadians had possessed at Amiens because tank losses had been too heavy. As a result, GHQ had "penny packeted" the remainder of the tanks out to formations.[7] New instructions were issued that the tanks were not to get in front of the infantry unless absolutely necessary.[8] As if under these conditions Currie's task was not already intimidating enough, Haig was impatient to keep pushing the Germans while they were on the run, and was demanding the attacks begin as soon as possible. "If we allow the enemy a period of quiet," Haig stated, "he will recover, and the 'wearing out' process must be recommenced."[9]

Fortunately, Currie had been prescient enough to shelve the plans made during the diversion prior to Amiens for the attack on Orange Hill; these now formed the basis for his orders. In Currie's words:

We [the Canadian Corps] were particularly benefited by all the reconnaissances and plans made for the capture of Orange Hill during the period of simulated activity at the end of July. The excellence of trench railways, rear communications, and administrative arrangements in the area were also of great value, and enabled the Canadian Corps to undertake to begin, with only three days notice, *the hardest battle in its history* (emphasis added).[10]

Currie met his divisional commanders the night of 22 August, and outlined his plan. His scheme was simple. The Second Canadian Division was to seize Chapel Hill, then push on to the southern end of Monchy Heights, while the Third Canadian Division would overwhelm Orange Hill, then Monchy, and exploit as far east as possible. The Corps would be without the First and Fourth Canadian Divisions, which were still en route from Amiens, but would have the excellent 51st (Highland) Division in reserve.[11] The most unorthodox aspect of the plan was the timing of the attack. Currie wanted to go at night, "in order to take advantage of the restricted visibility produced by moonlight and so effect a surprise; the attacking troops would thus pass through the enemy's forward machine gun defenses by infiltration."[12] Currie understood that night attacks entailed greater risk of complication, but felt the risk was necessitated. Moreover, he was confident in his Corps.[13]

Apart from its peculiar timing, Currie's plan was quite brutally simple:

It is essential to push the operations...with utmost vigour.... Leading Brigades must continue pushing on as long as possible and reserves must be close up, ready to push through as soon as leading troops are expended.

As far as possible, boundaries will be adjusted so that battle can be carried on with 2 Divisions in front line, each on a brigade front, thus enabling Divisions to keep fighting 3 days continuously.

We have three main systems of defense to penetrate [Monchy, Fresnes-Rouvroy Line, and the DQ Line]...These systems will mark definite stages in the advance, as it will probably be necessary to pause for 24 hours in front of each while fresh Brigades and Tanks are brought up and artillery moved forward.[14]

It seems from this statement that Currie expected German resistance in this sector to be similar to that at Amiens. This proved to be a gross underestimation on Currie's part of the tenacity with which the Germans would defend this critical sector, a mistake that would tell in the upcoming battle.

Currie's idea of a night attack frightened the staff officers at GHQ. Lieutenant Colonel John Dill (later a field marshal and Chief of the Imperial General Staff) rushed to Currie's HQ to protest, but to no avail. Currie's BGGS Brigadier General "Ox" Webber, simply rebuffed: "all we want from General Headquarters is a headline in the *Daily Mail* reading 'The Canadians in Monchy Before Breakfast.'"[15] Haig shared GHQ's apprehensions, and repeatedly visited Corps HQ throughout the planning period in order to personally urge forward and check up on the Corps' preparations. Despite Haig's anxiety to begin the attack as soon as possible, he wisely acquiesced when Currie requested an extra day to ensure preparations were complete for the attack. Currie would neither be stampeded by an impatient Haig, nor deterred by a timid GHQ; Currie would do it his way.

THE BATTLE OF ARRAS: 26-29 AUGUST

The battle of Arras[16] began on time at 3:00 a.m. 26 August. Currie's audacious night attack achieved overwhelming tactical surprise over the Germans. By daylight, the Second Division had taken Chapel Hill, and as Webber had prophesized, the Third Division had seized Monchy "before breakfast." In fact, the attack on 26 August was so successful that Haig recorded in his diary:

Today has been a most successful one. The capture of Monchy le Preux at the cost of 1500 casualties was quite extraordinary. The enemy knew the value of this position in his system of defenses, and so devoted much labour to strengthening it since he retook it from us [in March 1918].[17]

In a letter to his wife, Haig claimed that the Canadian victory, coupled with the gains to the south by the British Third and Fourth Armies, "was the greatest victory which a British Army has ever achieved."[18] Hyperbole, perhaps, but to a beleagured Commander of the BEF, the victories of late August, coming less than a year after Passchendaele, and only a few short months after the dark days of spring 1918, must have seemed nothing short of miraculous.

Despite their early triumph on 26 August, *two* enemies subsequently conspired to retard the Canadian Corps progress: the German Army, and the friction of war. By as early as 10:00 a.m., confusion created by the quick success was beginning to slow the rapid Canadian advance, and strong German counterattacks later in the day checked the Canadians' progress. By nightfall, the two lead divisions found themselves six kilometers deep within the maze of German defenses along the Arras-

Map 4.1
Arras Operations

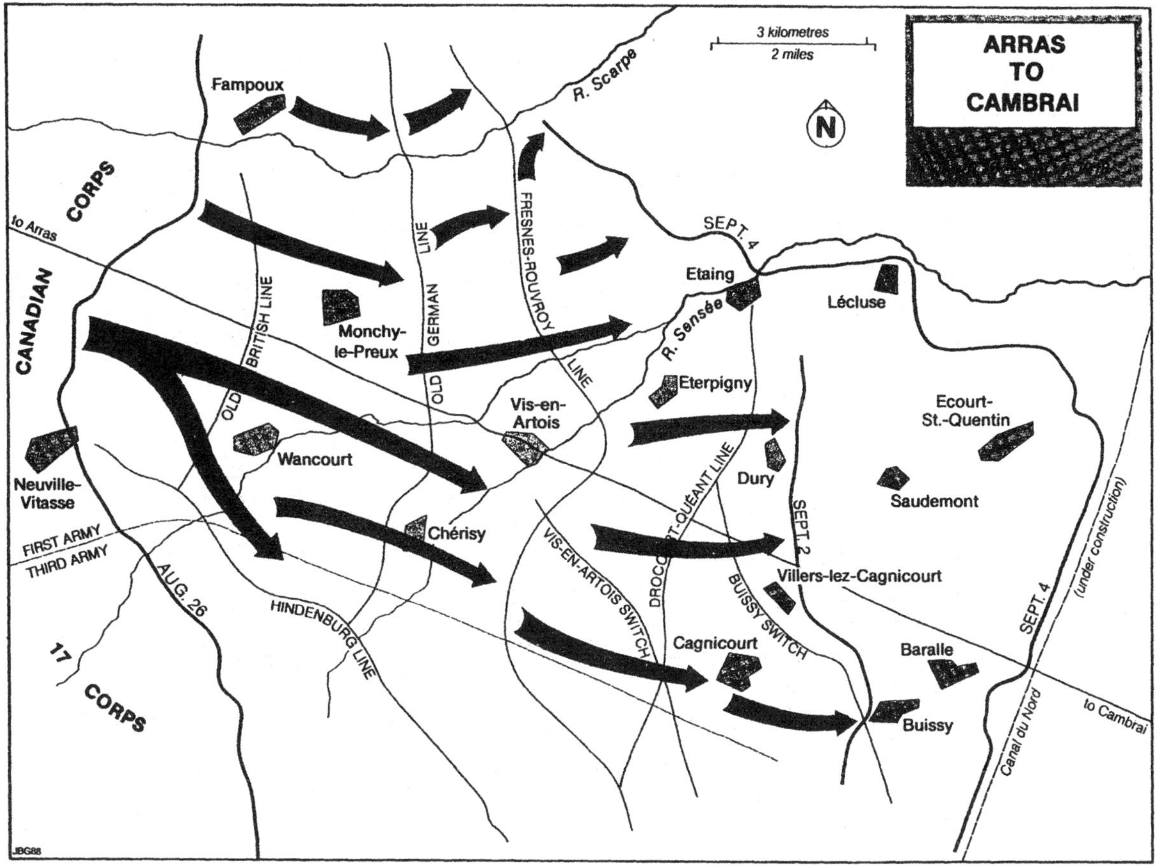

ARRAS
TO
CAMBRAI

N

3 kilometres
2 miles

to Cambrai

Canal du Nord

SEPT. 4 (under construction)

Ecourt-St.-Quentin

Saudemont

Villers-lez-Cagnicourt

Baralle

Buissy

BUISSY SWITCH

Cagnicourt

SEPT. 2

DROCOURT-QUÉANT LINE

VIS-EN-ARTOIS SWITCH

Dury

Eterpigny

Etaing

SEPT. 4

R. Sensée

Lécluse

FRESNES-ROUVROY LINE

R. Scarpe

Vis-en-Artois

OLD GERMAN LINE

Chérisy

Monchy-le-Preux

Fampoux

HINDENBURG LINE

OLD BRITISH LINE

Wancourt

AUG. 26

Neuville-Vitasse

FIRST ARMY
THIRD ARMY

CANADIAN CORPS

17 CORPS

to Arras

Cambrai road, and under heavy German artillery fire from guns that were out of range of the Corps' counterbattery assets. Nonetheless, at 8:00 p.m., Currie directed the divisions to continue their attacks in the morning, the objective being the Fresnes-Rouvroy Line, approximately two kilometers east of Monchy. The "24 hour pause" anticipated in Currie's orders of 25 August had now been shortened to a mere 12 hours.[19] (Map 4.1 shows the Arras operations.)

The attacks on 27 August were not as successful as Currie had hoped. As had happened at Amiens, coordination problems caused a late start, and lead elements of the Second Division did not begin their attack until 10:00 a.m. on 27 August. Furthermore, the Canadian divisions had pushed themselves beyond the range of most of their artillery support, and were therefore suffering grievously from the heavy weight of German defensive fire. Perhaps most important, the two divisions' attacks were not wholly coordinated, and therefore lacked the synergy achieved with proper orchestration. Command, control, and coordination methods during this period -- runners, field telephones, some wireless, or flags -- were simply too primitive to permit the different levels of command and staff to coordinate their efforts more effectively while engaged in operations. As the Third Division report stated: "the greater part [of the division was] ...in close touch [i.e. combat] with the en[emy].... In the continuous fighting the Brigades had got [sic] mixed. We were asked by the Corps...to capture the F-R [Fresnes-Rouvroy] Line... therefore,...to make a strong attack, the front had to be re-organized."As a result, by the night of 27 August, the Corps had not yet taken the Fresnes-Rouvroy Line.[20]

It was not just the poor coordination of the attacks that had foiled the Canadians. The Germans had recognized the danger forming on their flank, and had poured reinforcements into the threatened sector. Currie reported that by nightfall on 27 August, two more German divisions had been moved to counter the Corps advance, accompanied by trucked machine gun troops and additional artillery.[21] The Canadian Corps also received reserves, in the form of the First Canadian Division and the Fourth British Division, the latter substituting for the still-en route Fourth Canadian Division. Yet, despite the obvious fatigue that the men of the Second and Third Divisions must have been feeling, Currie chose not to relieve them with the two fresh divisions. The Fourth British Division had been delayed in arrival, and Currie thought that relieving only one of the exhausted divisions would create greater problems than it would solve; therefore, he declared that such an operation was "undesirable at this stage."[22] For Currie, this was a rare mistake, for he had underestimated both the ferocity with which the Germans were defending, and the exhaustion of his assaulting divisions. The Second Division reported that by 27 August: "[the] 4th Canadian Infantry Brigade was very short of troops and had to send forward what was practically a composite battalion from all 4 bns [battalions] of the Brigade, their reserve consisting of Headquarters details, batmen, cooks, etc."[23]

The divisional attacks continued on 28 August, achieving mixed results. General Lipsett's Third Division managed to take its objective, due to an "outstandingly innovative" plan. Lipsett concentrated the fire of all of his artillery resources along a very narrow axis, smothering the German machine gun nests. This clear, confined path allowed his forces to gain a lodgement in the Fresnes-Rouvroy

Line, and to begin clearing it. Unfortunately, as on 27 August, Lipsett's attack had not been fully coordinated with Burstall's exhausted Second Division, which had managed to pound its way in heavy fighting to its objective, but could not hold on when the Germans counterattacked. Ironically, the Second Division's "thin" artillery barrage inadvertently dried up when the Germans, quite by chance, sent up the prearranged flare signal to be used by the Canadian infantry to indicate success to their headquarters and guns. Simply stated, Second Division had been "used up." In the words of Daniel Dancocks, "there were too few troops taking part, and too many of them were killed or wounded, and they received too little help from their artillery."[24] One battalion, the 22nd, had lost 501 men in total, and all of its officers. At the infantry battalion level, especially for units like the 22nd, 28 August had to be as black as any single day during the war. By nightfall, Burstall reported that

our line [was] ...only a short distance in advance of the line reached by us on the previous night, with small parties of men as far forward as the front line wire of the Fresnes-Rouvroy line which they were still endeavouring to get through.... Our troops were both mentally and physically exhausted having had only a very few hours sleep in the preceeding eight days.[25]

If the advance had slowed in the two Canadian divisions' areas, it had come to an outright halt in the 51st Highland Division's sector. This formation had had the advantage of avoiding the heavy defenses astride the Arras-Cambrai road, but whereas the Canadian divisions had advanced four to five kilometers on Z day, the 51st had made only 1.5 to 2.5 kilometers. More telling was that even though its frontage was shortened in half by a rearrangement of Corps boundaries during the night of 26-27 August, it could only push its advance another kilometer forward on 27 August, whereas both Canadian divisions, despite their problems, pushed on nearly twice as far on a frontage nearly twice as wide.[26] As clearly seen by the results on the ground, even an "elite" British division such as the 51st Highland was no match, in terms of combat effectiveness, when compared to its bigger Canadian cousin. This was especially telling during days 2 and 3 of prolonged offensives, where the larger Canadian divisions simply had more endurance in sustained operations because they had more resources.[27]

The problem of endurance also dogged Sir Julian Byng's Third British Army to the south of the Canadian Corps. On 21 August, in the aftermath of the Amiens attack, Byng's Army had launched an attack toward Bapaume. After only one day, Byng called a halt to the attack to reorganize and bring in fresh troops. Although the advance was successfully resumed on 23 August, neither Byng's Third Army, nor Rawlinson's Fourth Army, now without the Canadian Corps, could sustain the advance and take advantage of the mental paralysis of the German High Command. Frustrated, Haig would now increasingly turn to a formation he knew could stand the prolonged "hard pounding" of offensive operations: the Canadian Corps.[28]

Currie's plan to keep his divisions driving forward for three days by having them use a one-brigade frontage and leapfrogging their brigades each day had been upset by the ferocity with which the Germans had defended. The result was that the divisional commanders had to narrow their frontages, and employ two brigades at a time in order to achieve the momentum necessary to overcome the enemy defenses.

Currie recognized the necessity of replacing the now-worn-down forward divisions with fresh troops, and the First Canadian Division and the Fourth British Division replaced the Second and Third Canadian Divisions on the night of 28-29 August.

It is crucial to note that the attack at Arras was a subtle departure from previous Corps attacks under Currie. Earlier Canadian "bite and hold" tactics set a deliberate pace derived from a limited objective outlook. At Arras, this had been replaced by a more urgent tempo, "pushing the operations with utmost vigour," toward a much deeper objective, in terms of both time and space. This sense of urgency no doubt reflected the pressure placed on Currie, and all formation commanders for that matter, by Haig and GHQ to continue pushing the Germans as quickly and as ruthlessly as possible. Yet the immediate effect of the more urgent approach was to steal time from lower formations and units for battle procedure, thereby forcing attacks to be launched without proper coordination, and eventually creating greater casualties. Currie was simply pushing too hard. He had little choice, however, as high casualty rates were inevitable, and to his mind it was probably better to take them quickly in a successful engagement, rather than slow the tempo of the advance, and give the Germans the time and opportunity to turn their formidable defenses along the Arras-Cambrai road into a *schlacthaus* [slaughterhouse]. Nonetheless, stung by the high casualty rates in the Second and Third Divisions, Currie was quick to search out an acceptable compromise between speed, violence, and coordination.

THE BREAKING OF THE DROCOURT-QUEANT LINE

The hard pounding of the Second and Third Canadian divisions had left Currie short of his ambitious goal by only the final objective, the D-Q Line. Pressure mounted from Haig and GHQ to continue the advance, and Currie received orders on 28 August that set the date for the assault on the D-Q Line as 1 September. Originally, GHQ had wanted to launch the assault earlier, but Currie had refused, needing time to consolidate his gains, rest his troops, and prepare a set-piece infantry-artillery attack on the strongly fortified position. Currie commented in his diary, "believing the Queant-Drocourt line to be the backbone of [enemy] resistance, we have decided... not to attack it until we are ready, then go all out."[29]

Currie wanted to secure his line of departure by completing the taking of the Fresnes-Rouvroy Line, and by clearing the approaches to the D-Q Line by capturing some heavily fortified villages to the Canadian Corps' front. These attacks were carried out by the First Canadian and Fourth British Divisions on 30-31 August. The attack in the First Division's area, carried out by the 1st CIB under Brigadier General William Griesbach, was described by Sir Archibald Macdonell as a "tactical masterpiece."[30] Turning an open flank to the south of the German positions to his advantage, Griesbach executed a converging "pincer" attack into the flank and rear of the German line. Instead of rolling west to east parallel to the German defenses, as most barrages did, the 1st CIB advanced behind an ingenious barrage that ran from south to north. The daring maneuver was highly successful, despite the short time allowed for its preparation.

Griesbach said later of the attack:

Thacker's [Brig.Gen. H.C. Thacker, 1 CDA] barrage is a masterpiece in any case, but it is to be remembered that he only had a few hours to do this job. He had several hundred guns under his orders and the execution of the complicated plan was perfect.... This matter of attacking in one direction and then facing in another calls for more than passing attention as a study in tactics.... Note that in taking the enemy in the flank and rear we escaped his protective barrage which fell wholly in front of Ulster Trench and bothered our people not at all.[31]

As Griesbach's success clearly points out, flank attacks against heavily defended trench lines were possible and successful on the Western Front. Contrary to a widely held belief, commanders in the BEF still recognized the advantages of the flank attack, and used it to their advantage when circumstances allowed.[32]

While the First and British Fourth Divisions carried out operations to secure attack positions, the Corps' heavy artillery attempted to cut gaps in the thicket of wire entanglements to the front of the D-Q Line. The gunners' work was made easier and more efficient by the use of the Number 106 instantaneous fuse, which detonated the round in the air, thus cutting the wire with shrapnel while flattening it with the force of the explosion. Despite the use of the new fuse, wire-cutting operations remained time and ammunition intensive. From 27 August to 2 September, the Corps' heavy artillery fired over 10,000 tons of ammunition, most of which went to wire cutting. The total artillery ammunition used during the battle of Arras amounted to more than 847,000 rounds, or 20,424 tons -- almost twice the tonnage expended by the Corps at Amiens, in only one-third the period. In the words of the Corps Artillery report, "the gunners may truthfully be said to have spent almost the entire eight days of August 26 to September 2 firing with one hand and hauling ammunition with the other."[33]

Owing to the amount of work required in wire cutting, Currie realized by 30 August that preparations would not be complete for the anticipated Z day of 1 September. Furthermore, roads had to be repaired, ammunition and supplies brought forward, and coordination completed for the attack. Currie therefore requested and was granted extra time to complete his preparations. The date of the attack had to be pushed back to 2 September.[34]

Currie's tactical plan was again uncomplicated. Essentially, the plan was similar to that of Amiens, only on a smaller scale. Given little room to maneuver, Currie's intention was to break the German line at its most critical point, the Arras-Cambrai road, and then fan outward north and south to capture the German defenses. The Corps would attack with three divisions forward, each division being reinforced with two companies of tanks. Unlike Amiens, only 50 tanks for the entire Corps would be available, as opposed to the over 300 that had been present August 8.[35] The Fourth British Division would be responsible for the north flank, attacking toward Etaing. In the center, the Fourth Canadian Division was given the difficult task of pounding straight down the heavily defended Arras-Cambrai road, and for taking the fortified village of Dury. The right flank of the Corps' attack would be made up of the First Canadian Division, responsible for seizing the Vis-en-Artois Line, and the critical villages of Cagnicourt and Buissy, and the Buissy Switch. Tactical surprise would have been impossible to achieve, and the Canadian Corps would instead have to rely heavily upon their artillery barrage to help the infantry achieve the breakthrough. In McNaughton's words: "The obvious solution [to] the difficulty lay in a preponderance of artillery sufficient to crush out of existence a wide section of the enemy's defensive system, entrenchments and defenders alike, thus creating a gap through which troops could be thrown to work around the exposed flanks."[36] Notwithstanding the presence of tanks, the Canadian Corps was relying once again upon the "traditional method" of infantry-artillery attacks that it had perfected during the previous two years of fighting.[37]

Despite the plan's simplicity, it again contained an innovative element: a return of the Canadian Independent Force, under machine gun tactics pioneer Brigadier-General Bruntinel. Like the cavalry at Amiens, the Independent Force's task was to exploit the initial breakthrough using truck mounted machine gun companies and armoured cars, in this case with the aim of capturing crossings over the Canal du Nord.[38]

Aware of the danger forming on their flank, the Germans moved to reinforce the position. By 1 September, elements of eight new German divisions were already moving to reinforce the D-Q Line and Canal du Nord.[39] Haig, too, had much at stake in the upcoming battle. On 1 September he had received an ominous note from Chief of the Imperial Staff, Sir Henry Wilson, that read: "Just a word of caution in regard to incurring heavy losses in attacks on the Hindenberg Line [which included the D-Q Line]... I know the War Cabinet would become anxious if we received heavy punishment in attacking the Hindenberg line without success."[40] In response, Haig commented to himself, "[i]f my attack is successful, I will remain as C.-in-C. If we fail, or our losses are excessive, I can hope for no mercy!"[41] Because Currie's attack on the D-Q Line, scheduled for just the next day, was a vital preliminary to the overall BEF onslaught on the Hindenberg Line, Haig once again found his future in the hands of the Canadian general and his Corps.

At 5 a.m., 2 September 1918, the Canadian attack began. The opening barrage came from 762 artillery pieces, the largest number to support a solo Canadian Corps operation during the war.[42] The rolling barrage was a masterful piece of planning, resembling the barrage at Amiens on 8 August, with a few subtle differences. First, the defenses at Amiens had been undermanned and ill-prepared, whereas the D-Q Line was fully manned and well-fortified, including deep lines of wire. The barrage, therefore, began rolling forward at the usual three minutes per 100 yard intervals until it reached the forward edge of the D-Q Line's main wire obstacles, whence it slowed to five minutes per 100 yard shifts. More important, the barrage followed the rough contours of the D-Q Line, a precision extremely difficult to coordinate and maintain, but successfully achieved by the Corps' artillery commanders. Once the initial objective, again denoted as the "Red line," had been seized at Z plus 152 minutes, the barrage would dwell 400 yards in front of the infantry for 30 minutes, allowing divisions to leapfrog forward brigades, and the artillery to lay on to its next targets. For the remainder of the attack, the Corps barrage was dispensed with, allowing divisional commanders to mass fires on targets as deemed necessary.

The toughest job in this sector would be the neutralization of the heavily fortified Buissy Switch, First Canadian Division's second objective, which ran south-

southeast toward the Hindenberg Line proper. Restricted Fire Lines* were planned to move forwards approximately 1000 yards every half hour until the third objective, again designated as the Blue Line, was seized, anticipated for Z plus 6 1/2 hours. The limit of exploitation, denoted by the Brown line, was beyond the crossings over the Canal du Nord, but no timings were given for this, as it was a contingency based on the success of Brutinels' Brigade. To ensure the Independent Force would be safe from friendly fire as it pushed down toward the canal, a restricted fire "box" was created around the Arras-Cambrai road from the Red line plus 1000 yards to the Blue line.[43]

Initially, the assaults went well, with the tanks clearing breaches in the wire where the artillery had failed to do so. Despite small pockets of fierce resistance, all three lead divisions continued to advance quickly behind the excellent covering fire of the artillery. The Corps staff reported that "the opposing infantry put up a poor fight, and surrendered in masses." Heavy fighting, casualties to officers, and the speed of the advance soon caused confusion, however, and once more the carefully planned attack began to stall for want of coordination and control.[44] A crisis occurred near midday, when the leading brigades advanced beyond the range of their artillery support, and the infantry were forced to continue the assault without it. As Currie later reported: "The enemy's resistance, free of the demoralising effect of our barrage, stiffened considerably, the open country swept continually by intense machine gun fire. In addition, the Tanks soon became casualties from enemy guns firing point blank, and the advance on the left and center was held up."[45]

As at Amiens, communications capabilities were the first vital artery to fail. As early as 6:55 a.m., 10th CIB reported that its telephone lines were out to divisional HQ, making it "impossible to render prompt reports to Divisional Hqrs and keep in touch with flank Brigade[s]." By 11:00 a.m., "the situation began to get obscure," and 10th CIB was forced to resort to runners in order to pass messages.[46]

10th CIB's plight was made doubly difficult by the often overlooked regularity of chemical warfare on the Western Front. At 10:00 p.m. "heavy enemy gas shelling of Brigade Hqrs" left the "staff working in gas masks." Despite this attack, 10th CIB's HQ managed to carry on with its mission, the communications breakdown posing a much greater problem than the gas attack, which seemed to be treated more as an inconvenience than a real deadly threat. In order to explain this almost nonchalant attitude toward the chemical menace, it is critical to remember that the Great War was the only conflict where both sides had chemical weapons and used them on a relatively unrestricted basis without international censure.[47] Instead of reacting with the near hysteria that modern Western armies often associate with chemical attacks, both sides in the Great War had come to accept such weapons, and learned to cope with their effects. Far from a deadly spectre, gas weapons on the

---

* A Restricted Fire Line is an imaginary line beyond which certain coordination measures have to be followed before indirect fire can be used on targets. It is primarily used to ensure the safety of one's own troops. In this particular case, no unobserved fire could be used in these areas, which meant that an artillery forward observer, spotter plane, or other person had to be able to physically see the rounds impacting in order to ask for artillery fire.

Western Front were treated with a practical respect, but not paranoid fear. Canadian Corps BGGS "Ox" Webber reflected his peers' practical, almost nonchalant view of gas weapons with his dryly humorous order at Amiens that, "all captured gas shells shall be returned to the enemy."[48]

It was the tactical limitations of chemical weapons that mitigated their overall terror effect. Once the British had developed a very good box respirator for personal use, the advantages to be gained by the German use of gas were temporary at best. At worst, gas became a double-edge sword that rebounded to wound its instigator, a lesson the Germans learned and regretted during the last part of the 100 Days because of the BEF's penchant (especially the Canadian Corps) for hurling captured stockpiles of "yellow cross" gas shells back on their previous owners. A gas attack remained a terrifying experience at the personal level, but by the 100 Days it could no longer provide a decisive breakthrough or breakdown.[49]

Other new technologies were similarly incapable of turning the tide of this pitched battle. The planned exploitation of Brutinel's Canadian Independent Force failed. Lack of cross-terrain mobility had confined the armored cars to the Arras-Cambrai road, leaving the force highly vulnerable to machine gun fire, and to artillery pieces firing in the direct mode. Brutinel later blamed the failure on the caution of his cavalry element, the 10th Royal Hussars, but given the cavalry's ordeal at Amiens, its caution was probably justified. He also blamed the ad hoc nature of his formation, claiming that it was "hastily put together only 24 hours prior to zero and was not properly welded. Its units were not endowed to an equal extent with boldness and resolution."[50]

McNaughton criticized Brutinel's attempt to push down the heavily defended Arras-Cambrai road as "ill-conceived," noting that a mistaken report from the Independent Force that one of its cars had reached the Canal du Nord had forced the artillery to stop firing on Dury. The result, reported a bitter McNaughton, was that the attacking infantry suffered heavily without the artillery support, and that a plan "carefully prepared and within our powers was sacrificed to a plan fantastic in conception, and...improbable of success."[51] McNaughton never forgot Brutinel's ill-fated attempt, nor did he let Brutinel forget. More significantly, this episode may have gone a long way in shaping the attitudes of not only McNaughton, but the whole generation of Canadian officers who "grew up" while McNaughton was CGS in the 1920s and 1930s, as to who rightfully deserved precedence on the battlefield: fire support or maneuver elements. Moreover, as the failure of the Independent Force exemplifies, innovation on the Western Front did not automatically mean success.

The First Canadian Division, using a more traditional approach, had been more effective than Brutinel's armored cars. The infantry-artillery assault of this formation had pushed through the Buissy Switch by early evening, 2 September. This advance meant that the Corps now dangerously outflanked the German positions to the north, compelling the Germans to pull back behind the Canal du Nord on the night of 2-3 September. Leaving behind strong rear guards of machine gunners, the Germans made a fighting withdrawal behind the Canal du Nord, and then destroyed the crossings over it to stop the pursuit of the Canadians. Currie paused the night of 2-3 September, and did not seriously pursue the Germans. After the war, First Army's

Chief of Staff Major General Sir William H. Anderson criticized Currie for failing to take advantage of the opportunity to seize the Canal du Nord.[52] Anderson, however, even with the benefit of hindsight, was wrong, and his remarks are indicative of how isolated from operational realities an Army HQ could be. Currie rightly believed such an attack would have been unwise, if not suicidal. The Canal du Nord was a formidable obstacle, and the defenses on it were too well prepared for the Canadians to attempt to storm in a hastily planned and executed attack.

Although the Canadian Corps advance had ground to a halt, the attack on the D-Q Line had achieved both its tactical and strategic purposes. Tactically, the Corps had managed to break into the D-Q Line and had overrun it on a frontage of seven kilometers. Strategically, this advance attained two results. First, the Germans were forced to pour what few reserves they had left in Crown Prince Rupprecht's Northern Group of Armies into the battle to shore up their sagging defenses. Second, the Corps' success at getting on the flank of the Hindenberg defenses forced Ludendorff to withdraw, from north to south, the German Seventeenth, Second, Eighteenth, Ninth, Sixth, and Fourth German armies, thereby surrendering all of the territory gained at such a huge cost during the spring and summer offensives. According to Ludendorff:

On the 26th of August the English offensive against the Arras-Cambrai road opened... On September 2nd a strong assault by English tanks over-ran obstacles and trenches in this line and paved a way for their infantry.[53] Shortly after two o'clock in the afternoon General von Kuhl...of the 17th Army...requested permission to withdraw. We had to admit the necessity...to withdraw the entire front from the Scarpe to the Vesle.[54]

Quite rightly, Currie considered the breaking of the D-Q Line an even greater triumph than that of Amiens: "it is a question whether our victory of yesterday [2 September] or of August 8th is the greatest, but I am inclined to think yesterday's was."[55] Both victories overshadowed the Canadian triumph at Vimy, at least in terms of strategic significance; the Germans did not have to withdraw six armies and surrender hundreds of square miles as a result of that victory. The Canadian Corps' conquest had unhinged Ludendorff's plan for a last stand on the Hindenberg line.[56]

NOTES

1. Dancocks, *Spearhead*, p. 89. There rages an academic debate over who deserves the credit for devising this front-wide strategy; see Terraine, *To Win A War*, pp. 139-159; Winter, *Haig's Command*, pp. 211-225; Travers, *How the War Was Won*, pp. 110-174; and Pitt, *1918*, pp. 222-235, to name just a few.

2. Marshal Foch, in a conversation with Brig. Gen. Brutinel, quoted in Dancocks, *Spearhead*, p. 91.

3. "Future Policy of Operations," dated 25 August 1918, "CCGS War Diary," Vol. 36, NAC, RG 9, Vol. 4789, File 2, (hereafter "Future Policy of Operations - 25 August 1918,").

4. Travers, *How the War Was Won*, pp. 176-177.

5. Haig, quoted in Dancocks, *Spearhead*, p. 91.

6. Nicholson, *CEF*, p. 426; See also Currie, *Corps Operations 1918*, pp. 44-45. Most of the Canadian Corps War diaries and post operational reports included maps and air

photographs of the impressive defenses on the Arras-Cambrai axis; see "CCGS War Diary," or the air photos in the Panet papers, Archives, Royal Military College of Canada, Kingston, Ontario.

7. On this point, see Johnson, *Breakthrough*, pp. 271-275; and Travers, *How the War Was Won*, pp. 138-143. Johnson makes the interesting point that it was not a shortage of tanks, but *tank crews* that negated a future "mass tank attack" for the BEF.

8. Currie, *Corps Operations 1918*, p. 47; Travers, *How the War Was Won*, p. 143; Nicholson, *CEF*, p. 427.

9. Haig, *Private Papers*, quoted in Nicholson, *CEF*, p. 425.

10. Currie, *Corps Operations 1918*, p. 44.

11. The Highlanders were another of the divisions - along with the Dominion troops, and some select others - who had achieved elite status in the BEF; see, Griffith, *Battle Tactics*, pp. 79-83.

12. Currie, *Report on Operations, 1918*, p. 47.

13. Ibid., pp. 45-47; Dancocks, *Spearhead*, p. 94.

14. "Future Policy of Operations-25 August 1918." Also see Currie, *Corps Operations 1918*, p. 45.

15. Dancocks, *Spearhead*, p. 94; Urquhart, *Currie*, p. 245.

16. The official name is "The Battle of the Scarpe 1918," (Nicholson, *CEF*, p. 427). The present author refers to it as the "Battle of Arras," in order to avoid confusion with the previous battles of the Scarpe.

17. Haig, quoted in Terraine, *To Win a War*, p. 128.

18. Douglas Haig, letter to Lady Haig dated 27 Aug 1918, quoted in De Groot, *Haig*, p. 388.

19. "Third Canadian Division Report on Operations, 26-28 August 1918," NAC, RG 9, III, D2, Vol. 4795, File 66 (hereafter "3 Can Div Report-Arras"); "Second Canadian Division Narrative of Operations-Battle of Arras, 1918," NAC, RG 9, III, D, Vol. 4794, File 54 (hereafter "2 Can Div Report-Arras"); "CCGS War Diary," Vol. 36, 25-27 August 1918; Currie, *Corps Operations 1918*, pp. 46-47; Dancocks, *Spearhead*, pp. 95-98; Nicholson, *CEF*, pp. 427-430.

20. "2 Can Div Report - Arras"; "3 Can Div Report - Arras"; Dancocks, *Spearhead*, pp. 98-99; Nicholson, *CEF*, p. 431.

21. See "Int on German Divisions Engaged," Section 2; Currie, *Corps Operations, 1918*, p. 48, and Nicholson, *CEF*, p. 430.

22. Currie, *Corps Operations 1918*, p. 49. No deeper explanation is given.

23. "2 Can Div Report - Arras"

24. Dancocks, *Spearhead*, p.103.

25. Nicholson, *CEF*, p. 432.

26. Canadian Corps Situation Map, 1:40000, Sheet 51B, edition 2 dated 29 August 1918. Panet Papers, RMC Archives, Kingston, Ontario.

27. Canadian historian Desmond Morton makes the same point about the relative endurance of British and Canadian divisions during the 100 Days; see Morton, *When Your Number's Up: The Canadian Soldier In the First World War* (Toronto: Random House, 1993), p. 179. The present author is loathe to make any such comparisons, but, given the mythology that has grown up around the Dominion Corps, one feels forced to address the reality and causes of it. This argument should by no means denigrate the record of the 51st Highland Division; rather one must point out that its efforts and achievements were made despite having had fewer resources to draw on than its Canadian neighbors; see Chapter 2 of this book for a comparison of Canadian and British formations.

28. On the Third Army attack, see Terraine, *To Win A War*, p. 125, or Dancocks, *Spearhead*, pp. 90-91.

29. Currie, quoted in Dancocks, *Spearhead*, p. 104.

30. Macdonell's full comment on Griesbach was: "He is the quickest officer that I have ever had anything to do with to grasp the tactical advantages or disadvantages of a given situation e.g. the breaking of the FRESNES-ROUVROY LINE. The way in which it was done was his own idea and was literally a Bde tactical masterpiece." "Confidential Report on Officers," Griesbach papers, NAC, MG 30 E 15, Vol.1, File 7.

31. Brig. Gen. W. Griesbach, Letter to Sir Archibald Macdonell, 2 February 1927, Griesbach papers, NAC, MG 30 E 15, Vol. 1, File 1.

32. Section II A, "First Canadian Division Report on Arras Operations, 28 August-5 September 1918," NAC, RG 9, III, D2, Vol. 4793, File 44, (hereafter "1 Can Div Report - Arras"); Nicholson, *CEF*, p. 433.

33. "Artillery Report-Arras and Drocourt-Queant Line," NAC, RG 9, III, Vol. 4807, File 174; Nicholson, *Gunners*, p. 355. Major General A.G.L. McNaughton's figures in "The Development of Artillery in the Great War," give the battle of the D-Q Line 27 days, but his figures include days until late September 1918.

34. "CCGS War Diary," 30 August 1918. See also Major-General Sir W. H. Anderson, "The Breaking of the Queant-Drocourt Line by the Canadian Corps, First Army," *Canadian Defense Quarterly*, Vol. 3, No. 1 (January 1926), pp. 120-127. Anderson had been the Major General, General Staff of the First Army. See also Nicholson, *CEF*, p. 432-436.

35. "CCGS War Diary," Vol. 37, 2 Sept 1918. At Amiens, approximately 150 tanks were directly under the control of the Canadian Corps, the remainder were with the Australian Corps.

36. McNaughton, "Development of Artillery," p. 160.

37. Travers, *How the War Was Won*, pp. 146-152.

38. Currie, *Corps Operations 1918*, p. 52.

39. Int on German Divisions Engaged, Section II; Currie, *Corps Operations 1918*, p. 53.

40. Sir Henry Wilson to Haig, 1 September 1918, quoted in Terraine, *To Win a War*, p. 139; Canadian historian John Swettenham claims that the reference to the Hindenberg Line meant specifically the D-Q Line, but it seems more plausible that it was a reference to the operations of the BEF as a whole; see Swettenham, *To Seize*, p. 216.

41. Haig, in Duff Cooper, *Haig* (London: Faber, 1938) Vol. 2, p. 361; quoted in Terrain, *To Win A War*, p. 139, and Swettenham, *To Seize*, p. 216.

42. McNaughton, "Development of Artillery", p. 169.

43. The best way to find this information is to look at "Canadian Corps Barrage Map A," Field Survey Battalion R.E. No. 6817. The best copy is found in the Panet papers, RMC Archives, Kingston, Ontario. Panet was the commander, 2 Division Artillery (2 CDA) during the 100 Days. His guns were placed under the control of 1st Canadian Division for the D-Q Line operation, and his personally marked map shows precisely how the barrage was to be carried out.

44. "CCGS War Diary", Vol. 37, 2 Sept 1918; "1 Can Div Report-Arras, Operations of September 2nd 1918." Other accounts are contained in Nicholson, *CEF*, pp. 436-440; Travers, *How the War was Won*, pp. 145-154; Dancocks, *Spearhead*, pp. 103-121; Currie, *Corps Operations 1918*, pp. 50-53. The number of guns is taken from McNaughton, "Development of Artillery," p. 169.

45. Currie, *Corps Operations 1918*, p. 52.

46. "10th Canadian Infantry Brigade Report on Scarpe Operations," NAC, RG 9, Vol. 4795, File 82 (hereafter "10 CIB-Scarpe").

47. The author has omitted the Iran-Iraq War of the 1980's, where allegations of chemical warfare were made against both sides, because the scale and constancy of use in this

conflict never reached the proportion it did during World War One.

48. "L.C. Instruction No. 2."

49. See Donald Richter, *Chemical Soldiers: British Gas Warfare in World War 1* (Lawrence: University Press of Kansas, 1993), for an excellent discussion of the BEF's development in this area. Griffith's *Battle Tactics* also provides a good overview of the development and limitations of chemical warfare in the BEF during the Great War, pp. 110-119.

50. "Report on the Independent Force, August 22 - September 11, 1918," NAC, RG 9, III, Vol. 4807, File 170.

51. See Swettenham, *McNaughton*, p. 151. McNaughton's criticism's of Brutinel's Brigade must also be considered as the criticism of the proponent of one nascent technology (modern artillery) against a rival (Brutinel's machine guns and "mechanized" formations.)

52. Anderson, "Queant-Drocourt," pp. 126-127.

53. There is a propensity by German historians and writers of this period to ascribe every successful attack to the presence of masses of tanks, as Ludendorff does here. As already discussed, the Canadian Corps possessed far fewer tanks than were seen at Amiens, and relied instead on artillery - infantry superiority for their success.

54. Ludendorff, *My War Memories*, Vol. 2, pp. 695-696.

55. Currie, quoted in Nicholson, *CEF*, p. 440.

56. Nicholson, *CEF*, pp. 438-440.

German prisoners, in gas masks, being used as stretcher bearers during the battle of Amiens. In the background is a Mark V tank advancing. *(National Archives of Canada / PA-2951)*

Prince Arthur of Connaught, Canadian Corps Commander Sir Arthur Currie, and Generals Watson and Odlum watching a rehearsal attack in preparation for the battle of Amiens. *(National Archives of Canada / PA-2121)*

A portion of the Hindenberg Defenses, just east of Arras. Notice the supply trucks in the background, and the masses of barbed wire. *(National Archives of Canada / PA-3280)*

Canadian troops resting in a trench during the "advance to victory," while others, in the background, move forward to continue the attack. *(National Archives of Canada / PA-3138)*

Canadian Corps' Heavy Artillery in counterbattery action against German guns just east of Arras, September 1918. It was heavy artillery like this that provided the bulk of the Corps' counterbattery firepower. *(National Archives of Canada / PA-3135)*

Canadian troops enter the smoke-filled ruins of Cambrai, October 1918. Cambrai was crucial to the German defenders as the northern nexus of their railway system. *(National Archives of Canada / PA-3270)*

The first Canadians enter Valenciennes, dashing westward toward the Canal, 1 November 1918. McNaughton said of the attack, "the Canadian Corps paid the price of victory in shells, and not in life." *(National Archives of Canada / PA-3377)*

5

"INTERMEZZO": THE PAUSE BEFORE THE CANAL DU NORD

Frequent periods of inaction remove war still further from the realm of the absolute and make it even more a matter of assessing probabilities.
Clausewitz, *On War*,
Book 1, Chapter 1

The breaking of the D-Q Line, and the subsequent withdrawal of a large portion of the German Army to the Hindenberg Line, had created an excellent opportunity for a rapid, Front-wide advance by the Allied armies. For almost the entire month of September 1918, the Canadian Corps stood on the near side of the Canal du Nord and waited for its logistical support and the remainder of the BEF to catch up. The time was not idly spent. Currie and the Canadian Corps used the much-needed break as an opportunity to reassess and critique the experiences of recent fighting, and to continue to train for the more fluid, dynamic style of warfare of the 100 Days. Ultimately, the pause before the Canal du Nord would give Currie not only the time he needed to rest and replenish his Corps, but also to modify the attack doctrine developed and practiced by the Canadian Corps.

The tactical considerations that necessitated a prolonged halt in front of the Canal du Nord were threefold. First, the Canal itself formed a formidable obstacle, a barrier made all the more daunting by the flooding of the low-lying areas in front of the Canal by the retreating Germans. Moreover, during their retreat, the Germans had destroyed every crossing over the Canal. It would now take the Corps considerable time to plan and amass the engineering resources necessary in order to repair the roads and tracks in the area, and to bring forward the necessary bridging and breaching equipment.[1] Second, the Canal was protected by its own thick defensive line, and in depth by the fortified positions around Bourlon Wood and Cambrai. These positions would have to be taken in one fell swoop, or the attacker would be left relatively isolated on the far side of the Canal, on a forward slope, subject to a murderous artillery and machine gun fire from the positions around Cambrai. Last, the Canadian

Corps' rapid advance had created a salient, and its flanks were now exposed. As the storming of the Canal could probably be achieved only as part of a larger operation, Currie was ordered to wait until the remainder of the BEF closed on the Hindenberg Line.[2]

From a logistical standpoint, the pause before the Canal du Nord was critical. The Corps, by 4 September, had pounded its way through 12 miles of the some of the densest defenses on the Western Front, and had overrun no fewer than five distinct defensive lines. It had inflicted heavy casualties on the German forces, and had captured 10,492 prisoners and 123 guns.[3] The shattered road and transport system in this area now had to be repaired before the Corps could push forward. More important, the Canadian divisions, exhausted by nearly a month of continuous offensive operations, had to be resupplied with men and materiel.

The vicious fighting of August 1918 had taken a grievous toll on the Canadian divisions. The Corps had suffered a total of 11,423 casualties since 26 August. Not surprisingly, almost 80% of these were suffered by the infantry battalions, some of which now stood below 50% strength.[4] For example, in the First Canadian Division, total losses from Arras operations alone were 163 officers and 3224 other ranks (ORs). Infantry junior officers suffered the highest casualty rates -- almost 85% of total officer casualties. Out of 163 officer casualties, only 25 were non-infantry, 12 of these being Machine Gun Corps officers (similar to infantry), and the remainder from the Field Artillery (4), Engineers (3), Trench Mortars (3), Medical Corps (2), and Canadian Army Pay Corps (1). First Division received replacements of only 95 officers and 1,325 other ranks, or less than half the total casualties. In the words of the First Division report: "The reinforcement situation from the standpoint of numbers became unsatisfactory...units [only infantry battalions were receiving reinforcements][were] only brought up to 966 OR's and Bexhill [Corps Officer Training Camp] needs to take in a greater number of cadets."

Casualties incurred in heavy fighting also placed a heavy drain on the medical service, and here a rare organizational oversight was reported. First Canadian Division quite rightly pointed out that "Canadian Divisions are much larger than British Divs, but they have the same number of Motor Ambulances. It is considered that each Field Ambulance [unit] should have *10* motor ambulances instead of 7."[5] Haig's decision to drive one of his "Cadillac corps" down the Arras-Cambrai road was beginning to strain Currie's replacement pool and his medical services.

Equipment losses during the battles of Amiens, Arras, and the D-Q Line were also large. The Canadian "Q" staff, however, once again displayed an outstanding grip on the situation. Weapons, such as Lewis and Vickers machine guns, were quickly replaced, but more mundane materiel often proved more of a problem. In the First Division alone, over 3,602 water bottles, 4,526 water bottle carriers, and 588 pairs of wire cutters had to be replaced. Mostly these "replacements" were found through careful battlefield salvage operations. As the divisional quartermaster noted, "in the midst of a big battle it is difficult...to prevent these losses.... The necessity of safeguarding Battle Eqpt has been impressed on all Brigades in this Division."[6] Ammunition placed the biggest strain on the logistics system. Most heavy lift was accomplished by light railway, but the Corps preferred to use trucks to haul the ammo during actual operations because of the flexibility and speed it provided in following the guns. The divisions, the end users of the Corps supply system, had nothing but glowing comments about the Corps logistics, one source commenting that "Corps 'Q' delivered our requirements the same evening, and no difficulties were experienced in getting all we asked for...rapidly."[7] Once again, as at Amiens, sound logistics had paved the way for tactical success.

The pause at the Canal du Nord was more than just an opportunity for Currie to "rest and refit" his divisions. He wanted to use the break in order to improve the Corps' performance in open warfare, and give his brigades a chance to do some refresher training to this end. On 5 September, Currie outlined his plan for the pause:

The present intention is that the Corps would mark time in its present position while operations are developed further South with a view to manouvering [sic] the enemy out of his positions behind the Canal.... In view of the above, the Corps Commander wishes the line held with a minimal number of men.... Divisions in front line should be disposed in great depth so that the reserve Brigades at least can carry on training...without drawing fire.[8]

Currie was aided in his plan by the excellent obstacle formed by the Canal du Nord, and by the existing fortifications of the D-Q Line, which alleviated some of the work required to make the Corps sector readily defensible. Nonetheless, Currie made it clear that this reversion to defense was only temporary, ordering that, "no extensive work will be undertaken." Ironically, Currie's defense scheme borrowed heavily from the methods used by the enemy, placing heavy emphasis on "machine gun nests disposed in depth and mutually supporting each other."[9] If imitation is truly the greatest form of flattery, then Currie was certainly paying homage to the tenacity and effectiveness of the German machine gunners his Corps had faced during August.

While the troops busied themselves with improving their defensive positions, and constant patrolling of the Canal and the German defenses opposite it so as to keep the enemy off balance, the senior leaders of the Corps began the formal feedback process necessary to improve their doctrine and tactics. Some universal problems in the Corps were quickly identified. Brigadier General Griesbach complained to his divisional commander, Macdonell:

I would say in the attack on the DROCOURT-QUEANT Line there was too much quick success, coupled with very heavy fighting which brought about a certain amount of disorganization.... Our Artillery also requires to be ginned up [improved] in the matter of offensive fighting. Trench warfare ideas still apparently prevail.... In future, I will assume the responsibility of ordering guns forward.... The training of officers in open warfare still leaves much to be desired.[10]

Griesbach's sentiments were echoed by the commander of 11th CIB, in Fourth Canadian Division, Brigadier General Victor Odlum. He claimed that despite an excellent beginning to the attacks, a breakdown in interunit coordination created confusion, to the point where he had to go forward for a "personal reconnaissance." Odlum asserted:

Communications were not satisfactory...between Battalions and forward Co[mpan]ys (owing to M.G. fire) they were bad, and from Brigade to Division they were just as bad. The Brigade wireless set was destroyed by a direct hit 5 minutes after it was set up; and wires could not be maintained.[11]

Brigadier General MacBrien, GOC 12th CIB, also commented that, "with the rapid and long advances made in our two most recent operations [Amiens and D-Q Line], it is impossible to carry sufficient wire to lay wire communication."[12]

The negative effects of these communications breakdowns were magnified by the inevitable time compression forced upon lower levels of command by the new urgency of "open warfare." GOC First Canadian Division Macdonell, commented:

Operations had to be decided upon quickly, and frequently, the tasks had to be set with insufficient time for full explanation. Commanders relied upon the ability of juniors to instantly grasp their plans and push them through successfully... In short, there was not sufficient time for the minute instructions which were thought necessary during the Trench Warfare phase.[13]

In reality, this was often a recipe for disaster, because, as historian Brereton Greenhous has noted, these types of orders were "more appropriate to apostles of *auftragstaktik*, unknown in the British Army."[14] What this usually meant was that attacks after the carefully coordinated set-piece phase of the battle were launched without enough co-ordination between flanking maneuver units, or fire support resources. As Tim Travers has pointed out: "The common thread in the conclusions of the two sets of Canadian brigades' reports was the failure to co-ordinate arms and weapons systems after the support of the artillery and tanks had been outrun, despite earlier training."[15]

In short, once the infantry advanced beyond the support of the artillery, the equivalency of firepower created a state of stasis on the battlefield. Under these conditions, the attacking infantry could advance only if they were willing to risk high casualties, or if some other form of firepower, such as the tank, forward artillery detachments, or a group of heavy machine guns, were available to tip the balance in the attacker's favour. In the words of one battalion commander: "Owing to the enemy present method of defense it is absolutely essential that either tanks be utilized for the entire advance or artillery barrage [be] employed to protect the advancing infantry."[16]

Griesbach and Macdonell advocated "boldness" and maneuver by the infantry as a solution to this dilemma; Macdonell said "the idea is to eliminate stickiness on the part of anyone: not to do away with necessary precautions, but to be bold -- always bold." Yet even they realized that this answer only went halfway.[17] It failed to take into consideration the fact that German defensive doctrine had evolved as well, mostly in order to solve the problem of the tank. The Germans were adapting to the tank by dispersion, spreading out their defense in even greater depth in order to absorb the tank assault, and incorporating special antitank artillery detachments and obstacles. This deeper elastic defense meant that the rear zone incorporated greater numbers of machine guns and antitank batteries.[18]

This change had two important effects on the Allies. First, it helped to counter the tank's effectiveness, thereby helping to force the readoption of the "semitraditional" method of infantry-artillery attack by the BEF.[19] Second, it meant that the set-piece phase of any deep offensive often ended leaving the infantry in the middle of a zone where the Germans could still concentrate large amounts of firepower. The report of 12th CIB reflected this new reality:

Rear Zone. This was an organized area defended by numerous Machine Guns and strong Artillery fire. It was in this Zone that the heaviest fighting took place, and where most of our casualties occurred. The Boche Machine Gunners [swept]...the crest of MONT DURY RIDGE... to a distance of 3000 yards (approximately) Eastwards.[20]

Odlum's report echoed 12th CIB's observation: "[One of] the lessons of the operation that struck me most forcibly [was] the helplessness of infantry on exposed ground when advancing against a line of distant machine guns, if unprotected by an artillery barrage."[21] In short, the problem facing the Canadian Corps was the need to maintain the momentum of the advance beyond the set piece, into what Griesbach described as the "third phase," open warfare.[22] Its symptoms manifested themselves as command and control breakdowns during days two and three of sustained offensive operations.

The solution to the problem of orchestration was "tempo."[23] In battle, like in music, tempo dictates the speed with which any given task is executed, and it affects both the synchronization and the fluidity of all the various instruments. An orchesta begins rehearsals slowly, and the tempo is increased as the composition is mastered. If a difficult piece were to be played at a rapid tempo without sufficient skill or practice, the result would be a musical disaster. This same allegory holds true for military operations. In the Canadian Corps' case, it seemed that attacks during open warfare failed because not enough time was being given to lower commanders to organize their assaults and bring forward the necessary firepower; in other words, the tempo of operations was too fast.

The solution hit upon, therefore, was to deliberately build in a four-to-six hour pause during the transition to open warfare specifically for battle procedure in order to reduce the friction of war. Time had to be allotted during the operations for a co-ordinated transition between the set piece attack on zero day, and operations on days two and three, thereby minimizing confusion and maximizing the synergistic effects of all arms. The pause would also help to solve some of the logistical difficulties incurred in high-intensity warfare, like overcrowded lines of supply. In effect, this interval would act much like the breaks an orchestra takes between movements of a symphony, or during rehearsals.

As with many wartime innovations, this solution sprang simultaneously from a number of sources. Brigadier General R.J.F. Hayter, GOC 10th CIB, stated: "In future, in an operation of this size...it is essential that a pause of quite six hours be allowed before the second advance commences.... Further, a longer pause would have given the Field Artillery Brigades more time to move up into new positions to cover the second advance."[24] MacBrien, GOC 12th CIB, made the same recommendation to his divisional commander: "A longer pause should be observed between two phases of an operation with such deep [o]bjectives.... 4 hours pause would have given time to bring up most of the Field Artillery and to have appreciated the situation before committing troops detailed to the second phase."[25]

Repeatedly, once the careful orchestration of the battle broke down, the advance stalled and casualties mounted. While technological advances, such as a reliable and robust battlefield wireless radio, could have provided some remedy for this problem, such systems were not available at the time. Lacking a technological means to overcome this breakdown in coordination, the Canadian Corps substituted a tactical solution. Currie recognized the limits of his ability to control and reorganize the battle once it had inevitably devolved into confusion. This point usually occurred after the first days successful assault. Currie's solution, then, was to pause after a successful attack, regroup his forces, and begin planning for what was in essence another set-piece attack. While this method may seem ponderous to those who have lived in an era of *blitzkrieg* or Desert Storm, it nonetheless allowed Currie to minimize confusion and, therefore, casualties, while allowing him to continue the offensive. In essence, Currie decided to trade space (ground gained) for time in order to maximize firepower effectiveness and minimize casualties. Happily enough, this combination of economy of force and offensive action was almost exactly what the Allied High Command had been looking for.[26]

The tactical response had another positive aspect. By anticipating and incorporating a break in the battle, Currie, and not the German defenders, controlled when the advance slowed. By dictating the tempo of the attack, Currie wrested away the initiative that elastic defense doctrine was supposed to bestow on the defender. Currie's divisions would stop when he wanted them to stop, and not when the Germans ground them to a standstill. Overlooked, however, was the loss of momentum that a preordained pause forced upon the attacker. The challenge for the Canadian Corps would be to keep the interruption brief enough to minimize the loss of momentum in the assault, thereby denying the German defenders the opportunity to take their own advantage of the break by reinforcing or counterattacking. As will be seen, it was this struggle against time and confusion that was to play a large part in the Corps' next engagement.

The solution also created another crucial problem: how to disseminate and incorporate these new ideas throughout the Corps. Macdonell had already pointed out that the "necessity for a suitable 'Offensive doctrine' well understood by Infantry, Artillery and Machine guns is apparent."[27] Currie now attempted to articulate and promulgate this new doctrine. On 19 September, Corps BGGS Webber issued a document outlining the use of "light troops," including Brutinel's Independent Brigade, entitled *Employment of Corps Mobile Troops*.[28] Currie and Webber followed this up with a much more important document that outlined the operational doctrine for the command and control of artillery units. *The Policy as to the Command of Artillery Units during Offensive Operations* (see Appendix at the end of this book) was released on 20 September. Like Griesbach had earlier done, it broke offensive operations down into three phases, and associated a state of control for the artillery for each one, as follows:

CORPS CONTROL
As soon as operations appear imminent, the order for Corps Control will be issued. This means that all artillery Units in the Corps will be directly under the orders of the

G.O.C., R.A. in order that he may co-ordinate barrages, bombardments and counter-battery work on the whole Corps front.

This phase will last normally until the conclusion of the set piece barrage....

DIVISIONAL CONTROL

This will come into force automatically, as soon as the set piece barrage is concluded....

Should it be necessary during the battle to arrange for a co-ordinated advance and barrage along the whole Corps front, ...the order for Corps control will be re-issued to enable the necessary co-ordination to be carried out.

NORMAL CONTROL

This comes into force as soon as the operations come to a standstill and the front begins to stabilize...[29]

These concepts were not new to the Canadian Corps; rather they were simply reflections of things that the Corps had been doing and working on since 1917. The significance of these outlines is that they were Currie's first attempts at codifying an operational doctrine based on the Corps' most recent experience with offensive operations. In short, these two documents are the fruit of the Corps' collective struggle to understand its success, and *re-create* it. Ironically enough, by the time the second document was ready, the Corps' attention was pulled away from this task by the upcoming attack on the Canal du Nord, and no other documents were completed, if they were even contemplated. The Canadian Corps' offensive doctrine remained narrowly understood within the Corps at the practical level, and largely unarticulated. Now this unwritten doctrine would face the ultimate test of the battlefield. The curtain was about to rise on the main event: the Canal du Nord and Cambrai.

NOTES

1. "CCGS War Diary," Vol. 37, 4 Sept.; see also Currie, *Corps Operations 1918*, pp. 54-55.

2. Currie, *Corps Operations 1918*, p. 54; Nicholson, *CEF*, pp. 442-443.

3. Dancocks, *Spearhead*, p. 119. Dancocks and other historians point out that by this point in the war, it was becoming increasingly difficult for the Germans to keep track of their killed and wounded, and apparently no official numbers were ever published. Griesbach noted that his men captured so many machine guns and trench mortars that they eventually just stopped counting; see "Report on Operations at the Drocourt-Queant Line," Griesbach papers, NAC, MG 30, E 15, File 33c, p. 5, (hereafter "Griesbach Report-D-Q Line").

4. Dancocks, *Spearhead*, p. 119; Nicholson, *CEF*, Appendix C. According to Nicholson's figures, the average "nonfatal" casualty rate for the Canadian infantry of the Great War was about 80% of the total (125,241 out of 159,472). Unfortunately, he does not break it down further into months, or include fatal casualties.

5. "1 Canadian Division Report-Administrative Arrangements for Operations at Arras, 28 Aug-4 Sep 1918," NAC, RG 9, III, Vol. 4793, File 44 (hereafter "1 Can Div Administration-Arras").

6. Ibid., p. 7.

7. Ibid., p. 8.

8. "Future Policy," memo dated 5 September 1918, "CCGS War Diary," Vol. 37, September 1918.

9. "Canadian Corps Provisional Defense Scheme," dated 5 September 1918, "CCGS War Diary," Vol. 37.

10. "Griesbach Report-D-Q Line."

11. "11 CIB Report-Narrative of Operations Carried out Sept 2 and Sept 5 1918 against DURY Hill and the Canal du NORD" (hereafter "11 CIB Report - Dury Hill") NAC, RG 9, III, D2, Vol. 4797, Folder 82.

12. "12 CIB Report-Scarpe Operation-Capture of the Drocourt-Queant Line, 2 Sept 1918" (hereafter "12 CIB Report-Scarpe,") NAC, RG 9, III, D, Vol. 4797, File 82.

13. Lt. Gen. Archibald Macdonnel, "First Canadian Division Report on Arras Operations 28 August-5 September 1918" (hereafter "1 Can Div Report-Arras") NAC, RG 9, III, D2, Vol. 4793, File 44.

14. Brereton Greenhous, "Chiefly," p. 74. Greenhous's comment was aimed at Rawlinson's change of objective at Amiens, but his point is nonetheless valid in this case.

15. Travers, *How the War Was Won*, p. 152.

16. Lt. Col. C. Edwards, CO 38 Canadian Infantry Battalion, "12 CIB Report - Scarpe."

17. "1 Can Div Report-Arras."

18. Wray, *Standing Fast*, pp. 6-8; Travers, *How the War Was Won*, pp. 134-145.

19. Travers, *How the War Was Won*, Introduction.

20. "12 CIB Report - Scarpe."

21. "11 CIB Report - Dury Hill."

22. See Figure 2.1 of this book for more details.

23. Numerous writers have pointed to tempo as a key to military operations. Martin Samuels has argued that the German Army understood the efficacy of tempo by this period; see *Doctrine and Dogma*, p. 83. Richard Simpkin examines the role of tempo in modern warfare in great depth in *Race to the Swift: Thoughts on Twenty-First Century Warfare* (London: Brassey's, 1985), see especially the introduction and p.p. 106-161.

24. "10 CIB Report-Scarpe Operation" NAC, RG9, III, D, Vol. 4797, File 82. (hereafter "10 CIB Report - Scarpe"), p. 17.

25. "12 CIB Report - Scarpe."

26. See Tim Travers, *How the War Was Won*, pp. 110-148, especially p. 148.

27. Macdonell, "1 Can Div Report-Arras."

28. Canadian Corps G. 528, "Employment of Corps Mobile Troops," dated 19 September 1918, "CCGS War Diary," Vol. 37.

29. "Policy as to Command of Artillery Units During Offensive Operations," dated 20 September 1918, "CCGS War Diary," Vol. 37 (September 1918), NAC, RG 9, III, D2, Vol. 4789, File 3. Ian Brown also mentions this document in "Not Glamorous," p. 440. The same general information can be found in the Canadian War Narrative Section draft on "Artillery Doctrine," Brutinel Papers, NAC, MG 30, E 414, Vol. 1.

6

"MAGNUM OPUS": STORMING THE CANAL DU NORD AND THE BATTLE OF CAMBRAI

...only the element of chance is needed to make war a gamble, and that element is never absent.

Clausewitz, *On War*,
Book 1, Chapter 1

The Canadian Corps was certainly not alone in its successes of August and early September 1918. Allied armies across the Western Front had been on the advance, grinding forward in the face of increasingly desperate and increasingly weakening German resistance. By mid-September, however, the German Army had been able to mount an orderly, if costly, withdrawal to its last fully developed line of defense: the Hindenberg Line. The stand here would be a desperate one, and the Allied military leaders knew it. In order to maintain the crushing momentum of their Front-wide advance, Haig and Foch now agreed on a series of attacks that, like repeated hammerblows, would crack the German Army once and for all. Their strategy was outlined thusly:

26th September: Attack by Franco-American forces between the Meuse and Reims (American First and French Fourth Armies);
27th September: Attack by the British Third and First Armies (towards Cambrai);
28th September: Attack by the G.A.F (Flanders Group of Armies, between the coast and the Lys);
29th September: Attack by British Fourth and French First Armies (on the Hindenberg Line).[1]

The sequence of the attacks was crucial. Haig had hoped that the Franco-American drive might draw German strategic reserves southward before his own precious BEF flung itself onto the heavily defended Hindenberg Line. Haig knew full well that his troops faced a daunting task that would be the ultimate test faced by the

BEF. If the line cracked, the German Army could fall back only on hastily organized positions far to the rear; if it held, the Allies would have suffered a costly reversal that would probably not only cost Haig his job, but also drag the slaughter into 1919.[2]

Despite having tacitly promised it a rest after its success at the D-Q Line, Haig turned once again to the Canadian Corps to help break a crucial part of the German line.[3] If Byng's Third British Army was to be successful in its bid to overrun the Hindenberg Line, then it would need a secure left flank. This meant Cambrai would have to be cut off, for it formed the northern nexus of the German Army's railway system. To get at Cambrai, the Canal du Nord would have to be stormed, and Bourlon Wood, a thorn in the side of the BEF since 1916, would have to be taken. For this complicated and crucial task, Haig looked to the Canadian Corps.[4]

It would have been difficult to overstate the importance of Cambrai to its German defenders. It was not only the hub of the German logistical system in the Flanders theater, but also the northern pin of the Hindenberg system, securing the line as far south as Reims. It had been the scene of heavy fighting in November 1917, where a successful attack by Byng's British Third Army, using tanks, had turned into a reverse by an aggressive, German counterattack employing "stormtroop tactics."[5] As Daniel Dancocks has noted: "There was no doubt that the Germans would defend Cambrai with ruthless, even fanatical, determination; its loss would be disastrous for the enemy because it would render the rest of the Hindenberg Line untenable."[6]

THE GAMBLE

Currie had grudgingly anticipated the prospect of having to storm the Canal du Nord, and had been preparing his Corps for the task even before the formal notification came in the form of verbal orders from General Horne, commander First Army, on 15 September 1918. Logistical preparations were already well-advanced for this operation. The engineers and special railway troops had been very busy constructing roads, bridges, and waterpoints, and pushing light railways as far forward as possible. Ammunition dumps had also been established, and the artillery had carried out a vigorous harassing fire and counterbattery program against its adversary opposite the Canal, including extensive gas shelling in response to German gas use. More important, Currie had already ordered a detailed reconnaissance of the Canal and its defenses, and the Corps Intelligence unit was already assembling a good picture of what faced the Corps on the other side of the steep banks of the Canal. Much of this came from special air patrols who took hundreds of air photos. Ground sources were provided by the constant patrols sent out by the forward infantry battalions, including German prisoners taken in raids. Engineer parties also went out to probe for possible crossing sites, and to determine how much work would be involved in the vital bridging operations. Through the diligent efforts of the Corps Intelligence units, and their "collection agencies," Currie and his staff had a good picture of the intimidating task that faced them.[7]

Though the intelligence portrait was clear, Currie could not but find it daunting. The Canal itself, and the flooded areas that surrounded it, made his available approaches limited and replete with complications. Moreover, as already seen, the

Map 6.1
Canal du Nord and Cambrai Operations

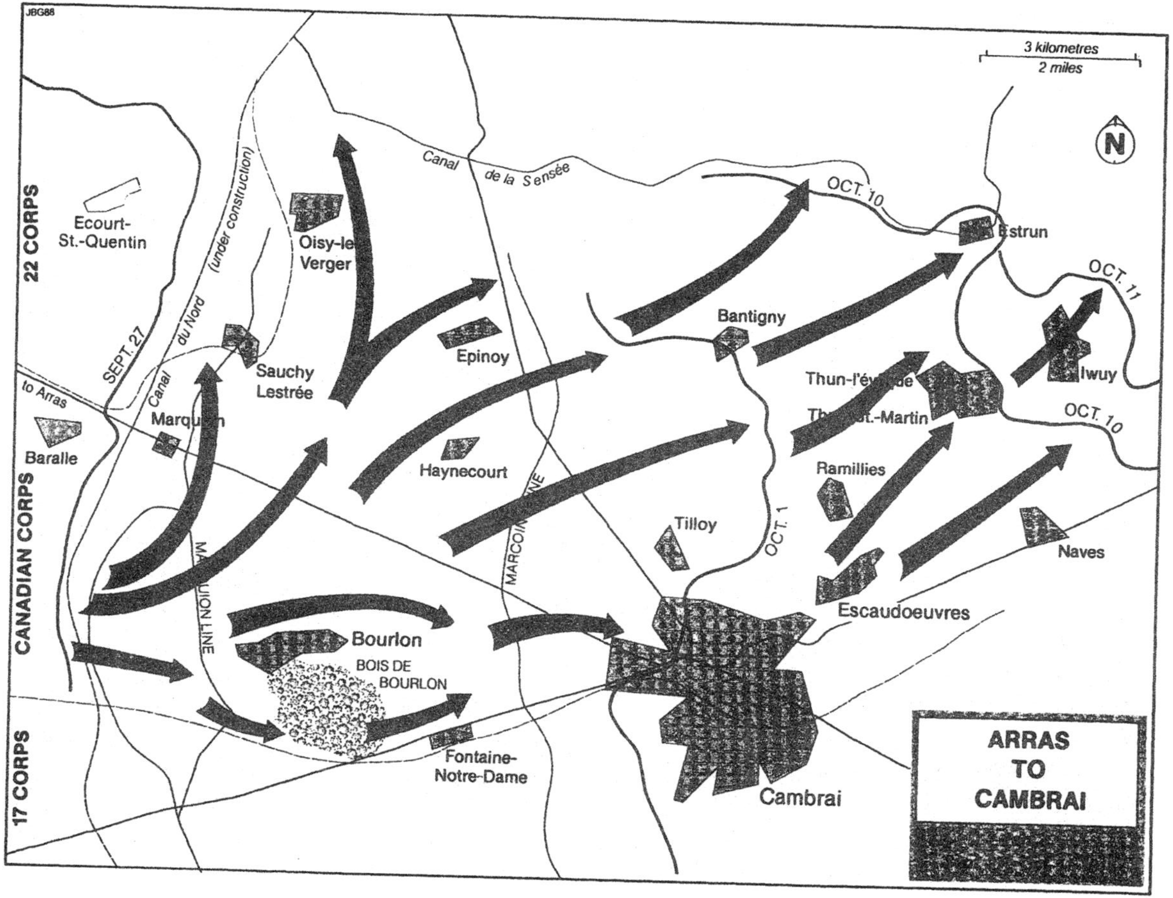

ARRAS
TO
CAMBRAI

N

3 kilometres
2 miles

OCT. 11

Iwuy

OCT. 10

Naves

Estrun

OCT. 10

Thun-l'Évêque
Thun-St-Martin

Ramillies

Escaudoeuvres

OCT. 10

Bantigny

OCT. 1

Cambrai

Tilloy

Canal de la Sensée

MARCOING LINE

Epinoy

Haynecourt

Bourlon
BOIS DE BOURLON

Fontaine-Notre-Dame

Oisy-le-Verger

Sauchy
Lestrée

Marquion

MARQUION LINE

Canal du Nord (under construction)

SEPT. 27

to Arras

Ecourt-St-Quentin

Baralle

22 CORPS

CANADIAN CORPS

17 CORPS

Canal was protected by its own line of defenses, and two lines further in depth around Bourlon Wood and Cambrai, the Marquion and Marcoing Lines (See Map 6.1). In Currie's words: "A thorough reconnaissance of our front had shown that the frontal attack of the Canal du Nord was impossible.... The whole of our forward area was under direct observation,...and any attempt to bring guns forward...was severely punished."[8] The Germans had come to the same conclusion about the likelihood of an assault in this sector, and had therefore disposed their forces with the majority north of the Sensee River. Of the 21 German divisions that were facing the First Army, 13 were north of the Sensee River, while only 8 (3 in line and 5 in reserve) were opposite the Canadian Corps' front.[9] In anticipating a British frontal attack elsewhere on the Canal, however, the Germans had opened a window of opportunity for Currie.

Currie's audacious solution to his tactical dilemma made maximum advantage out of the bad hand of cards he had been dealt. Realizing that his only hope of successfully crossing the Canal was through a narrow, dry corridor only 2,600 yards wide, Currie proposed to push his divisions, nose to tail, down this defile. Once clear of the Canal, the divisions would then fan out north and east, one division rolling up the Marquion Line along its flank, while the others pounded eastward, enveloping Bourlon Wood from the north and south, and isolating Cambrai by smashing the Marcoing Line. According to Currie:

This attack was fraught with difficulties. On the Corps battlefront of 6,400 yards the Canal du Nord was impassable on the northern 3,800 yards. The Corps had, therefore to cross the Canal du Nord on a front of 2,600 yards, and to expand later fanwise in a north-easterly direction to a front exceeding 15,000 yards. This intricate manoeuvre called for the most skillful leadership on the part of the commanders, and the highest state of discipline on the part of the troops.

The assembly of the attacking troops in an extremely congested area known by the enemy to be the only one available was very dangerous especially in view of the alertness of the enemy. A concentrated bombardment of this area prior to zero, particularly if gas was employed, was a dreaded possibility which could affect the whole operation and possibly cause its total failure.[10]

Currie's gamble was one that might have proved too intimidating for other corps commanders. Once again, as at Orange Hill and Monchy in late August, the boldness of Currie's plan disturbed his superiors. General Horne was adamantly opposed to the turning movement, claiming that it was too complicated, and fearing the heavy losses that may be incurred if something went awry.[11] Currie refused to revise his plan, however, and Horne took the matter up with Haig. Having had faith in Currie's ability to work miracles before, Haig backed the Corps commander. Horne remained unconvinced however, and tried one last ploy. He asked Currie's close friend, and the commander of the Canadian Corps at Vimy, General Sir Julian Byng, to check on Currie's plan. After inspecting Currie's plan, Byng commented to the Canadian: "Do you realize that you are attempting one of the most difficult operations of the war? If anybody can do it, the Canadians can do it, but if you fail, it means home for you.[12] Currie remained undaunted. He mollified General Horne by making a small modification in the timing of the second phase of his attack plan, and then concentrated on supervising the detailed preparations. Again, Currie would do it his way.[13]

Currie's willingness to accept the risks of such an audacious attack was based on an honest confidence in his Corps' operational ability, and an understanding that the other option -- a frontal attack almost certain to result in heavy casualties -- was unacceptable. By using a sword instead of a sledgehammer, Currie sought to achieve his tactical objectives without jeopardizing Canada's most valuable military asset, the Canadian Corps. Horne's unwilling acquiesence to Currie's plan also firmly underlined Currie's primacy in operations where his Corps formed the "spearhead." Haig's refusal to overrule Currie on Horne's behalf supports the position that Haig trusted Currie's judgment in operational matters more than some of his own Army commanders.[14] Moreover, it was indicative of the growing realization that the Canadian Corps, and by extension Canada, was now a "junior but sovereign ally."[15]

Horne made Currie's plan official in written orders issued by First Army HQ on 22 September. These orders reflected the primacy of the Canadian Corps in the operation, stating that, "the operations of the First Army will be carried out by the Canadian Corps, with the co-operation of XXII and VIII Corps." The British formations had a very important role to play, for they were to draw the Germans' attention away from the Canadian Corps by feigning an attack to the north, thus holding the bulk of the enemy's forces in this area until the Canadian Corps could secure its foothold on the far side of the Canal.[16]

Currie had initially anticipated seizing only the Canal du Nord and Bourlon Wood. The operation, however, was expanded by GHQ orders on 22 September to include the high ground further east dominating Cambrai, and up to the Canal de l'Escaut. To assist in this additional task, Currie was given under command the Eleventh British Division and the Seventh Tank Battalion. The latter unit could only muster 28 Mark IV tanks, so Currie could not count on mechanical superiority, as at Amiens, to carry the day for him.[17]

The paltry number of tanks available were further dispersed throughout the Corps, one company (8 tanks) being allotted to each of the First, Third, and Fourth Canadian Divisions. The technological limitations of the tanks during this period were clearly indicated by the Corps orders, which noted that "in view of the obstacle created by the Canal, it is doubtful if the tanks ...can get forward fast enough to be of any material assistance before the Red Line is reached.... In any case, they cannot be counted on for Z plus 1 Day."[18] Instead of tanks, Currie would be relying on the infantry-artillery attacks that had proved so successful for the Canadian Corps in the past.

Currie's maneuver plan reflected the audacity of the attack. He broke the operation down into two phases, the first being the set-piece crossing of the Canal du Nord and seizure of Bourlon Wood, the second, the capture of the bridges over the Canal de l'Escaut and the high ground dominating Cambrai on the north.[19] During the first phase, the First Canadian Division would roll up the Marquion Line along its flank from south to north. Simultaneously, the Fourth Canadian Division would "envelope Bourlon Wood from north to south, leaving the center of the wood to be mopped up later." Once this was accomplished, the Third Canadian and Eleventh British Divisions would be brought into the bridgehead, and the attack pushed outward for phase two. According to the Corps' orders:

Corps Commander's intention is to gain as much ground as possible beyond Blue line on Z day, provided the resistance is not more than can be overcome by open warfare tactics, i.e manoeuvre, supported by a limited amount of artillery.

If, however, the enemy resistance cannot be overcome without considerable artillery support...Divisions will devote the remainder of Z day to...making all the preparations for a co-ordinated advance under a barrage along the whole Corps front on the early hours of Z plus 1 day.[20]

In other words, if resistance stiffened, Currie planned to stop, reorganize, and try another setpiece, thus attempting to control the tempo of the battle.[21]

Despite its failure at the D-Q Line, Currie again included Brutinel's Independent Force. Its task was to exploit success along the Cambrai-Valenciennes road, with a view to, "securing the crossings over the Canal de l'Escaut between Cambrai and the Sensee." Brutinel's Brigade was "free to operate on any road suitable for its purpose," providing that it did not interfere with the flow of artillery ammunition, which was "vital to the success of the operation."[22]

Currie's proviso to Brutinel baldly pointed to the absolute necessity of workable supply lines if the attack was to be successful. It was under these conditions that Currie's earlier reorganization of the Corps Engineer resources paid huge dividends. Currie's orders made absolutely clear the crucial role of engineers in the operation: "the success of the whole operations beyond the Blue Line depends on the speed with which the Canal is bridged, and therefore all units must be prepared to give the engineers every possible facility and assistance."[23] This placed a heavy responsibility on Corps Engineer (CE), Major General Lindsay, who had been given under his control "the whole of the Corps resources in Engineer units, including the field companies and pioneer battalion of 11th Division."

The summer reorganization made Lindsay confidant that he could complete the myriad of tasks he was now given. No fewer than nine crossing sites over the Canal du Nord had to be built, three of which were to be "heavy" bridges capable of sustaining the light railway traffic necessary for artillery ammunition resupply once the divisions had started fighting in earnest on the far side of the Canal. A failure to complete these vital arteries would leave the infantry, and their supporting field artillery, on the far side of the Canal, cut off from the umbilical cord of artillery ammunition and supplies on the near side, a logistical breakdown of potentially catastrophic proportions. No other British corps, however, had the resources necessary to complete these tasks so readily at hand. The Canadian Corps not only had an existing engineer organization almost three times as large as a similar British formation, but also had four specialist bridging units already incorporated into its order of battle, perfect for just such a task as the Canal du Nord. It was almost as if Lindsay and Currie had anticipated the attack on the Canal du Nord during the summer of 1918.[24]

Like any good gambler, Currie found a way to hedge his bet; as Clausewitz said: "even in daring there can be method and caution."[25] Currie would once again be relying on his favorite trump card -- the artillery. The nature of the maneuver plan and the terrain created some complicated problems for the GOCRA, Canadian Corps, Major General Morrison. To cover the assault during phase one, Morrison devised an innovative yet practical relay barrage, in which the rolling barrage beyond the Canal du Nord was fired in relays by mobile field artillery units who crossed with the forward divisions, but remained under control of the Corps. This barrage also incorporated a "back barrage," a tactic developed and widely used throughout the war, in which a certain number of guns would begin at the far end of a barrage area, and creep slowly back toward the attacking troops until it met the forward rolling barrage. This created the impression on the enemy that he was being shelled by his own guns, seldom a morale booster for troops already under attack.

Because of the confined nature of the terrain during the early part of the attack, the barrage would be extremely dense to begin with, having approximately one 18-pounder gun firing for every 14 yards of frontage, but would later fan out in accordance with the maneuver plan, slowly reducing density to about one 18-pounder per 40 yards. The barrage also changed speeds, slowing as the troops crossed the Canal du Nord. In all, nearly 785 guns of all calibers, not including the trench mortars, were to be used by the Canadian Corps. Most of these guns would remain under Corps control throughout the first phase of the attack because, according to Morrison's report, "the depth of the rolling barrage necessitated employment of practically all the field artillery in the Corps and subsequently rendered impossible the releasing of any [field] brigades for close support [i.e. under the control of infantry brigades].[26] Providing some compensation for the lack of field artillery at the brigade-level would be the use of machine gun brigades to help "thicken up" the artillery barrage, and to provide close support direct fire to the infantry if necessary.

McNaughton, as head of the CBSO, and de facto commander of the Corps' heavy artillery, was given the vital task of providing security for the highly vulnerable Corps as it made its way into its congested assembly areas. The concerted intelligence- gathering effort throughout September had furnished the CBSO with excellent information on the location of German artillery batteries and ammunition stockpiles. The counterbattery plan for the Canal du Nord resembled that for the Amiens operation, in that once again, if the Germans began to shell the Corps before it could get clear of its assembly areas and the long, dangerous defile created by the dry bed of the Canal, McNaughton had authority to unleash his "steel rain" early. If the Corps was not compromised prior to zero hour, then the counterbattery effort would coincide with the initial onslaught of the divisions, again timed to steal away the German means of retaliation and defense at the exact moment they needed it most.[27]

Despite the Canadian Corps' ability to effectively strike back, it remained vulnerable to a German chemical attack, especially as part of a spoiling effort. The threat of a German preemptive strike, particularly their potential use of gas, was very real. The Germans had been employing chemical weapons generously throughout September in order to harass and wear down the Canadians, although these efforts mostly had a nuisance effect.[28] In fact, it appears that the Germans consistently lost chemical warfare duels with the Canadian Corps during this period, as any German shelling was usually met with a substantially greater number of gas rounds fired with good accuracy at German artillery positions. On 23 September, in response to a week of desultory German gas shelling, the Canadians responded with 3,434 rounds of gas and 563 drums of gas projected into the enemy's lines; as the Canadian Corps War Diary succinctly puts it, "there was no retaliation."[29]

Chemical warfare's greatest limitation remained its double-edged nature, as indicated by the Fourth Canadian Division's order that "the gassing of BOURLON WOOD will be stopped in sufficient time before the operations so as to enable the 11th C.I.B. to push troops through it on Z day without experiencing any ill-effects."[30] Nonetheless, a gas attack on the congested assembly areas, or as it moved through the tightly packed corridor, remained the Corps' worst nightmare as it awaited Z hour.

On the night of 26-27 September, the First and Fourth Divisions moved into their cramped assembly areas. It was to be, in Currie's words, "for everybody a night full of anxiety." The die had been cast.[31]

THE PAYOFF

Currie's gamble paid off magnificently. Once again, as at Arras, audacity had enabled him to achieve tactical surprise over the Germans. The diversionary attack to the north by XXII Corps had completely fixed the Germans' attention. The Canadian attack began at 5:20 a.m., 27 September, and by midday they had captured all of their objectives less Bourlon Wood. Here, on the right flank of the Corps, XVII Corps had been unsuccessful in its attack on Notre Dame de Dammery. This left the Fourth Division open to enfilade fire from the flank as it attempted to envelope Bourlon Wood. Despite this setback, the 11th CIB, under Odlum, pushed on to take the southern flank of the woods. By 1:01 p.m., the Fourth Canadian Division reported that it had made the Blue line.[32]

At this point, some six hours after the battle had opened, the Germans began to launch a number of strong counterattacks against both the First and Fourth Divisions. These were repulsed, but the heavy fighting took its toll on the leading formations. The Germans, nevertheless, found that by rapidly mounting counterattacks, they themselves fell prey to confusion and attrition, thus allowing subsequent attacks by the Third Canadian and Eleventh British Divisions to push deeper into their defenses. An attack was launched against the last line of defense, the Marcoing Line, on the evening of 27 September, but the Canadian Corps had simply gone too far too fast, and had outrun its artillery and logistical support. The Germans were able to hold off the last attack and, by late on the night of 27 September, the Canadian assault abated, if only temporarily.

The Corps Engineers had proven worthy of the great faith that Currie had placed in them. By 9:00 a.m. on 27 September, four two-way bridges had been constructed over the Canal. Three more elaborate trestle bridges were completed by 6:00 p.m., and the vital and complicated heavy bridges were ready for use by the morning of 28 September.[33] The Corps' artillery had also justified the faith placed in it, especially McNaughton's counterbattery effort: "Heavy casualties inflicted by our artillery has been apparent by an inspection of the battlefield. Time after time enemy batteries in the open were engaged and their crews and teams destroyed...at one position, 5, 77's [guns] were found, some still limbered, their crews and horses all dead. " Those German guns that did survive were quickly denied to the defenders by their capture. Greisbach's 1st CIB alone accounted for more than 50 German guns captured in their attack on 27 September.[34] Aside from a few unfortunate incidents of fratricide, where rounds fell short or troops advanced into their own barrage, the Canadian artillery had once again paved the way for its infantry.[35]

The tanks played a more controversial role. According to most reports, the tanks proved to be quite helpful.[36] In at least one instance, however, the tanks proved to be of more dubious assistance. In the 3rd CIB's area, two tanks that had been detailed to crush the wire in front of the Marquion Line in fact refused to go forward even when personally led and accompanied by the infantry they were sent to support. Despite the pleas of the exposed infantry, "the officer [commanding the tanks] replied that he was short of petrol -- [h]e climbed in his tank and shut the door. All four tanks then went back over the hill and out of sight."[37] The brigade commander, Brigadier General Tuxford, was livid, because the result was that "many casualties were incurred in cutting this wire, [and] the enemy,...given the opportunity to rally by the hours wait...now stiffened."[38]

This was not the only disappointment for the Canadian Corps. The failure of the Third Army's XVII Corps, under Lieutenant General C. Fergusson, to keep up with the spearhead allowed the Germans to bring enfilade fire to bear on the flank of the Fourth Canadian Division, causing heavier casualties than had been expected. Edmonds, the British official historian, later admitted:

Thus the final objective [of XVII Corps] was not secured and at night the left of XVII Corps was some three thousand yards behind the flank of the Canadian Corps. It was a matter of regret that a first class and well rested division could not have been provided to operate alongside the Canadian 4th Division.[39]

Similar problems with flanking formations would continue to haunt the Canadian Corps throughout the remainder of the war.

The Corps' achievements on 27 September easily rivalled its earlier triumph on 8 August. In a single day, the Corps had crossed and bridged the Canal du Nord, had broken two defensive lines and threatened a third, and had seized the wooded height that had proved a bane to the BEF for more than a year. Edmonds noted that the Canadian Corps' operation had resulted "in complete success," with some formations even "beyond the line suggested for exploitation."[40] The advance in some places was as much as eight kilometers, and this against well-prepared fortifications with the advantage of an excellent natural obstacle, totally unlike the pathetic defenses around Amiens on 8 August. The defenders were well prepared and certainly far more desperate than those at Amiens. Moreover, the Corps had triumphed without the weight of tanks, and without the advantage of having another elite corps, like the Australians, on their flank to help cut through these better defenses and share the brunt of the assault. The most significant difference between Amiens and Canal du Nord, however, was that the surprising success of the latter could not be attributed to anything but sound planning, intricate coordination, and the aggressive execution of an audacious plan devised by a practical, yet innovative military mind.

Interestingly enough, the German reaction to both diasters was similar. Crown Prince Rupprecht's Army group moved quickly to reinforce around Cambrai in order to stem the onrushing tide of British and Canadian forces, while Ludendorff, removed from the immediate physical danger in his HQ at Spa, had the luxury of collapsing into a deep depression. Once again, the de facto German supreme commander informed his political superiors that the war would have to be ended.[41] In his memoirs, Ludendorff specifically singled out the triumph at the Canal du Nord as the single biggest threat facing the German Armies in late September, despite the many Allied attacks across the entire front. He recorded:

> In the direction of Cambrai, on the 27th, a strong enemy attack gained ground beyond the Canal, *although every possible step had been taken to resist them*. Further south, up to the Vesle, the front held.
> In Champagne and on the western bank of the Muese a big battle had begun on the 26th of September, French and American troops attacking with far-reaching objectives. West of the Argonne we remained masters of the situation, and fought a fine defensive battle...[and] held their thrust.[42]

At Army level, every available reserve formation was being rushed in to plug the gap and stop the attackers. The rolling, open terrain around Cambrai would now become the stage for a struggle, a *schlact*, between an irresistible force and an enemy desperate to be an unmovable object.

"DEJA VU ALL OVER AGAIN"

The German reaction to the breach in this highly sensitive part of their defensive position was to "firewagon" in a large number of reserves, by railroad, if possible. The ferocity of the attack led German intelligence to mistakenly believe that they were facing not four, but *twelve* divisions of Canadians, and the Germans reacted accordingly, reinforcing with three divisions on 28 September, and four more on the 29th.[43] More important than the infantry divisions, whose combat capability had already been tremendously eroded by casualties and morale problems, were the marksman machine gun companies. The Germans, like the Canadians, had created special units of machine gunners to help reinforce thier infantry divisions. In the German case, these marksman machine gun companies were usually made up of above-average soldiers specially trained in the sighting and use of machine guns. They proved remakably cohesive, and the morale problems that affected German infantry regiments toward the end of the war seemed not to have affected the machine gun companies. Still near full strength and manned by determined soldiers, these troops would prove to be the Canadians' nemesis throughout the last half of the 100 Days.

The startling Canadian success on 27 September detonated a knee-jerk reaction from the Germans that now drew large numbers of reserves away from other sectors. In short, by the time that Rawlinson's Fourth Army began its attacks on 28-29 September, the German strategic reserve in northern France had already been committed to stopping the assault on Cambrai. Currie's gamble, in concert with Byng's operations south of the vital railway link, had paid off for all the Allied forces, as the British First and Third Armies now gnawed their way through the German counterattacks.

Although the first phase of Currie's plan had been a complete success, the transition to the second phase would be much more difficult. On 28 September, the Third Canadian Division was successful in breaking into and clearing a portion of the Marcoing Line, but by midday its advance had been brought to a halt by heavy machine gun fire. After a pause to coordinate another artillery barrage, the 7th and 9th CIB of the Third Division continued the assault into the area east of Sailly, but were again eventually frustrated by a fierce counterattack.

In contrast, the attack of the First Canadian Division was a failure, owing in large part to a poorly planned barrage which necessitated a daylight withdrawal of troops from the 10th Canadian Infantry Battalion, resulting in many unnecessary casualties. When their assault did commence, it was found that both flanks were exposed to heavy German artillery and machine gun fire. The divisional report recorded:

It became apparent that the attack could not succeed... The attacking troops however went bravely forward against the enemy entanglements, and in spite of his heavy fire calmly commenced cutting passages through by hand. For two hours this unequal fight went on in spite of swiftly dwindling numbers.[44]

This tragic episode clearly showed that despite the Corps' increasing proficiency at the combined arms battle, the infantry nonetheless occasionally found itself fighting alone against German defenses that were still formidable if not properly softened up with firepower. Attacks by the Third and 11th British Divisions also met with limited success, again checked by the spiraling weight of German machine guns and artillery.[45]

29 September saw an ever-increasing entropy in the Canadian Corps' efforts. To the south, XVII Corps under the Third Army had once more been unable to match the pace of advance, again leaving exposed the right flanks of both the First and Third Canadian Divisions. As a result, the Third Division found it necessary to clear the northern part of the Marcoing Line in Third Army's area.[46] Two assaults on Epinoy by the 11th British Division were unsuccessful, forcing the First Division to surrender progress made earlier in the day toward Abancourt, which, in turn, endangered the flank of the Fourth Division.[47] The widening attacks brought the Corps beyond the Marcoing Line and into the outskirts of Cambrai. Operations on 30 September had captured Tilloy, but the second phase of the attack had to be cancelled, again because of heavy counterattacks.

As at Amiens and at the D-Q Line, the deadly cycle of diminishing returns began to repeat itself. The initial assaults, under a relatively well-organized barrage, would be successful. When the barrage ended, or became ragged, the direct firepower of the German machine gunners would reassert its superiority over the flat terrain around Cambrai, and the infantry advance would stall. The Germans would then counterattack, and the Canadian and British infantry would be forced to beat back these counterattacks. By early afternoon, these first two acts had been played out, and the attackers would attempt to resume the offensive, only to fall prey again to the problems of advancing against superior volumes of direct firepower. The progress would come to a standstill in the late afternoon, the attackers would consolidate their gains while beating off repeated counterattack attempts, and, by nightfall, HQ staffs at brigade and divisional level would begin planning for the next day's assault.

The familiar pattern would be repeated. Success early in the day was followed by "confusion caused by inconsistent communications and unavoidable delays which resulted in a series of piecemeal attacks."[48] Battle procedure broke down as commanders, or their replacements, received increasingly shorter notice of attacks and objectives. The result was attacks that were being launched with poor reconnaissance, incomplete planning, and only minimal coordination. As battle procedure became more ragged, casualties mounted. The solution of deliberately building in a pause for battle procedure was for the most part ignored as Currie and his divisional commanders sought to pound their way down into Cambrai against an ever-increasing tide of German defenders. Moreover, even when time was allowed for detailed coordination, Currie could not control the high rate of casualties, and he could not control the Germans' dogged will to stop the breakthrough to the Scheldt. Tempo, therefore, was only a partial solution to the tactical problems of attacking a stubborn and talented defender when the attacker possessed only marginally superior forces in terms of numbers and firepower.

The dilemma came to a head on 1 October. Currie realized his divisions were exhausted after four days of continuous assaults, but he hoped that one more push might cause a German collapse, and allow the Corps to reach the Canal de l'Escaut.[49] It was therefore decided that one last set-piece attack of all four divisions, under a Corps Control barrage, would be planned for 1 October. The Corps War Diary claims that this "attack made excellent progress in the early stages," but in reality there were problems from the outset. The attack of the 11th British Division had been held up at the start line by wire obstacles, and this forced elements of the First Division to abandon their assault. Elements of the Third Division raced ahead, pushing beyond Bantigny and to the Canal bank by 8:00 a.m. At 10:00 a.m., however, "the decision of the enemy to resist to the last quickly manifested itself." Heavy counterattacks, supported by artillery concentrations, fell on the Third Division, forcing them to withdraw from Bantigny and Blecourt. The Fourth Division was similarly counterattacked. The seesaw fighting was so vicious that even an experienced Brigade commander like Victor Odlum, whose 11th CIB led the Fourth Division's attack, commented that the fighting of 1 October was, "the hardest battle in which the brigade ever engaged."[50]

Tuxford's 3rd CIB provides an excellent example of the effects of these four days of sustained operations on units. He reported that in his battalions, by 1 October, "there was evidently a certain amount of disorganization owing to

    (1) Loss of Officers....
    (2) Lack of detailed knowledge of places by all ranks, owing to lack of time.
    (3) Darkness, and lack of knowledge of the ground.
    (4) The heavy accession of new men...due to heavy losses."[51]

More important, Tuxford reported, "there can be no doubt that owing to the short time to arrange details, that the artillery...firing on our front were very much at sea [confused] regarding the barrage." As a result, the 3rd CIB advanced behind a "ragged" barrage, inevitably suffering casualties and further disorganization. It was a vicious circle. Moreover, German reinforcements continued to teem into the area.

Currie reported that the enemy reinforced the four original divisions in the Canadian sector with 6 others, plus extra artillery and 13 marksman machine gun companies, while south of Cambrai, on a British portion of front twice as wide, the enemy reinforced with only 3 divisions. Currie's decision was inevitable: "to continue to throw tired troops against such opposition...was obviously inviting a serious failure, and I accordingly decided to break off the engagement."[52]

By 2 October, Currie had halted his push toward Cambrai in order to allow fresh troops to be rotated into the line. From 3-8 October, the Canadians got a brief respite in order to prepare for the final phase of the drive to Cambrai. The Canadian Corps exchanged places with the British XVII Corps, and during a night attack on 8 October, the Corps found itself at the Canal de L'Escaut, outside of Cambrai. The battle of Arras-Cambrai was over.

It is probably best to let Currie's own words speak for what the Canadian Corps had accomplished. In his report on *Canadian Corps Operations in 1918*, Currie said:

Since August 26 the Canadian Corps had advanced 23 miles, fighting for every foot of ground and overcoming the most bitter resistance...[the Corps had] engaged and defeated decisively 31 German divisions in strongly fortified positions and under conditions most favorable to the defense. 18,585 prisoners were captured...371 guns and...over 116 square miles of French soil containing 59 towns and villages.[53]

Given the circumstances, these figures were quite a testament to the Canadian Corps' ability, but these gains were not purchased without a heavy price.

The Canadian Corps paid a high premium for its primacy in the operations of the First Army. No other formation had been tasked with taking part in three major engagements under two different armies in the same time span as the Canadian Corps. Casualty figures point dramatically to how lopsided the effort truly was. The XXII Corps, also under command of the First Army, was on the flank of the Canadian Corps between 27 September and 7 October; it sustained 86 officer and 1,840 other rank casualties. During the same period, the Canadian Corps casualty rate was nearly *ten* times as high: 707 officers and 12,913 other ranks were killed, wounded, or missing.[54] Between 2 August and 11 October, the Corps had sustained a total of over 30,000 casualties.[55]

The lopsided contribution of the Canadian Corps to the Allied attacks of late September is made even more glaring when compared to the efforts and effects of the much larger First American Army in the Meuse-Argonne region. Here, an American Army of nine large divisions[56] faced only five weak German divisions. This gave the American Army a numerical superiority of at least two to one in terms of divisions, and possibly as high as seven to one in terms of actual infantry. Yet, as already seen, the American attack at Meuse-Argonne, 26 September, was relatively unsuccessful, and created few problems for the German High Command. On the other hand, on the Canadian Corps front during the breaking of the Canal du Nord and the push to Cambrai, three Canadian and one British division defeated between seven and ten German divisions -- a superiority, at least in terms of divisions, that was precisely the reverse of the American situation![57]

The after action reports of the Canadian Corps show that despite its success, Currie, Griesbach, McNaughton, Brutinel and others continued to search for a tactical solution to the problem of maintaining momentum during sustained offensive operations. The Corps was simply unable to escape the technological restrictions it faced.   The most serious of these problems remained communications and coordination. Once again, a litany of complaints surfaced about the inadequacy of the communications systems of the era to stand up to the demands of high-intensity offensive operations day after day. One battalion CO commented:

The need of improving communications is on[c]e more emphasized. In the battle of the 29th, situations changed so fast that by the time instructions had been received from Brigade, issued in view of a certain reported condition of affairs, the circumstance had completely changed, rendering the course of action proposed altogether inapplicable.[58]

Another battalion commander agreed: "communications...still leave much to be desired. The use of...[s]ignal lines to Brigades was impossible."[59]

Communications difficulties made the already daunting task of overcoming the "fog of war" even more perplexing. Virtually every divisional report commented on the inability of commanders and staffs to coordinate support fire for forward troops in a timely and effective manner because of communication breakdowns. Human errors compounded these predicaments, as reflected by this recommendation in Fourth Division's report: "The use of Scouts by Machine Gun batteries is imperative, as nearly all situation reports appear to err considerably. In one case, the Machine Guns were asked to fire at a suppos[e]dly enemy counter-attack, which was found to be our own troops retiring."[60]

Command, control, and communications problems, confusion, and the tenacity of the German defenders created rapidly changing tactical situations, making it increasingly difficult for Currie or his divisional commanders to anticipate future events. As a result, they were forced to push operations much faster than was truly effective and efficient; in effect, the tempo set by the conductor was too fast for at least some of the orchestra members to properly keep up. To put it another way, in the time-space equation, the Canadians were now shortchanging themselves on time in order to gain space, but in some cases, the fast tempo had the opposite effect, resulting in ineffective attacks. A good example of this was the 11th CIB's attack on 30 September. According to Odlum, the brigade commander, "the failure of the attack was due to the haste with which it was thrown in and the failure to protect the exposed left flank."[61] Another formation, 6th CIB, reported: "Above all, the operations were planned and carried out on short notice, and on some occasions conferences were not even possible. Notwithstanding these difficulties, the spirit of all ranks ensured success."[62]

Tuxford, GOC 3rd CIB, reported that for his attack on 1 October, the barrage map arrived late, contained unexpected and unexplained changes, and that runners had to be used to advise the infantry battalion commanders of these last-minute changes because only one copy had been sent.[63] It seems that throughout the Canadian Corps, the quick tempo of the operations meant that orders were late in arriving, counterorders were passed too late to stop actions, and artillery barrages went astray; yet the Canadian Corps triumphed. One may rightly ask, how? The solution was simple. First, the Canadian Corps offensive tactical doctrine, including its infantry, machine gun, and artillery tactics, continued to be superior to that of the counterattacking Germans. Second, Currie's resolute will to continue the advance, and the ability of his divisions, brigades and battalions to persevere despite casualties and increasing disorganization continually wrested the initiative away from the Germans. The defender never got a chance to properly recover or reorganize after the blow of 27 September, because the fast tempo of the Canadian Corps' operations created greater command and control problems for the Germans than it did for the Canadian Corps. Odlum, almost sympathetically, recounted the story of a captured German regimental commander who had been ordered to counterattack Bourlon Wood on 28 September. The German was quite surprised to be taken prisoner, because "he stated that his battalions had counter-attacked Bourlon Wood, and he believed the counter-attack to have been a complete success!"[64]

The battle around Cambrai, from 28 September to 7 October, is probably best understood in an operational context as three distinct but intimately interconnected "battles within battles."[65] In the first place, it was a duel between the Canadian artillerymen and the German machine gunners. Whichever force could win the firefight by establishing firepower superiority usually controlled that piece of the battlefield. The second trial took place at the brigade, battalion, and company headquarters; that of the commanders and staffs at these levels to keep their units and attacks organized enough to continue advancing or defending. This was a struggle against the natural entropy of war. As one Canadian GOC noted:

The outstanding feature of the operations of the 28th was the fact...that when a Brigade has put in all its reserves and is hung up by hostile machine guns on front and flanks, it is not possible to get them forward again that day without adequate preparation; that is to say, <u>orders</u> must be got to units in the most forward zone, and this cannot be done until after dark.[66]

Last, but perhaps most importantly, the operations outside of Cambrai were a test of *will*: whose knees would buckle first, the Canadian and British infantry, or the German machine gunners? The ferocity of the four days of fighting, from 28 September to 1 October, paid homage to the courage and toughness of the soldiers of both sides, but, in the end, the "irresistable force" wore down the "immovable object."[67]

In their historical context, the Canadian Corps' operations of 27 September to 7 October must be seen as two separate but connected events, pointing to two different lessons. The crossing of the Canal du Nord and the seizure of Bourlon Wood is an excellent example of the potential for success of an intrepid plan. But audacity and maneuver cannot always ensure a decisive victory, especially if the enemy, as around Cambrai, remains relatively intact and displays a tenacious will to survive. Such battles, at least in the age of modern Western warfare, have become affairs won *extensively* but not *exclusively* by "hard pounding."

One hundred years earlier at Waterloo, Napoleon had "humbugged"

Wellington by stealing a day's march, much the same way Currie surprised German defenders of the Canal du Nord. Yet these acts were only the opening movements in a tragic and violent symphony. The second lesson, as demonstrated by the Canadian Corps' push towards Cambrai, is that *tenacity* also plays an important role in deciding the outcome of a battle. The Battle of Cambrai, 1918, like the Battle of Waterloo, is an example of a contest where two relatively equally matched forces are pitted against each other, under strategic conditions which demand a decision. In such cases, perseverance, the willingness and ability to "pound harder," may be the hallmark of not just good soldiering, but also of good generalship. Tenacity, however, does not guarantee victory if not coupled with other factors. At Waterloo and Cambrai, both the opposing sides displayed a tenacious will to win. What made the difference for the Canadian Corps at Cambrai was its superior ability to coordinate effective efforts at short notice, thereby seizing and maintaining the initiative from the Germans. In short, to paraphrase historian Ian Brown, Cambrai was a perfect example of the success of operations that were "not glamorous, but effective."[68]

For military historians, Currie's successful crossing of the Canal du Nord and the vicious fight toward Cambrai deserve greater recognition because they contain some very important lessons. First, Currie's gamble, and its payoff, proves that audacity, when coupled with tactical competence and proper organization, can be a true "force multiplier" by allowing an attacker to gain and maximize the advantages of tactical surprise. Moreover, the Canadian Corps was one of the few corps on the Western Front capable of storming and bridging the Canal as rapidly as it did. It was almost as if it was custom built specifically for such an offensive operation, with its larger engineering and logistical organizations, and an outstanding indirect fire support capability.[69] The lesson here then, is that operational formations must constantly and consciously be metamorphosizing their organizations in order to stay prepared for the *next* battle or conflict, and not the *last*.

For the Canadian Corps, the operations around Cambrai in late September-October 1918 confirmed the validity of the lessons and innovations the formation had incorporated throughout 1917 and 1918. For Currie, the Canal du Nord was his operational masterpiece, the culmination of his education as a general. Both Vimy and Amiens are more familiar to students of history, but at the Canal du Nord, Currie faced more a difficult task, and won a greater victory. He devised and stuck to an audacious plan in the face of the objection of his superiors. Whereas both Amiens and Vimy were simple frontal attacks, the Canal du Nord incorporated risk and maneuver, belying the popular myth that all major BEF attacks on the Western Front were unimaginative and predictable. The Corps' ability to arrange the attack in such a short period of time was a masterwork of coordination and staffwork. Last, as part of the greater Allied thrust, the attack unhinged Ludendorff's plan for a last stand on the Hindenberg Line, and signalled the inevitable defeat of the German Army on the Western Front.

Currie had hoped that the second phase of the Battle of Cambrai would be fought in conditions of "open warfare." But Currie also understood that after four bitter years of war, offensive operations against such a determined and well-prepared enemy were bound to be bloody, and that there was simply no escaping the "hard pounding" inflicted on the Canadian Corps. Although his hopes for "open warfare" were thwarted by the tenacious German defense of the Hindenberg system, that system now lay broken before the Allies. For Currie and the Canadian Corps, the "hard pounding" was almost over.

NOTES

1. These timings were set down in an official agreement between Foch and Haig on 23 September 1918; Edmonds, *BOH*, Vol. 5, p. 7; Terraine, *To Win a War*, pp. 153-155.

2. Dancocks, *Spearhead*, p. 127; Terraine, *To Win a War*, pp. 150-156.

3. Dancocks, *Spearhead*, p. 123.

4. See Edmonds, *BOH*, Vol. 5, pp. 14-19.

5. This famous attack has only recently been deeply examined; see, for instance, William Moore, *A Wood Called Bourlon* (London: Leo Cooper, 1988); Travers, *How the War Was Won*, pp. 19-33; and Gudmundsson, *Stormtroop Tactics*, pp. 139-155, for the German side.

6. Dancocks, *Spearhead*, pp. 127-128.

7. "CCGS War Diary," Vol. 37, 5 September -15 September 1918; Currie, *Corps Operations, 1918*, pp. 55-56, Travers, *How the War Was Won*, p. 158.

8. Currie, *Corps Operations, 1918*, p. 55.

9. These figures come from Maj. Gen. Sir W. Hastings Anderson, "The Crossing of the Canal du Nord," *Canadian Defense Quarterly*, Vol. 2, No. 1 (October 1924), p. 65.

10. Currie, *Corps Operations, 1918*, p. 57.

11. Dancocks, *Spearhead*, p. 133.

12. Quoted in ibid., pp. 2-3.

13. It is to Currie's credit that he makes no mention of this dispute in his *Corps Operations, 1918*. The episode is recounted in Urquhart, *Currie*, pp. 252-253, and Dancocks, *Spearhead*, pp. 132-134.

14. Haig was not the only one to recognize Currie's ability; ironically enough, at almost the exact same time that Haig was tacitly encouraging Currie to shape the operations of the First Army, Haig's political superiors were seriously considering Currie for Haig's job. On 14 September, Lord Milner, Secretary of State for War, met with Currie and told the Canadian that if the war went on until 1919, Currie would be placed in command of the British Army. (Letter, Currie to McGillicuddy(?), n.d., in Currie Papers, NAC, MG 30 E 100, Vol. 27, File 7.) Lloyd George confirmed this by stating that "my later idea, after I had got to know Monash [GOC Australian Corps], was to make him Chief of Staff and Currie Commander-in-Chief" (Urquhart, *Currie*, p. 227). It seems that this idea, then, was more than just an idle poke by Lloyd George at his British generals after the war; see also Dancocks, *Spearhead*, pp. 125-126.

15. Morton, *Military History of Canada*, p. 161.

16. An excerpt of these orders is quoted in Edmonds, *BOH*, Vol. 5, pp. 17-18.

17. Travers, *How the War Was Won*, p.157.

18. "B.W. Instruction, No.1," NAC, RG 9, III, D3, Vol. 4789, File 3; ("B.W." stands for Bourlon Wood), paragraph 21.

19. "B.W. Instruction No. 1," Edmonds, the British official historian, thought the attack so significant that he included these orders, whole and verbatim, as Appendix V to his *BOH*, Vol. 5. For ease of reference, the present author will refer to the Edmonds Appendix where possible.

20. "B.W. Instruction, No. 1," paragraph 9.

21. A good analogy to what Currie envisioned is that of the basketball coach who calls for a time-out when the momentum of a game swings against his team, in order to reorganize his players and reassert his gameplan.

22. "B.W. Instructions No. 1," paragraph 17.

23. "B.W. Instructions, No. 2," paragraph 1.

24. "B.W. Instructions, No.2," paragraph 25; see Chapter 2 of this work for details on the Engineer reorganization in the Canadian Corps.

25. Clausewitz, *On War*, Book 1, Chapter 1, p. 86.

26. "Artillery Notes -- Bourlon Wood, 27 September-1 October 1918," NAC, RG 9, III, D, Vol. 4807, File 176 (hereafter cited as "Artillery Notes -- Bourlon Wood.").

27. "Artillery Notes - Bourlon Wood."

28. "CCGS War Diary," Vol. 37, 10 - 25 September 1918.

29. "CCGS War Diary," Vol. 37, 23 September 1918.

30. "Fourth Canadian Division B.W. Instructions, No.2," contained in "Fourth Canadian Division Report on Operations Around CAMBRAI, 27 September-1 October 1918," NAC, RG 9, III, Vol. 4797, File 10. The latter is hereafter referred to as "4 Can Div Report-Cambrai."

31. Anderson, "The Crossing of the Canal du Nord by the First Army, 27th September, 1918," *Canadian Defense Quarterly*, Vol. II, No. 1 (Oct. 1924) pp. 63-77; Currie, *Corps Operations, 1918*, pp. 59-59.

32. "CCGS War Diary," Vol. 37, 27 September 1918; see also Nicholson, *CEF*, pp. 445-448, and Edmonds, *BOH*, Vol.5, pp. 19-29.

33. "CCGS War Diary," Vol. 37, 27 September 1918; Edmonds, *BOH*, Vol. 5, pp. 24-25 .

34. Letter, Griesbach to Sir Archibald Macdonell, n.d., Griesbach papers, NAC, MG 30, E15, Vol. 5, File 33D.

35. "Artillery Notes - Bourlon Wood."

36. See "CCGS War Diary," Vol. 37, 27 September 1918, and Nicholson, *CEF*, p. 447.

37. Statement of Major I.H.R. Sinclair, 13th Canadian Battalion, to 3rd CIB, dated 30 September 1918, NAC RG 9, III, D2, Vol. 4793, File 46.

38. Brigadier General Tuxford, "Operations of 3rd Canadian Infantry Brigade - October 1918," NAC, RG 9, III, D2, Vol. 4793, File 46, p. 5. The same information is contained in "1st Canadian Division Report on Canal du Nord-Bourlon Wood-Cambrai Operations (September 27th to October 2nd 1918, inclusive) Section II (C)-Attack of 3rd Canadian Infantry Brigade," NAC, RG 9, III, D, Vol. 4793, File 46, p. 3. (The entire 1st Division Report will hereafter be referred to as "1 Can Div Report - Bourlon Wood".)

39. Edmonds, *BOH*, Vol. 5, p. 36. In fact, the very good 63rd (Royal Naval) division had been on the Fourth Division's flank for the first part of the day, but was later "leap-frogged" by the 57th (West Lancashire) Division, about which Edmonds' comments were made. Neither proved able to keep up to the Fourth Canadian Division.

40. Edmonds, *BOH*, Vol. 5, p. 29.

41. See Ludendorff, *My War Memories*, pp. 718-722. Popular myth has it that upon hearing of the German Armies' setbacks, Ludendorff had a complete nervous breakdown, even foaming at the mouth. This has been denied by Ludendorff's personal physician at the time, Dr. Hochheimer; see Parkinson, *Tormented Warrior*, pp. 178-183.

42. Ludendorff, *My War Memories*, pp. 718-719.

43. The divisions brought in on 28 September were the 22nd and 207th German Divisions, and the 1st Guards Reserve Division; on 29 September, 26th Reserve, 234th, 35th,

and elements of the 49th and 18th Reserve Divisions; Nicholson, *CEF*, p. 454.

44. "Narrative of 28th September 1918," Section III C, "Subsequent Operations," "1 Can Div Report - Bourlon Wood," p. 2.

45. For reports on the attacks on 28 September, see "CCGS War Diary," Vol. 37, 28 September 1918; Nicholson, *CEF*, pp. 449-50; Edmonds, *BOH*, Vol. 5, pp. 53-55; "1 Can Div Report-Bourlon Wood," section III.

46. Currie, *Corps Operations 1918*, p. 60.

47. Ibid., p. 60.

48. Dancocks, *Spearhead*, p. 148.

49. Currie, *Corps Operations 1918*, p. 61.

50. Odlum diary, NAC, MG 30 E300 Vol. 57, File 20, p. 20.

51. Tuxford, "Report on Operations, of 1st October 1918," p. 3.

52. Currie, *Corps Operations 1918*, p. 62.

53. Ibid. , p. 68.

54. Edmonds, *BOH*, Vol. 5, p. 155.

55. Nicholson, *CEF*, p. 460.

56. American divisions were roughly twice the size of British divisions - 28,000 men versus 14-16,000 - the primary difference being in infantry; see David Trask, *The AEF in Coalition Warmaking, 1917-1918* (Lawrence: University Press of Kansas, 1993), p. 18.

57. I have borrowed this comparison from the papers of Brig.Gen. William Griesbach, who made this point in rebuttal to an article written by American Brigadier Henry O'Reilly in *Liberty Magazine*, 29 January 1927, that claimed that the American Army won the war for the Allies; Griesbach papers, NAC, MG 30 E15, Vol. 1, File 2. Griesbach uses the figure of 21 American divisions. David Trask, an American historian, also makes this comparison in *The AEF and Coalition Warmaking*, p. 172. It must be kept in mind that these American forces had nowhere near the experience or training that the Canadian Corps did, and the difference between a seasoned, veteran formation and a "green" army are painfully exhibited by this disparity.

58. Lt. Col. J .L. Ralston, CO 85th (Nova Scotia Highlanders) Infantry Battalion, "4 Can Div Report-Cambrai."

59. Lt. Col. M. Scott, in ibid.

60. "4th Battalion Canadian Machine Gun Corps - Lessons," in ibid.

61. Brig. Gen. Victor Odlum, GOC 11 CIB, "Narrative of Operations of 11th Canadian Infantry Brigade, September 27th to October 2nd, 1918," in ibid.; see also Travers, *How the War Was Won*, pp. 162-163.

62. "Narrative of Operations-Sixth Canadian Infantry Brigade, October 1st to 12th 1918" NAC, RG 9, III, D, Vol. 4794, File 53, p.14.

63. "3 CIB Report-1 October 1918," p. 2.

64. Odlum Papers, NAC, MG 30 E 300, Vol. 57, File 20.

65. This idea of "battles within battles" is taken from John Keegan's *The Face Of Battle* (London: Penguin, 1976).

66. Brig. Gen. Hayter, GOC 10 CIB, "10 CIB Report-Cambrai, dated 11 October 1918," NAC, RG 9, III, D, Vol. 4797, File 10.

67. It was a testament to the ability of the German Army that they were able to mount so many counterattacks throughout those four days, especially considering the mauling many units had taken throughout the spring and summer of 1918.

68. Brown, "Not Glamorous, But Effective," pp. 443-444.

69. One must also note that the Australian Corps, again under Rawlinson, breached

the equally formidable Somme Canal on 2 September, and that the British IX Corps crossed the difficult St. Quentin Canal on 29 September; they had, however, fewer engineering resources, in some cases crossing the Canal using lifebelts. See Bean, *AOH*, Vol. 6, pp. 772-1043; Terraine *To Win A War*, pp. 162-174, and Edmonds, *BOH*, Vol. 5, pp. 95-111.

7

"ALLEGRETTO": THE PURSUIT TO VALENCIENNES

> . . . the importance of the victory is chiefly determined by the vigor with which the immediate pursuit is carried out. In other words, pursuit makes up the second act of the victory.
>
> Clausewitz, *On War*
> Book 4, Chapter 12

Even as the first Canadian troops were entering Cambrai, the Germans were making clear their intention to make the Allied advance as costly as possible. Finding the center of the city ablaze, soldiers from the Second Canadian Division captured German troops who claimed to be under orders to set fire to Cambrai in order to destroy anything the Allies might use, and to delay their advance. Like a tsunami receding back into the ocean, the German Army left in its wake a shattered countryside of blown bridges, cratered roads, and destroyed railway lines. All this had been done in hopes of delaying, and if possible stemming the onrushing tide of Allied forces. The Germans now pinned their hopes on the Hermann Line, an incomplete and only loosely connected set of positions anchored by the built-up area around Valenciennes in the north on the BEF front. The German Army was now fighting a desperate yet stubborn rearguard action in hopes of forestalling its collapse.

Desperate times called for desperate gambles. On 11 October, only two days after surrendering Cambrai, the Germans launched a counterattack from the village of Avesnes le Sec, approximately 5 kilometers northeast of Cambrai, toward the Canadian Corps. Accompanying the attacking force were seven tanks: three German and four captured British machines. The Canadian response was one of mixed incredulity and morbid curiosity at finally being on the receiving end of a tank assault; one soldier reportedly mistook the tanks for "moving houses." Once over their surprise, however, the Canadians quickly applied the German solution to tank assaults, called up a battery of field artillery, and, firing over open sights, put all but one out of action. The counterattack eventually failed, no doubt confirming for the Germans what the Canadians already knew: tanks themselves did not guarantee success in offensive operations, nor were they even particularly effective when used in small numbers.[1]

More effective than the tanks were the ubiquitous German machine gunners. Heavy machine gun fire from well-camouflaged, mutually supporting "shellholes" now became the chief impediment to the Corps' advances. The Canadians responded by emphasizing the use of infantry patrols and hasty flanking attacks in order to outmaneuver the German machine gun positions. Once outflanked, isolated machine gun detachments usually retired to a rearward position. This cat-and-mouse game continued throughout middle and late October, as the Germans doggedly traded space for time in their retreat to the Hermann Line. In essence, the depth of elastic defense's forward zone had become so deep that it in itself almost became elastic defense.[2]

The breaching of the Hindenberg Line did not bring the breakthrough into "open green fields" that the senior Allied commanders had for so long hoped for. The "open warfare" envisaged by men like Haig, Horne, and even Currie fell prey to the same technological and tactical advances and limitations that had so drastically and irrevocably changed the face of battle from 1916 to 1918. It could not and did not return to the stage after a hiatus of four years for a number of reasons, the primary ones being the tenacity of the German machine gunner, the change in terrain, and, most important, the operational restrictions faced by the BEF. For most of October, the Canadian Corps found itself hindered by the Canal de l' Escaut, an obstacle which ran diagonally through its area and caused repeated problems, primarily because the waterway required bridging resources, and because the Germans had blown its locks and flooded the lowlands that surrounded it. Currie reported:

> The enemy's demolition had been very well planned and thoroughly carried out, all bridges over the canals and streams being destroyed, every cross road and road junction rendered impassable...and the railways...blown up at frequent intervals. The enemy also considerably impeded our progress by his clever manipulation of the water levels in the canals which he controlled.[3]

Furthermore, the Canadian Corps was now advancing into the heavily populated coal producing region of France, and the large industrial areas and well built towns that filled this region created their own unique operational challenges.

Throughout almost the entire war on the Western Front, the combatant armies had fought over a virtual wasteland devoid of any civilian presence, with built-up areas reduced to nothing more than formless rubble. Now, however, the Canadians were progressing into territory where the danger of inflicting casualties on innocent civilians increased with almost every kilometer advanced. This created problems heretofore unknown for the Canadian Corps. It placed restrictions on its use of artillery, especially the use of high explosive rounds, near inhabited areas. This restriction, accepted as absolutely necessary from a moral and humanitarian perspective, nonetheless made the Corps' job much more difficult and dangerous as the German defenders, especially the machine gunners, began to seek refuge in the excellent concealment provided by buildings on the outskirts of towns. The recommended method for dealing with this limitation was to "shell approaches and the edges of such places, and [use] smoke [within] the village itself." This method often left counterattack forces concealed inside the built-up area untouched, creating further difficulties and dangers for the assaulting forces. It was precisely this problem that allowed the Germans to mass and counterattack from Avesnes on 11 October.[4]

A more pressing problem was how to cope with the needs of the growing numbers of refugees and newly liberated civilians. The population in this area of France had been stripped of their food by the retreating German Army, and many villages now turned to their liberators for food and protection. On 18 October, Currie reported that 2,000 civilians from the town of Auberchicourt, "had been left by the retiring enemy without food," placing an additional burden on an already overtaxed supply system. By 21 October this number would swell to over 90,000 civilians.[5] Currie's report continued:

Faced as we were with an ever lengthening line of communication, and with only one bridge available...the work of the supply services was greatly increased. This additional burden was, however, cheerfully accepted, and the liberated civilians...as well as our rapidly advancing troops, were at no time without a regular supply of food.[6]

A large part of the "regular supply" came from the soldiers themselves, as Currie pointed out: "Many of the units have voluntarily given up 15% of their rations to the inhabitants."[7] Overall, the Canadians were greeted enthusiastically, and Currie went out of his way to ensure that his Corps maintained friendly relations with the locals.

The Canadian Corps was now reaching the limits of its logistical capabilities, and its administrative lifeline became more of a tether. Since August, the Corps had advanced over 40 kilometers from its original supply bases. Food, ammunition, medical supplies, and replacements now had to be transported relatively long distances over a shattered transportation network. The Corps Engineers made a huge contribution through their efforts to keep the supply lines open. The Engineers not only had to cope with the tactical requirements of dismantling a large number of German "booby traps," but also with the logistical necessity of repairing cratered roads, demolished bridges, and sabotaged canals. The work schedule for Lindsay's men was nothing short of frenetic, and Currie reported that "their resources in men and material were taxed to the utmost." Despite the engineers' herculean efforts, Currie conceded: "It was clear from the wholesale destruction of roads and railways that the reconstruction of communications would be very slow and that it would be difficult to keep our troops supplied."[8] Not surprisingly, there was little sympathy from those nearer the front who could not, or would not, understand the staggering logistical problems the Corps now faced; said one antiaircraft officer:

Our HQ...are at present at least 30 miles behind the line & we have to draw our rations from them....Such insanity as drawing rations for 5 sections 30 miles over bad roads when HQ could easily be with second line section....Too much whisky and fast life is responsible for it all. It is nothing short of criminal.[9]

Even Currie became frustrated, complaining bitterly in his diary that:

> the enemy is making a very orderly and practically unmolested retirement. Our trouble is that the troops are very tired and that the getting forward of supplies is becoming difficult owing to the distance away of railheads. Our Higher Authorities do not seem well enough organized to push their railheads forward fast enough.[10]

The rapid retreat of the main body of the German forces created a new tactical challenge for the Canadian Corps, and for most of the other formations in the BEF. The Canadian response was initially cautious. From 12 to 17 October, the pursuit was really a mopping-up operation in and around the Canal de l' Escaut. The Corps would begin the advance every morning with "test barrages" on suspected enemy positions in order to ascertain their intentions. If the Germans failed to respond in strength, which was usually the case, infantry patrols were sent forward to make contact with the enemy and report on their disposition. What these patrols usually found was that the German positions of only the night before had been abandoned, and that the enemy had successfully broken contact with the Canadians. This loss of contact with the enemy concerned Currie, for it allowed the Germans too much operational freedom. The infantry patrols would then have to push forward rapidly in order to reestablish contact, this occurring usually during midday.

From 17 October onwards, the Germans began their retreat in earnest, and the test barrage-infantry patrol method was found to be too ponderous. The leading divisions were augmented by the attachment of cavalry, and of armored cars and machine gun batteries from the Motor Machine Gun Brigades. The mobility and speed of these elements proved more effective at maintaining contact with the enemy, but they remained too vulnerable to the machine gun fire to clear away the rearguards. Moreover, the armored cars remained limited to open terrain and roads, and were easily stopped by the cratered roads and blown bridges in the area. Once again, a technological shortcoming would have to be overcome with a tactical solution.[11]

The Canadian Corps response had as its genesis the open warfare exercises of the summer training period. The solution emphasized the close cooperation of all arms, including the Air Force. In the particular case of the pursuit to Valenciennes, the forward divisions advanced with one brigade forward, where possible, leapfrogging the brigades as they became exhausted. The brigades followed suit, pushing forward a new battalion roughly every day. The infantry were usually preceded by a forward screen of cavalry, cyclists, and armored cars, as well as trench mortars and some field artillery detachments, whose job it was to maintain contact with the enemy rear guard, and push them aside if possible. The ground captured by the armored cars would then be occupied by the infantry, and the gains consolidated. This use of the armored cars and cavalry as a forward screen had the added advantage of keeping the infantry relatively safe from direct fire while continuing to push the advance.

The artillery, especially the CBSO, was assisted in its task of harassing the main body of the enemy by the use of air contact patrols. Able to fly above the German rear guard, and therefore with a better opportunity to spot targets of primary importance such as troop concentrations, artillery positions, and resupply facilities, the aircraft would act as spotters for the artillery shoots in depth. The aircraft had a further advantage of speed and, therefore, if contact was lost, the Air Force could quickly scan the area for the enemy's rearguards and report back. This air-to-ground coordination was extremely successful, providing not only near real-time intelligence and target acquisition capabilities, but doing so in an economical manner in terms of friendly casualties and ammunition. By mid-October the Canadian Corps had put these elements together and, necessity being the mother of invention, developed a largely unwritten doctrine for limited pursuit operations.[12]

Daily operations took on a predictable rhythym during this period, 18-25 October. A rapid advance could be made every morning because the enemy had retired during the night, in some cases succeeding in breaking contact with the forward elements of the Canadian Corps. Contact with the enemy would be regained by midmorning, and resistance would slowly increase as the Corps' forward elements moved deeper into the machine gun-dependent rear guard. At some point in the early afternoon, the advance would stall, and the lead infantry battalions would consolidate their gains. A weak German counterattack was often launched at this point, followed by a evening of vigorous patrolling by the Canadian infantry. During the night, the Germans would once more slip away like ghosts, and the whole cycle, beginning with the advance to contact, would recommence the following morning. Currie, hoping to reduce casualties, discouraged his brigades from becoming heavily engaged during the pursuit; it would have been senseless anyway, as the Canadians only had to wait until the next morning to find the German position abandoned. The pace of these operations became so predictable that Burstall, GOC Second Division, even went so far as to predict a precise time for the German counterattack: "during recent operations, the enemy has most frequently attacked about 1500 hours." The result was, as Travers has put it, "mobile warfare had thus become a structured science rather than an art."[13]

Currie would have preferred to push the pursuit faster, but did not do so for some good reasons. First, the Corps was far in advance of its lengthening and weakening supply lines, and its logistical tail became more of a drag the further it advanced. Second, the Corps lacked the technological means for a more rapid pursuit; the vulnerability of the armored cars and cavalry limited their usefulness. Moreover, a more aggressive pursuit would probably have generated a higher casualty rate, a situation Currie and other leaders were loath to permit, especially since the Corps had already suffered over 35,000 casualties since early August. The tenacity and bravery of the German machine gunners, and their success in trading space for time, could not be underestimated. Last, it must be pointed out that despite all these problems, the Canadian Corps still maintained an average advance of over 4 kilometers per day throughout the period 11 to 24 October.[14] Economy of effort, a sensitivity to needless casualties, and a looming logistical breakdown conspired to keep the Canadian Corps, like the rest of the BEF, from taking full advantage of the opportunity for "open warfare" that presented itself in October 1918.

As October wore on, and the Canadian Corps neared the border of France and Belgium, a subtle change occurred in the pursuit operations. From 25 October onward, German resistance stiffened, and a large number of concentrated enemy artillery batteries reappeared.[15] The BEF was now closing with the Hermann Line, the last resort of the shattered German Army. In the First Army sector, the Germans had concentrated their forces around the city of Valenciennes, and the dominant terrain feature of the region, Mount Houy. It would be here that the Canadians would fight their last grand battle of the Great War.

NOTES

1. " CCGS War Diary," Vol. 38, 11 October 1918; "Report on Independent Force," NAC, RG 9, III, D, Vol. 4807, File 170; Dancocks, *Spearhead*, p. 178. A controversy over the actual number of tanks appears to be a problem of perspective; that is, not all units saw all the tanks.

2. See Wray, *Standing Fast*, pp. 6-8, for the modification of elastic defense.

3. Currie, *Corps Operations 1918*, p. 75.

4. "First Army No. G.S. 1290-Notes on Conference of Corps Commanders Held at First Army Headquarters on 27th October, 1918." "CCGS War Diary," Vol. 38, (October 1918).

5. "CCGS War Diary," Vol. 38, 21 October 1918.

6. Currie, *Corps Operations 1918*, p. 74.

7. Currie, quoted in Dancocks, *Spearhead*, p. 184.

8. Currie, *Corps Operations 1918*, pp. 73-75.

9. Lt. James McRuer, E Battery, Canadian Anti-Aircraft Artillery, quoted in Travers, *How the War Was Won*, p. 172.

10. Currie, diary entry, 20 October 1918. NAC, MG 30 E 100, Vol. 43.

11. "CCGS War Diary," Vol. 38, 11-28 October 1918; see especially the entries for 17 -21 October; Currie, *Corps Operations 1918*, p. 72; Report on Independent Force-Brutinel`s Brigade, NAC, RG 9, III, D, Vol. 4807, File 170; Travers ,*How the War Was Won*, pp. 172-173.

12. See Nicholson, *CEF*, pp. 461-470, and Travers, *How the War Was Won*, p. 172.

13. " CCGS War Diary," Vol. 38, 16-25 October 1918; Maj. Gen. Henry Burstall, GOC 2nd Division, "General Staff Instructions, 2nd Canadian Division, G.S. 190. dated 5 November 1918," Burstall Papers, NAC, MG 30 E6, Vol. 4, File 28; Travers, *How the War Was Won*, pp. 172-173.

14. For these figures, see Currie, *Corps Operations 1918*, p. 83.

15. See "CCGS War Diary," Vol. 38, 25-30 October, 1918. The number of hostile batteries engaged increased from 3 on 25 October to 12 on 26 October, and 25 on 27 October. See also Currie, *Corps Operations 1918*, pp. 75-77.

8

"CODA": MOUNT HOUY TO MONS

It is with artillery that war is made.
Napoleon[1]

After nearly two weeks of pursuit, the British First Army closed up to the determined German rearguard in the area of Valenciennes and Mount Houy, the key to the Hermann Line. Here, the First Army paused in order to stabilize its front and sort out its lengthening logistical tail.[2] It would be difficult to understate the value of Mount Houy and Valenciennes to its German defenders. Mount Houy is a long, low ridge rising about 50 meters above the flat plains that surround it, overlooking them for a distance of nearly 20 miles. From a military perspective, it is an almost ideal place for a large defensive position because it dominates all of the surrounding area, while its convex slopes allow for excellent fields of fire on its forward slope, and abundant areas for defensive works in depth, artillery gun positions, and counter attack assembly areas on its wide reverse slopes.

From this perspective, Mount Houy is probably more of a dominating terrain feature than Vimy Ridge, for it is both larger in size and overlooks a wider area. Coupled with the bottleneck created by the built-up area of Valenciennes, and the obstacle of the Canal de l'Escaut, it is little wonder why the Germans chose Mount Houy and its environs to nail down the Hermann Line in this sector of the Western Front. By the last week of October, the Germans had elements of *five* divisions on or around Mount Houy, with further counterattack forces essentially hiding in Valenciennes, using the city's large civilian population and its many buildings as improvized cover from Allied attack. More tellingly, the Germans had decided to mass their artillery resources in the region near Mount Houy.[3]

Haig's overall plan was to have Horne's First Army take Valenciennes as a preliminary to a general attack on the Hermann Line. To this end, Horne outlined a plan on 27 October that had General Godley's XXII Corps capturing Mount Houy, while the Canadian Corps supported this attack by securing the southern and eastern approaches to Valenciennes. This would turn the flank of the German positions from the south, and avoid the more serious natural water obstacles to the north of Valenciennes.[4]

Horne also chose this meeting to proselytize to Currie and Godley on his conception of future operations. For the most part, Horne's comments point to the fact that he was out of touch with what was happening inside his own Army. Horne felt it necessary to lecture Currie with the statement: "I wish to draw attention to the importance of organising good covering fire at the commencement of an attack." This direction was probably meant more for Godley than for Currie, as Horne would not just have been preaching to the converted had he directed his remarks to the Canadian, but would have seemed to be quoting scripture and verse to one of the apostles. Horne emphasized one of his last points, "the importance of pressing the attack where resistance is weakest...thus turning and enveloping the strong points," by pointing to two examples -- the D-Q Line and the Canal du Nord -- which were actually designed and executed by Currie.[5] More tragically, it appears that Horne's advice -- however well-intentioned or profound -- may have missed the real target it was intended for, falling on the deaf ears of Godley.

While Horne's plan to take Valenciennes from the south was sound in theory, its attainment rested almost completely on the success of the XXII Corps' attack on Mount Houy. It has been suggested by Andrew McNaughton that XXII Corps misunderstood the value of Mount Houy to the German defenses, and therefore underestimated the tenacity with which they would defend the high feature.[6] Currie was also skeptical of the success of Godley's plan, especially because the division tagged to make the attack, the excellent 51st Highland, had already made one unsuccessful attempt on the slope. As a result, McNaughton, newly promoted to brigadier general and now in command of the Canadian Corps' heavy artillery, was directed by Currie to offer the Corps Artillery's expertise in wire cutting to the GOCRA XXII Corps. When McNaughton did so, he was hastily rebuffed by his somewhat insulted opposite in XXII Corps. This ill-considered reaction was to lead to tragic consequences.[7]

The XXII Corps attack, conducted by the 51st Highland Division on the morning of 28 October, was a failure. Despite the tenacity and bravery of the Highlanders, and their early success, the Germans managed to regain possession of most of Mount Houy after a vicious, day-long, see-saw battle. By nightfall, Currie realized that the Canadians would "have to take that damn hill," and requested that a planned relief of the 51st Highland Division by the Fourth Canadian Division be postponed.[8] Currie was subsequently criticized after the war by Major-General, General Staff (MGGS) of the First Army Sir W. H. Anderson, for not coming to the rescue of the Highlanders.[9]

In retrospect, however, it seems that Currie made a wise choice. First, as any infantry soldier can attest, a nighttime relief in place is a difficult operation to carry out, even under the best conditions, and virtually impossible if the force to be relieved is still under heavy enemy contact and unsure of the status and location of all its subunits; these were precisely the conditions the Fourth Division would have found themselves in had Currie allowed the relief to take place. Moreover, as McNaughton later pointed out in Currie's defense: "to do so would have involved us in continuing an operation badly deranged without any chance of organizing for the effective use of our artillery in support of our infantry; would have invited a fourth failure, and... inevitably a bloody price would have been paid."[10] Much of the blame for the failure must inevitably rest not on the shoulders of the Highlanders, who fought heroically throughout 28-29 October, but on Godley and the HQ staff of XXII Corps for failing to understand the importance of the position, and for failing to employ overwhelming indirect firepower, despite Horne's admonitions and McNaughton's offer of assistance.

In contrast, the Canadian Corps attacks on 28 October in support of the Highlanders' assault on Mount Houy went off successfully. These operations, against much less imposing positions, it must be noted, left the Canadian Corps in possession of terrain on *three* sides of Mount Houy. Given this advantageous position, Horne agreed to Currie's request for a postponement of subsequent operations, and new orders were issued. As usual, under Horne's revised plan, the Canadian Corps became responsible for carrying out virtually all of the First Army's attack. In the words of Major General Anderson, "the standby of the First Army in all the operations from Vimy... to the end of war was the Canadian Corps."[11]

Currie accepted the challenge, but not gratefully. Calling McNaughton to a conference, Currie said: "The war must nearly be over now and I do not want any more fighting or casualties than can be helped... I told Andy McNaughton that I thought this would be the last barrage I would ask him to make in the war."[12] McNaughton's reply was to plan and execute what might be one of the most effective fireplans yet devised.* Some *eight* brigades of Field Artillery and *six* brigades of Heavy Artillery, totalling more than 300 guns, were available and would be used, compared to the four brigades of field artillery and a single brigade of heavy artillery that XXII Corps had employed.[13] Despite the protests of First Army Headquarters and GHQ, McNaughton brought forward and fired more than *two thousand tons* of ammunition, roughly the same amount as fired during the entire Boer War. Moreover, because the Canadians held the ground surrounding three sides of Mount Houy, McNaughton's artillery could "give not only overhead and oblique fire, but enfilade and reverse as well."[14] The plan called for a single infantry brigade, Brigadier General J.M. Ross' 10th CIB, to assault the hill once McNaughton had completed his artillery program. The infantry would be assaulting virtually in the wide open up a hill, with the firepower of the artillery creating artificial cover by fire for the infantry's assault (see Map 8.1). In only two days the requisite supplies and ammunition were brought forward, and the preparations were complete. Zero hour was set for 5:15 a.m., 1 November.[15]

The indirect fireplan for the attack on Mount Houy begs a closer examination, because it proved to be the virtuoso performance of the Canadian Corps' artillery planners, especially McNaughton, now GOCRA Corps Heavy Artillery, and

---

* The only one that the author can think of that was more effective was Desert Storm.

Map 8.1
Mount Houy Operations

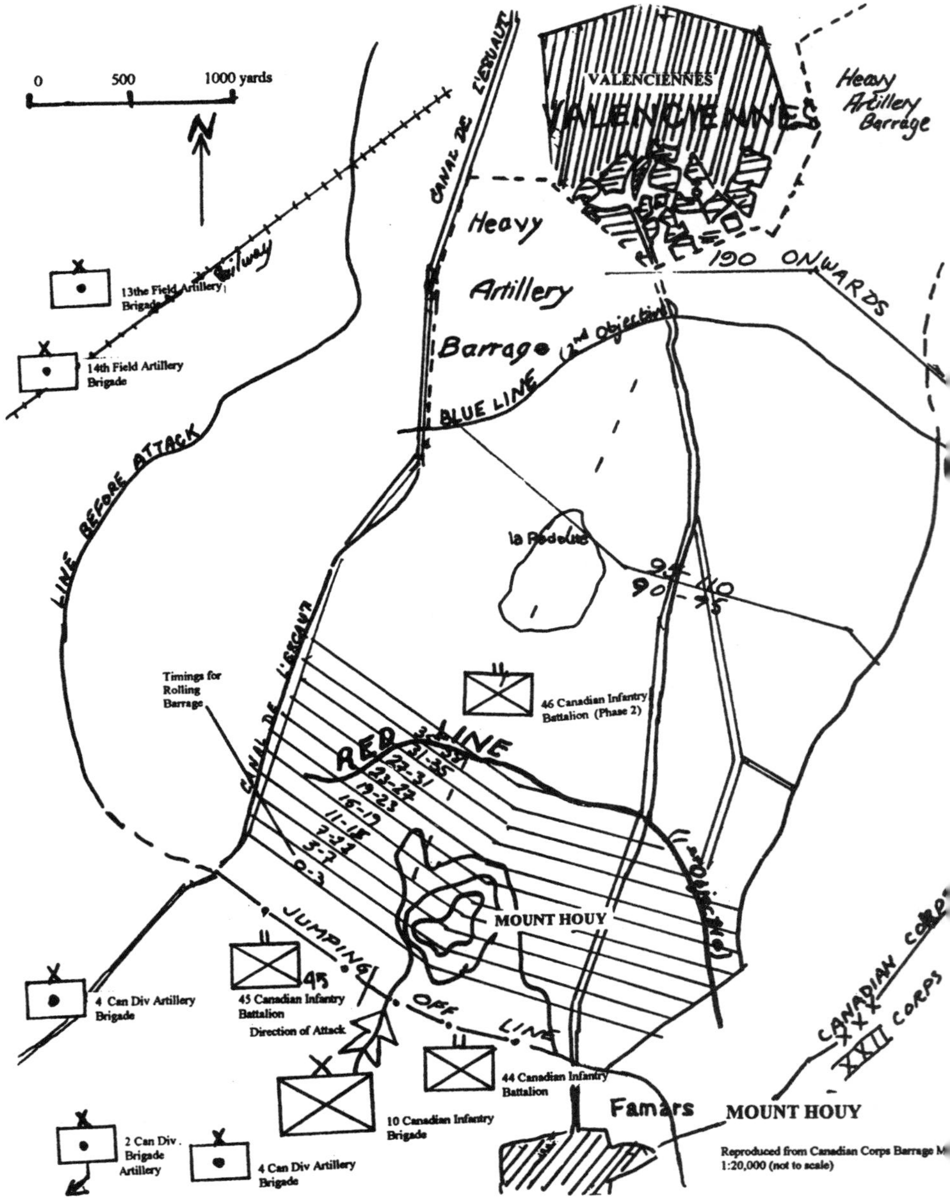

CANAL DE L'ESCAUT

VALENCIENNES
VALENCIENNES

Heavy
Artillery
Barrage

190 ONWARDS

Heavy

Artillery

Barrage (2nd Objective)

BLUE LINE

la Podelue

95-110
90-95

46 Canadian Infantry
Battalion (Phase 2)

13the Field Artillery
Brigade

14th Field Artillery
Brigade

LINE BEFORE ATTACK

Railway

Timings for
Rolling
Barrage

CANAL DE L'ESCAUT

RED LINE
27-31
24-27
18-23
11-17
3-10
0-3

MOUNT HOUY

(Objective)

JUMPING

OFF

LINE

4 Can Div Artillery
Brigade

45
45 Canadian Infantry
Battalion
Direction of Attack

44 Canadian Infantry
Battalion

Famars

MOUNT HOUY

CANADIAN CORPS
XXII CORPS

10 Canadian Infantry
Brigade

2 Can Div .
Brigade
Artillery

4 Can Div Artillery
Brigade

Reproduced from Canadian Corps Barrage M
1:20,000 (not to scale)

0   500   1000 yards

N

Brigadier General W.B.M. King, CDA Fourth Division. McNaughton had been scrimping and hoarding shells from a bewildering number of sources in anticipation of just such an opportunity as Mount Houy. The barrage map itself shows that the Canadian and British artillery allotted to the Corps would fire a "box" barrage that would swing in and out over the German positions, fired entirely by 18-pounders using shrapnel rounds. As was becoming typical, no preliminary registration or bombardment was to be used, and this restriction was made all the more onerous because the Canadian Corps had advanced beyond the sectors surveyed and gridded by the BEF, and now had to rely on its own survey to produce accurately gridded "shooting" maps for the attack. A further restriction was the necessity to avoid the bombardment of civilians in Valenciennes and the outlying villages. Only a few houses, where the enemy were positively known to be defending, were targeted, but these were to be literally drenched with heavy artillery fire. In for just as rough a treatment were the German batteries in the vicinity of Valenciennes and Mount Houy, who were again expertly targeted by the CBSO.[16] By nightfall of 31 October, McNaughton reported: "Our vast, widespread, powerful and intricate organization set ready in co-ordination to help the attacking infantry; each part assigned to the task it could best do, and no dangerous possibility overlooked."[17]

The results of all this coordination were devastating. McNaughton's carefully planned blizzard of steel obliterated the German defenses on Mount Houy, and silenced the German artillery around Valenciennes. Isolated outposts held out against the infantry assault for short periods, but on the whole, the advance was only lightly opposed. German troops, many still stunned from the barrage, surrendered *en masse*, in groups of between 20 to 50.[18] One captured German company commander stated "that as it was impossible to see or even know from which direction his attackers were coming, he could do nothing but surrender with his whole company."[19] The totality of the defeat inflicted upon the Germans was evidenced by the casualty figures. The Germans had lost over 800 killed, 75 captured wounded, and over 1,300 prisoners, not mentioning the wounded who were evacuated before capture. The Canadians, on the other hand, lost only 80 men killed and 300 wounded.[20] In terms of ratios, the defending German infantry had held a superiority of numbers of at least three to one over the attacking Canadian brigade, but suffered a casualty rate of nearly ten to one. Elements of five German divisions had been occupying Mount Houy, and a single Canadian brigade had been sent to attack them. A report forwarded to Currie after the battle looked at the attack in a different light: "Total expenditure field and heavy [artillery] was 87,700 rounds or 2,150 tons. This was an allowance of approximately a ton and a half of shells in support of each infantry soldier attacking."[21] In short, it was a completely lopsided contest. In McNaughton's words:

The barrage and bombardment had left scarcely a yard of ground untouched. Enemy dead were everywhere.... By the most intense barrage in history a single infantry brigade, weak in numbers...had broken through a German key position...the Canadian Corps had paid [the price] of Victory..."in shells and not in life."[22]

THE LEGACY OF MOUNT HOUY

The Mount Houy operation was to be the last full-fledged attack the Canadian Corps would undertake in the Great War, but its results would have a lingering impact on the Canadian approach to land warfare for years to come. The ease with which the infantry took the hill after the devastating bombardment of the artillery confirmed in many minds the supremacy of firepower over maneuver on the modern battlefield. McNaughton, as chief of staff of the Canadian Army in 1933, would publish an influential article describing the Canadian attack at Mount Houy as a "study in co-ordination" and the proper use of artillery.[23] It may be that the Canadian Army, having found its salvation not in the tank and "mechanized warfare," but in artillery and set-piece battle, would look to the same methods during the interwar period and the early part of World War Two. Many of Canada's higher ranking generals in World War Two, men like the First Canadian Army's commanders, Generals McNaughton and Crerar, were artillery officers in World War One,[*] and may have seen at Mount Houy what they perceived to be the "wave of the future." Overwhelming firepower seemed omnipotent, and therefore firepower, as opposed to maneuver, would allow the soldier of the future to close with and destroy the enemy. As a result of the influence of men like McNaughton and Crerar, technocratic "artillerists" came to dominate Canadian military thinking during the interwar period.[24] Perhaps what historian John English has described as the elusive "Amiens Alchemy" -- the search for another decisive victory like Amiens -- that haunted the First Canadian Army in its Normandy campaign in 1944 can be more properly understood, at least in the Canadian context, as the "Holy Grail of Mount Houy," or the quest for an illusive bloodless victory achieved through a devastating superiority in firepower.[25]

ENDGAME

As a result of their loss of the vital ground at Mount Houy, the German positions in the vicinity of Valenciennes and along the Hermann Line became untenable. During the night of 1-2 November the Germans withdrew from the City of Valenciennes, and began abandoning the Hermann Line. Currie launched his pursuit, but cautiously. On 2 November the Canadian Corps liberated Valenciennes, and pushed its way forward toward Belgium. The final hours had begun.

With the Canadian triumph at Mount Houy, the way had been cleared for Haig to launch his general attack on the Hermann Line, but this proved unnecessary as the opposition melted eastward toward Germany. Again the pattern seen in middle and late October repeated itself. The Germans would withdraw deeply at night, and the forward elements of the Canadian Corps would not regain contact until early afternoon. Late afternoon would see an increase in fighting as the main body of the

---

[*] McNaughton was GOCRA Heavy Artillery at Mount Houy; Crerar, his protege, had just taken over from McNaughton as head of the Canadian Corps CBSO, so both figures played key roles in the inception and execution of the artillery plan on 1 November 1918.

Corps came into contact with the German rear guard. Not wishing to become decisively engaged, Currie ordered that the main body of the leading brigades avoid becoming entangled in regular actions unless absolutely necessary, thereby avoiding needless casualties. At night, the Germans would retreat again, and the next morning the Canadians could advance relatively easily again until the afternoon. Currie continued to use a combination of cavalry patrols, motor machine guns, forward artillery, and armored cars as a "forward screen," thus keeping his infantry relatively safe from direct fire while continuing to push the advance.

Necessity was the mother of tactical invention, and it was in this period, 2-11 November 1918, that Tim Travers claims that the Canadian Corps developed an unwritten doctrine for, "fairly rapid mobile warfare."[26] Unwritten, because there was neither the time, nor perhaps conscious recognition that what seemed to the Canadian Corps as simply a short term, practical solution to the unique problem of the pursuit of a crumbling army, was a tactical evolution. In most cases, commanders and soldiers alike were already looking beyond the tactical problem of following up the Germans to the happier prospects of the end of the War. Nonetheless, by November 10 this evolutionary style of warfare had brought the Canadian Corps to the outskirts of Mons, the Belgian city where the British troops had fired their first shots of the Great War.

After the war, Currie would be criticized by bitter ex-Minister of Militia Sir Sam Hughes for wasting the lives of Canadians in the taking of Mons during the final days before Armistice. Hughes (and later a Port Hope, Ontario, newspaper) claimed that Currie's sole motive had been personal glory. In reality, Currie had directed "that if the town [Mons] could be captured without many casualties, the pressure should be continued."[27] Currie's desire to take Mons stemmed from two considerations, one symbolic and the other tactical. The symbolic reason was that Currie felt that it would be "befitting that the capture of Mons should close the fighting records of the Canadian Troops," thus ending the war where the BEF began it.[28] The pragmatic, tactical reason was in order to secure a satisfactory line for defense of the area in case the cease in the hostilities was only temporary.[29] Canadian Corps HQ had received word on 10 November that a cease-fire would go into effect at 11:00 a.m. 11 November. Currie should have suspected, but could not have known, that this truce would hold. The truce notwithstanding, Currie opted to take the ground that would give him the best chance of defense should hostilities recommence. Despite the *ad hominem* arguments of a disgruntled politician after the fact, Currie certainly cannot be faulted for thinking like a soldier up to the very last minute of the war.[30]

Currie had planned an encircling maneuver of Mons, hoping to avoid the bombardment of the city because it was still filled with its civilian population. Early on the morning of 11 November, however, patrols from the Royal Canadian Regiment and the Royal Highlanders of Canada (The Black Watch) moved into Mons, and by daylight had secured the far outskirts. The German defenders had again melted away during the night, leaving the Canadian Corps in possession of the same ground that the British Expeditionary Force had begun the war on in August 1914. The 100 Days, and the Great War they had helped to end, had come to a close.

Prophetically enough, when told of the armistice, Andrew McNaughton cursed: "Bloody fools! We have them on the run. That means that we shall have to do it all over again in another twenty-five years."[31] And when the Canadians returned to face the Germans again, it was McNaughton who was to be their leader.

NOTES

1. Napoleon, quoted in *Warrior's Words*, ed. Peter Tsouras (London: Cassel, 1992), p. 31.

2. Currie, *Corps Operations 1918*, pp. 72-76; Nicholson, *CEF*, pp.465-469.

3. This terrain analysis is based on a number of sources, including Lt. Col. M. Festung, "Report on Mount Houy Operations, November 1st, 1918," dated 28 Dec 1918, NAC RG 9, III, D2, Vol 4790, File 10 (hereafter referred to as "Report-Mount Houy"); Major General A.G.L. McNaughton, "The Capture of Valenciennes: A Study in Co-ordination," *Canadian Defence Quarterly*, Vol. 10, No. 3 (April 1933), pp. 280-281. The author has visited and extensively walked both battlefields, and these conclusions are based to a great extent on these studies; see also Nicholson, *CEF*, pp. 470-471.

4. Edmonds, *BOH*, Vol. 5, p. 395; Major General Sir W.H. Anderson, "The Operations Round Valenciennes by the First Army, October-November, 1918, A Study in Co-Operation," *Canadian Defence Quarterly*, Vol. 2, No. 3 (April 1925), pp. 289-303; "First Army No. GS 1290, Notes on a Conference Held at First Army Headquarters on 27 October 1918," "CCGS War Diary," Vol. 38, October, 1918.

5. "First Army No. G.S. 1290, Notes on Conference Held at First Army Headquarters on 27 October 1918." "CCGS War Diary," Vol. 38, October 1918.

6. McNaughton, "Valenciennes," pp. 279-294.

7. Dancocks, *Spearhead*, p. 185.

8. Currie, quoted in Dancocks, *Spearhead*, p. 185.

9. Anderson, "First Army - Valenciennes," p. 292.

10. McNaughton, "Valenciennes," p. 281.

11. Anderson, "Queant-Drocourt," p. 120.

12. Currie, quoted in Dancocks, *Spearhead*, p. 187.

13. No comparisons of the number of *rounds* fired, a much more important statistic than guns used when determining the weight of a bombardment, are available, but given First Army's shock at the amount of ammunition McNaughton used, one can assume that the Highlanders could have been better served by XXII Corps HQ. See Edmonds, *BOH*, Vol. 5, p. 396.

14. McNaughton, "Valenciennes," p. 282.

15. The orders for the attack on Mount Houy are contained in "Canadian Corps Operations Order No. 245," dated 27 October 1918 "CCGS War Diary," Vol. 38, October 1918.

16. H.M., "Outline of Report of Artillery in Connection with Mont Houy Operation-November 1st, 1918," n.d., NAC, RG 9, III, D2, Vol. 4790, File 10 (hereafter "Artillery Report - Mount Houy"); Currie, *Corps Operations 1918*, pp. 77-78; McNaughton, "Valenciennes," pp. 283-289; Nicholson, *Gunners*, p. 368.

17. McNaughton, "Valenciennes," p. 289.

18. Ibid., p. 290; Dancocks, *Spearhead*, p.190.

19. "Artillery Report - Mount Houy," p. 2.

20. Currie, *Corps Operations 1918*, p. 78.

21. "Reports - November 1918: Artillery Report on Mount Houy," n.d., n.a., p. 14.

Currie papers, MG 30 E 100 Vol. 38, File 169.

22. McNaughton, "Valenciennes," p. 293. For another view of McNaughton's actions, see Swettenham, *McNaughton*, pp. 161-166.

23. McNaughton, "Valenciennes," pp. 279-294.

24. See J. L. Granatstein, *The Generals: the Canadian Army's Senior Commanders in the Second World War.* (Toronto: Stoddart, 1993), pp. 3-178, 258-267. Brereton Greenhous alludes to the same criticism of General Guy Simonds in his review of Dominick Graham's biography, *The Price of Command*, in *Canadian Defence Quarterly*. Vol. 23, No. 4 (December, 1993) pp. 38-40.

25. See John English, *The Canadian Army and the Normandy Campaign: A Study of Failure in High Command* (New York: Praeger, 1991).

26. Travers, *How the War Was Won*, p. 172.

27. Currie, quoted in Dancocks, *Spearhead*, p. 201.

28. Currie, *Corps Operations 1918*, p. 84.

29. Ibid., p. 83.

30. Dancocks includes an excellent discussion on the entire affair of these allegations, *Spearhead*, pp. 241-245.

31. McNaughton, quoted in Swettenham, *McNaughton*, p. 168.

9

"POSTLUDE": AFTERMATH

Without the cautionary examples of the destructive power of war unleashed, theory would preach to deaf ears. No one would have believed possible what has now been experienced by all.

Clausewitz, *On War*,
Book 8, Chapter 2

COUNTING THE COSTS

Wars, even in the modern industrial age, are neither planned nor waged by accountants, and a campaign's cost cannot simply be quantified in terms of resources spent and profits gained. Yet it seems almost an almost inevitable question for observers of history to ask: "was it worth it?" In the case of the Canadian Corps and the battles of the 100 Days, an objective, material cost-profit comparison can be made, but it provides but cold comfort. One must first balance the real costs, those unrecuperable assets spent in attaining any goal -- casualties -- with what was ultimately achieved.

Often lost sight of in the historical literature on the subject is that for the Canadian Corps, the final 100 Days were far and away the most costly period of the Great War. Casualties, owing to the virtually continuous nature of the offensive operations, were extremely heavy: a total of 45,830 of all ranks killed, missing and wounded from 8 August to 11 November. This figure is nearly *twenty* percent, or one-fifth of the total number of casualties sustained by the Canadian Expeditionary Force for the *entire* First World War. During no other time -- not during the agony at Ypres in 1915, the slaughter on the Somme in 1916, or through the momentous battles of 1917 -- had the Canadian Corps suffered the same casualty rates as were inflicted during the hard pounding of the final 100 Days. Although the CEF's official historian has pointed out that "by First World War standards [the number of casualties] were not excessive in the light of their task,"[1] the high loss rate nevertheless left the Corps exhausted by the end of operations on 11 November. The Second Canadian Division still had not yet fully recovered from its days of agony along the Arras-Cambrai road, and the remainder of the divisions were falling short of infantry replacements.

The casualty rate for the Canadian Corps in the 100 Days would also eclipse the losses suffered by the First Canadian Army during the next World War. For the whole of the Northwest Europe campaign, from D-Day to VE day, a period of nearly one year (333 days), the total number of Canadian casualties in the First Canadian Army were 3,680 officers and 44,272 other ranks, for a total of 47,952 all ranks, compared to the Canadian Corps losses of 45,830 for the 100 Days. The casualty rate, the number of casualties sustained per day, was therefore *three* times as high during the 100 Days as it was during the Northwest Europe campaign.[2] Thus, the 100 Days remains the bloodiest period yet in the annals of Canadian arms.

And for what? What was achieved at such a huge cost in life and limb? It would be unfair not to let those who were closest to the sacrifice speak for themselves. In material terms, Currie pointed out:

Between August 8th and November 11th the following had been captured [by the Canadian Corps]:

Prisoners	31,537
Guns (Heavy and Field)	623
Machine Guns	2,842
Trench Mortars (Heavy and Light)	336

Over 500 square miles of territory and 228 cities, towns and villages had been liberated, including the cities of Cambrai, Denain, Valenciennes, and Mons.
From August 8th to October 11th not less than 47 German Divisions had been engaged and defeated by the Canadian Corps, that is, nearly a quarter of the total German Forces on the Western Front [about 200 divisions].[3]

This record eclipsed even that of the other "spearhead" dominion formation, the Australian Corps. Sir John Monash, GOC Australian Corps, reported that from Amiens onwards, his corps had captured 29,144 prisoners and 338 guns, and had defeated 39 German divisions.[4] Thus, between them, the two Dominion Corps encountered elements of nearly 40 percent of the German Army on the Western Front. The Canadian Corps' *Intelligence Report on the German Armies*, added:

During the period 8 August - 11 November the Corps had engaged 68* German Divisions out of a total of approximately 200.... [I]n spite of all the efforts of the Enemy Higher Command to maintain his strength on the Western Front, the steady drain caused by enormous casualties made itself felt not only in the reduction of the [numbers] of Divisions, but in the reduction of the effective strength of every unit in the field.[5]

---

* This figure contrasts with the one given in Currie's *Corps Operations 1918* because the Intelligence Reports' figures reflect a wider definition of "engaged."

Despite these seemingly herculean feats, many Canadian generals were stung by criticism over the seemingly high casualty figures. In response to challenges about this after the war, McNaughton and Brigadier General J.A. Clarke, commander of 7th CIB, were quick to point to a comparison between the Canadian Corps' achievements during the final 100 Days, and those of the American Army in the Meuse-Argonne offensive, related most dramatically in the following table:

	American	Canadian
Troops engaged	650,000	105,000
Duration of Operations	47 days	100 days
Max. Distance Advanced	34 miles	86 miles
German Divisions Defeated	46	47
Average Number of Casualties suffered per German Division defeated	*2,170*	*975*
Total Casualties	*100,000*	*45,830* [6]

McNaughton, not unsurprisingly, attributed this "success" rate to the Corps' skillful and generous use of artillery, having an average ammunition expenditure, in terms of per gun per day, that was roughly twice the American rate (23 rounds per gun per day versus 42 rounds per gun per day).[7] McNaughton further assured his countrymen:

No Canadian need fear a comparison of these figures with the corresponding results obtained by any similar organization, allied or enemy, for I know of no other organization in the history of the war which was able to produce such a high ratio in shell to troops, nor any in which the price paid for victory was lower in personnel.[8]

As these figures well attest, the ultimate conclusion that must be drawn is that at the *operational* level, the Canadian Corps was able to make a highly significant contribution towards the defeat of the German Army on the battlefield at precisely *half* the cost, in terms of life and limb, as the American Army. But for all of these figures, the real answer to the question "was it worth it?" remains unanswered.

FORGETTING TO WIND THE CLOCK

The answer to the question "was it worth it" should have been at least partly answered after the war by the creation of an official record and history of the Canadian Corps operations. Unlike its success on the battlefield, however, the Corps failed to ensure that an official history of its operations would be published. This point is critical when considering the 100 Days from a historical perspective because much of the Corps unwritten doctrine would have found expression had the writing of a detailed official history had been completed. As an intellectual exercise, it could have provided the opportunity to clarify what the Corps had learned from their experiences, and point the way to the future. This would have been especially true for the compressed experiences of the final 100 Days, which left little or no time for reflection before the rush to occupy Germany, repatriate, demobilize and resume normal life overtook the minds of the Corps' soldiers and leaders.[9]

The story of the Canadian War Narrative Section (CWNS) is an interesting study in the failure of an official history process. Established by agreement between Currie and the Overseas Ministry in late 1918, the CWNS had a mandate to complete an official history of the Canadian Forces Overseas during the Great War. Initially the CWNS fell under the keen direction of Brigadier General Raymond Brutinel. Currie actively encouraged its work, paying close personal attention during the hectic demobilization period of late 1918 and 1919. Currie recommended:

the persons responsible [for writing the history] must...commence the task at once.... Immediate action is desirable in order that documents which are not always correct or complete may be supplemented by the personal knowledge of participants. It is [my] belief that only by immediate action can full use be made of the careful work of research and compilation which was done at the end of the war.[10]

Brutinel, for his part, threw himself wholeheartedly into the task, but the difficulties in preparing the official history were many. One of the first obstacles to overcome was deciding what should be included, and what tone and style the work should adopt. Brutinel outlined his approach in a memorandum to Currie and the other members of the CWNS:

Clearness and accuracy are essential in a work of this character and every other consideration must be subordinated to the attainment of these qualities.... Regarding [t]roops attached or formations operating on the flanks of the Canadian Corps, and in co-operation with it... no adverse comment need be made respecting the leadership or conduct of the formation or Troops acting in conjunction with the Canadian Corps.[11]

Although this outline reflected a relatively similar style that was adopted by the British official historian Brigadier General Sir James Edmonds in his now controversial *Official History of the Great War*, its direction to avoid "adverse comment," meant that, at least to some degree, the record would be sanitized, although the original intention of Brutinel's comment was less to distort history than it was to ensure that excellent wartime allies would not suffer offense.[12]

One of the major hurdles was the sheer volume of material the CWNS had to sort through -- literally a blizzard of documents. Coupled with the necessity to try to check every possible fact where possible in order to avoid an injurious slight to some person or unit, this made the preparation of any official history a daunting task. In some cases, unit histories were unavailable, and sources expected to provide the necessary information proved unusable; therefore, the accomplishments of these units virtually slipped into the quicksands of history unseen and unexamined. Such was the case with the history of the innovative Canadian Machine Gun Corps (CMGC), whose full story was never "officially" told.[13] Major H. Logan, a CMGC officer given the task of compiling a CMGC narrative from the various unit histories, lamented to Brutinel:

Each unit...was asked...to prepare a history of its own activities. These histories were to form the chief material out of which the Machine Gun narrative was to be constructed.... They [the unit histories] have proved quite unsatisfactory in most cases, and, in fact, almost useless for my purposes.[14]

The ultimate demise of the plans for the official history, however, was the *malaise militaire* that gripped Canada in the wake of its great exertions in World War One. Demobilization commenced rapidly after November 1918, and many officers' minds turned almost immediately to thoughts of peacetime pursuits. As the Corps repatriated and demobilized throughout 1919, access to documents, key personalities, and support resources such as manpower, editors, and office supplies became more difficult for the CWNS. Relegated to a tiny office at 286 Sparks Street in Ottawa, the CWNS was literally abandoned by the government, having to fight for such basic items as typewriters and even office supplies like paper.[15] These difficulties were compounded by the selection of people to write the official monograph who were neither trained as historians nor were completely objective about the subject.[16] Despite these obstacles, Colonel Fortescue Duguid, Brutinel's eventual successor, gamely planned an eight-volume in-depth history of high quality. Only two volumes were ever published: *The Official History of the Canadian Forces in the Great War, 1914-1919, Volume 1*, covering 1914 to mid -1915, published in 1938, and a volume on the medical services.[17] A full official history of the CEF would have to wait until 1962, with the publishing of G.W.L. Nicholson's excellent one-volume work.[18]

The Canadians were not the only ones to fall prey to the unique problems of writing a detailed official narrative of the Great War, especially the 100 Days.[19] The decision to complete works in a random order meant, for instance, that the portion of Edmond's excellent British Official History on the 100 Days was not published until *1947*, far too late for it to be available to teach any lessons to the soldiers of World War Two about the experiences of the 100 Days. More critically, the events that most riveted the attention of soldiers and scholars alike were the disastrous and controversial earlier battles of the Great War, like the Ypres battles, or the Somme battle of July 1916. Again, little of real value could be learned from these that would help modern soldiers face the mechanized battlefield of the Second World War.[20] By then, a whole generation of pundits -- men like Liddell-Hart, J.F.C. Fuller, and Hugh Trenchard -- painted scenes of a future war that were so different from 1918 that the past seemed totally irrelevant. The mantra of mechanized warfare and the fear of the trenches gripped the minds of British and Canadian soldiers alike, and often blinded them to the deeper significance of their own experiences on a high intensity battlefield.

It would be wrong and unfair to say that Canadian generals learned nothing from their experiences in the 100 Days. Even had the official history process been completed as foreseen by Currie and Brutinel, there can be no guarantee that this process would have arrived at the "correct" conclusions about the future of tactics and operations. But in failing to create an official history, by failing to undergo the ultimate exercise of examining the whole of its operational development, the Canadian military inhibited its intellectual growth. It must be noted that the military that thought hardest about its operational experiences of World War One -- Germany -- perceived some very profound lessons from the events of the 100 Days.[21]   By forgetting to examine closely enough where they had been, the Canadians could not know where they were going. The price for this failure would be paid by the next generation of Canadian soldiers, again in France, and again fighting Germans.

NOTES

1. Nicholson, *CEF*, p. 460.

2. Canadian Corps casualty figures are from Nicholson, *CEF*, pp. 548; World War Two casualty figures are from C.P. Stacey, *The Canadian Army, 1939-1945: An Official Historical Summary.* (Ottawa: Kings Printer, 1948), p. 272.

3. Currie, *Corps Operations 1918*, pp. 84-85.

4. Lieutenant General Sir John Monash, *The Australian Victories in France* (Sydney: Angus and Robertson, 1936), p. 284. Because they had fought beside each other at Amiens, the Australian and Canadian Corps "shared" the defeat of some German divisions, although the figures cited do not reflect this.

5. "Conclusion - Int on German Divisions Engaged," CCGS War Diary, Vol. 37.

6. These figures were cited by Brigadier General J.A. Clarke in the *Debates, House of Commons, Session 1922*, II, 2 May 1922. The table is found in Swettenham, *To Seize the Victory*, p. 238.

7. McNaughton, *Canadian Artillery Association Summary No. 1* (April 1921), p. 2, contained in the Currie Papers, NAC, MG 30 E100, Vol. 41, File 185.

8. McNaughton, "Development of Artillery in the Great War," p. 170.

9. "Forgetting to wind the clocks" is a reference to the last words of the captain in Joseph Conrad's *The Nigger of the Narcissus.* Ship's captains used clocks in order to navigate to determine longitude. They are also the way in which man can understand and orient himself in the infinity of time. Symbolically speaking, forgetting to wind the clock is a metaphor for making a mistake that would result in losing one's way; without remembering to "wind the clock," one would know neither where they had been, nor where they were going.

10. Memorandum, n.d., "Recommendations from the Advisory Board on the Preparation of the Official History," Currie papers, NAC, MG 30 E100, Vol. 41, File 186.

11. Raymond Brutinel, "General Directions for guidance in the compilation of detailed narrative of operations of the CANADIAN CORPS." 15 Sept 1919, NAC RG 9, III, D2, Vol. 4809, File 196. The papers contained in Vol. 4809, File 196 shall hereafter be referred to as CWNS Papers.

12. Griffith says of Edmonds' *BOH*, "Either despite or because of its often irritatingly close grain, it would not be too much to say that ...[it] is positively the best book ever written, or ever likely to be written, about the Great War on the Western Front." *Battle Tactics*, pp. 258-261. Winter claims that Edmond's account is simply "fraudulent," especially in showing Haig in only the best of light; Winter, *Haig's Command*, pp. 240-257. Bean's *AOH* set the standard for future "official histories." For more on the official histories, see the "Note on Sources" at the end of this work.

13. Eventually, a good "semiofficial" history of the Canadian Machine Guns was written by Lt. Col. C.S. Grafton, *The Canadian "Emma Gees": A History of the Canadian Machine Gun Corps* (London, Ont: Hunter Publishing, 1938).

14. Letter, Major H. Logan to Brutinel, 5 August 1919, CWNS papers.

15. Evidence for this is contained in numerous administrative memoranda contained in the CWNS Papers, RB4. See also, for instance, the wrangle over pay for CWNS staff, letter from Company Sargeant Major James Duff, dated 31 July 1919, CWNS Papers, RB1.

16. This point was made by A.M.J. Hyatt in a personal conversation with the author at RMC Kingston, May 1994.

17. Col. A.F. Duguid, *The Official History of the Canadian Forces in the Great War, 1914-1919, Volume. 1* (Ottawa: Department of Militia and Defense, 1938); A. McPhail, *The Medical Services* (Ottawa: Department of Militia, 1924); Nicholson, *CEF*, p. xiii. It must be noted that an excellent 5 volume series entitled *Canada in the Great World War* (Toronto: United Publisher's, 1920), by various authorities (mostly journalists and historians) was published in 1920, but it was never intended as an official history, and the authors lacked the same access to documents and insight into personalities that the CWNS was supposed to have. The Corps Intelligence Service wrote its own excellent "semiofficial" history, which stands as an excellent example of how techniques learned during war can be codified and passed on; Maj. J.E. Hahn, *The Intelligence Service Within the Canadian Corps, 1914-1918* (Toronto: Macmillan, 1930).

18. Nicholson, *CEF*.

19. Johnson nicely sums up the failure by almost every major combatant to produce a high quality official history; see *Breakthrough*, pp. 295-296. Bean's efforts in Australia produced what is perhaps arguably the best and standard setting Official History in his six-volume *AOH*.

20. Bidwell and Graham make the same point in *Firepower*, pp. 131-132, 145-146.

21. That the events of the 100 Days left a haunting legacy in the minds of some of Germany's brightest officers is obvious in some of their writings, especially the official history, and, for example, in Guderian's *Achtung! Panzer*. For more on how the German Army profitted from their experiences, see Trevor Dupuy, *A Genius for War: The German Army and the General Staff, 1807-1945* (Englewood Cliffs, NJ: Prentice-Hall, 1977), or the superlative essay by Michael Geyer, "German Strategy in the Age of Machine Warfare, 1914-1945," in *Makers of Modern Strategy*, ed. Peter Paret (Princeton, NJ: Princeton University Press, 1986).

10

"FINE": CONCLUSIONS

Lastly, even the ultimate outcome of a war is not to be regarded as final.
The defeated state often considers the outcome merely as a transitory evil
for which a remedy may still be found.

Clausewitz, *On War*,
Book 1, Chapter 1

There are seven main points that have been illustrated by this examination of the Canadian Corps' involvement in the 100 Days campaign. *First*, the Canadian Corps, for a number of reasons, was operationally and organizationally better prepared than most of the other corps in the BEF to undertake sustained offensive operations in late summer of 1918. *Second*, recognizing the superiority of both the Corps organization and Currie's operational ability, Haig deliberately used the Canadian Corps to lead the assault on some of the toughest and most vital points of the German defenses, including Amiens, the D-Q Line, the Canal du Nord/Cambrai, and finally, Mount Houy. *Third*, the Canadian Corps' repeated success in the role as "spearhead" of the BEF's advance allowed the Corps to make a military contribution to the defeat of the German Army on the Western Front out of all proportion to its relatively small size. *Fourth*, as a result of executing sequential large-scale high-intensity offensive operations in rapid succession, the Canadian Corps developed its own innovative and unique operational approach even further, despite the fact that much of the innovation was never formally articulated as written doctrine. *Fifth*, because of its battle experiences and superior resources and organization, and as evidenced by its success throughout the 100 Days campaign, the Canadian Corps was by late 1918 one of the best, if not *the* best Allied corps on the Western Front. It had not only survived the brutal hard pounding of three large-scale offensives in three months, but, in doing so, had defeated a relatively disproportionately large number of German divisions. *Sixth*, the Canadian Corps' experience in the campaign of the 100 Days had a significant residual effect on Canadian military thought, especially during World War Two. *Last*, but certainly most important from a didactic perspective, the story of the Canadian Corps in the 100 Days reveals critical lessons for both soldiers and scholars alike about the nature of World War One and about future high-intensity conflicts in general.

Let us look at each one of the assertions in turn. The Canadian Corps tactical and organizational superiority to most other BEF corps in 1918 derived from its unique status as a semiautonomous "national army." This allowed it, from 1917 onward, to maintain a relatively stable, homogeneous structure of the four Canadian divisions overseas, and to develop its own doctrine, training schools, organization, and operational procedures. At both divisional and corps levels, Canadian formations were significantly larger than their British counterparts, having greater numbers of infantry, indirect fire, engineer, and service support resources. In effect, the Canadian Corps in 1918 actually packed the operational punch of a small British Army-level formation, and this provides an important clue as to how it was employed by Haig. More important, the Canadian Corps was commanded by an intelligent yet practical general, Sir Arthur Currie, who encouraged advice and innovation from his very able subordinates, men like Webber, Brutinel, McNaughton, Macdonell, and Griesbach, to name only a very few. Travers has pointed out that these talents did not go unnoticed or unused by Haig; by 1918, "Haig gave [or, was forced by circumstances to give]... good corps commanders such as Currie, Haldane, and Monash greater freedom."[1] Having been spared from the German offensives of spring and summer 1918, and having had the summer to hone their offensive skills even further, the Canadian Corps was almost ideally suited to undertake the gruelling offensive operations envisioned as necessary by Haig and Foch in order to end the war in 1918.

Haig had recognized early on the political and operational advantages of employing the Canadian Corps in a spearhead role. In effect, he used it much like a separate "shock" army in order to propel some of the most critical BEF offensive operations. Haig eagerly allowed Rawlinson to use the Canadian Corps for the important attack at Amiens, and was equally happy to move Currie and his troops northward to the First Army on short notice in order to make use of the Canadian Corps to break the hinge of the Hindenberg Line, the D-Q Switch. Again, at the Canal du Nord and Cambrai, Haig placed the utmost faith in Currie and the Corps, going so far as to allow Currie virtual veto power over Horne's protest as to the method of attack. In short, throughout the final months of the war, Haig looked to Currie and the Canadian Corps, as well as to a small handful of other elite formations, such as the Australian Corps and the 51st (Highland) Division, to act as the battering rams for the BEF's Front-wide assault.

Haig's faith in Currie and the Canadian Corps was well founded. At four critical points, the Canadian Corps acted as a vanguard for the Allied advance to victory: at Amiens, the D-Q Line, Canal du Nord/Cambrai, and, finally, at Valenciennes. Time and again, as a result of its success in the spearhead role, the Canadian Corps created the conditions and opportunity necessary for the Allied armies to drive the German military machine to collapse in 1918. The Corps was instrumental in leading the Allied onslaught of successive, set-piece attacks that effectively devoured the German Army's strategic reserves in repeated and rapid succession, pushing the already exhausted and demoralized German forces to near collapse, and eventually leading to confusion and despair at the highest levels of the German military command. This commenced with *der Schwarze Tag* (the Black Day), 8 August at Amiens, where the Canadians and Australians, under Rawlinson's Fourth Army, surprised and overwhelmed the German defenders, leading to a veritable rout in that sector. It was followed by the widescale attack on the Hindenberg defenses in late August and early September, in part made possible by the Canadian Corps attack on the D-Q Line, which secured the flank of the Third and Fourth British armies. In early October, the Canadian Corps played the primary role in the breaching of the Canal du Nord, and the capture of the vital rail center of Cambrai. This victory directly resulted in the withdrawal of nearly two entire German Army Groups, and the abandonment of Germany's last fully prepared defensive line. Finally, the Corps' stunning victory over the German forces at Mount Houy and Valenciennes in early November rendered the last German defenses in northern France, the Hermann Line, untenable, and precipitated the wholesale retreat which ended in an armistice on 11 November 1918. No other Canadian Corps battles, and certainly not Vimy Ridge, ever came close to having as decisive an impact on the outcome of the war as did the 100 Days campaign.

As a result of their participation in almost continuous, large scale, high-intensity offensive operations throughout the 100 Days, the Canadian Corps developed and refined their tactical and operational abilities even further. The limited-objective, set-piece attack used so successfully throughout 1917 was transformed into a nearly continuous cycle of rapid pace, coordination-intensive attacks that aimed at reducing the friction of battle by controlling the *tempo* of the advance. Communications, command, and control methods available at the time, however, limited the Canadian Corps ability to coordinate complex plans in short time periods, and therefore restricted operational efficiency once the set-piece portion of these attacks was complete. Nevertheless, the Canadian Corps' tenacity and its ability to absorb punishment and continue with the advance because of its larger divisions helped to overcome these problems and led to its success at Cambrai. When conditions changed as a result of its success, the Corps' tactics also changed, with the rapid adoption of an ad hoc but reasonably effective means of "mechanized" pursuit based on a combination of all arms, including tactical air support, forward maneuvering artillery, and armored cars. In short, the repeated battle experiences endured throughout the 100 Days by the Canadian Corps made it an even better formation than it had been in early August 1918.

As a result of its seasoning and continual improvement, the Canadian Corps, by the end of the Great War, was one of the most successful, if not *the* most successful Allied corps on the Western Front. This conclusion is based not only on the Corps' "undefeated" record, but also on the fact that it survived some of the most ferocious fighting of the Great War and repeatedly emerged successful. Moreover, in terms of sheer numbers, the Canadian Corps had engaged more German divisions -- 68 out of approximately 200 -- than any other corps, including the excellent Australian Corps, can claim to have faced and defeated during the 100 Days.[2] The 100 Days campaign must therefore be considered as the Canadian Corps' *aristeia*[3], a period in which it made a contribution to the military resolution of the war out of all proportion to its relatively small size. The 100 Days are probably the highest point, as well as the bloodiest, achieved by Canadian arms in the twentieth century; neither before nor since have Canadians played such an effective, crucial, and decisive role in land warfare.[4]

Not surprisingly, the experience of the 100 Days campaign had a lingering effect on Canadian military thought. During the 100 Days, Currie and other Canadian commanders attempted to minimize the "friction" of war through detailed planning and consecutive set-piece attacks in rapid succession. The in-depth coordination for these attacks was also necessitated by a heavy reliance upon artillery to create "artificial cover" for maneuver on terrain easily dominated by the machine gun. This focus on "ordering the disorder" in an attempt to maximize firepower and thereby minimize casualties was to become a lasting legacy to the "Canadian way of war."[5] Currie's pattern of repeated, deliberate set-piece battles, relying heavily on the firepower of the artillery, and culminating in the dramatic taking of Mount Houy, proved highly attractive. In fact, the success of such tactics may have provided the paradigm for Canadian generals to follow in World War Two. Choosing to focus on the success of Currie's set-piece battles, with a massive dependence upon the firepower of the artillery, Canadian military leaders, especially the highly influential Andrew McNaughton, ignored Currie's consistent efforts to incorporate movement and surprise in his attacks, and his repeated experiments with mechanized forces.[6] Mesmerized by the relatively cheap success of Mount Houy, Canadian generals in World War Two may have overlooked the lesson learned by Currie in the 100 Days that offensive operations in the face of well-prepared enemy positions are costly, bloody affairs, won eventually, but not exclusively, by "hard pounding." Indeed, cheap and quick victories, such as the one achieved by the Canadians at Mount Houy, are the exceptions and not the rule in land warfare. Firepower could give the attacker the edge, but inevitably it was audacity, innovation, and good staffwork, coupled with the inexorable push of infantry, assisted at times by tanks, that most often won the victories. Unfortunately, Currie's perceived prudence proved to be the bane of the Canadian Army during World War Two, and the "Amiens Alchemy" eluded it in 1944 during Operations TRACTABLE and TOTALIZE. As successful as the Canadian Corps under Currie had been during the 100 Days, their mastery was not be repeated by Canadian troops a generation later.[7] Ironically enough, it may have been Canadian success during the 100 Days that was to pave the way for the Canadian Army's lackluster showing in Normandy in 1944. Having learned the wrong lessons, the generals of the First Canadian Army made the old mistake of fighting the last war.

This investigation of the Canadian Corps experience during the 100 Days has also revealed some important lessons for both modern soldiers, and for students of the Great War. First, the campaign reveals that by 1918, the Great War had become a truly *modern*, high intensity conflict incorporating almost every aspect of battle that contemporary soldiers deal with today -- indirect fire artillery, tactical air support, chemical weapons, electronic deception plans, tanks and mechanized forces, C3I challenges, and the paramount importance and difficulties of logistics in modern war. In short, in the Canadian Corps' experiences of the last 100 Days of the Great War, one can see foreshadowed what was to come to pass in the next major land war in

Central Europe, and perhaps even draw some lessons about what to expect in any future high-intensity land conflicts.

The Canadian Corps' story points to the speed at which tactical and doctrinal changes have to be made in any war in general, and were made during World War One in particular. Griesbach, while instructing at the Allied Tank School at Fontainebleau in late October 1918, noted that the course, even though newly established, was "about three months behind the times... the whole program [was therefore] poor and out of date." His opinion was, of course, based on his own recent personal experiences working with tanks at Amiens and the Hindenberg Line, and the tactical innovations that had already been adopted by the Corps as a result of this experience.[8] Moreover, as already discussed, in less than a week, the Canadian Corps swiftly adopted a more mechanized form of warfare when faced with the challenge of keeping up with the rapid German withdrawal of late October 1918. As historian Bruce Gudmundsson has argued, in the hothouse conditions of the Western Front, ideas and innovations erupted so quickly, and in so many different areas, that "written" doctrine was simply unable to keep up with the pace of tactical adaptations.[9] The same frenetic pace of technological and tactical development on the battlefield has not seen been since 1917-1918.[10]

The set-piece attack as practiced by the Canadian Corps provided a practical solution to the unique temporal-spatial problem posed by the conditions of the Western Front.[11] In short, given relatively little *space* within which to maneuver, Currie compensated by using additional *time* to organize the firepower superiority, tactical deception, and massing of forces that consistently resulted in victory over enemies of roughly the same strength. Moreover, despite the incredibly cramped conditions of the Western Front, where armies fought cheek by jowl, Currie nevertheless repeatedly attempted to incorporate maneuver into his plans, the best example of this being the attack on the Canal du Nord. The Corps' experiences seem to point to the efficacy of the set-piece attack, and the effects of synergy created by careful coordination of all forces and arms on the battlefield. In the final analysis, the Canadian Corps' success stemmed from its ability to orchestrate the effects of an ever-increasing number of battlefield assets, creating a synergistic effect that resulted in the unleashing of a symphony of destruction on bewildered German defenders.

The consistent supremacy of the Canadian Corps artillery resources over their German counterparts, and often over German machine gunners, may also point to the contemporary dominance of indirect fire weapons systems over direct fire in the modern "battle space." Ironically enough, Napoleon's famous adage that, "it is with artillery that war is waged," was more true for the Canadian Corps than it was in Napoleon's time, because the emperor's artillery remained essentially a direct fire weapon. The Canadian Corps' emphasis on using the new science of indirect fire gunnery to engage and destroy the enemy's most valuable assets -- such as *eingrief* divisions, artillery batteries, ammunition dumps, and other logistical installations -- foreshadows the current military doctrine of "Deep Battle" and the engagement of "follow on forces."[12] Furthermore, the exertions of the Corps "Q" staff, and the Corps Engineers point to the importance of logistics and logistical mobility on a high-intensity battlefield, and to the vital role Engineers play in this through their efforts to maintain and repair transportation networks, and camouflage and protect logistical installations.

The Canadian Corps' experiences and the place of the 100 Days in Canadian military history point to another crucial truth: the need to learn from past ordeals and the vital need to train *in* war. During the war, the Corps developed an effective method of feedback and postoperational examination, leading to rapid and effective adoption of innovative tactics. Unfortunately, in their haste to return to peacetime life, the leaders of the Corps neglected to insure that the same would be done for the entire war, in the form of an official history, thereby literally abandoning many of the hard learned lessons paid for at such a dear price during the war. The reality of high infantry casualty rates when assaulting even hastily prepared positions manned by seasoned troops, the requirement for simple and durable command and control capabilities, the advantages of surprise, tactical air support, the need for innovative plans, and the reality of "hard pounding" -- all these lessons were seemingly pushed to the back of the minds of Canada's military leaders during what has been called the "long forgotten winters" of the interwar period.[13] Moreover, despite a predilection for conventional methods, the Canadian Corps also experimented with mechanized warfare, but could not develop a successful written doctrine because there were not enough tanks, not enough training opportunities, and not enough time to reflect on and record the lessons learned. The Canadian Corps may have been on the verge of discovering a mechanized warfare doctrine, but the war ended before a tactical innovation in a distinct set of circumstances could be developed into a comprehensive doctrine, and the Corps' experience was quickly forgotten in the rush to return to peaceful life.

While modern soldiers may dismiss the operational lessons of the Great War as irrelevant, they do so only at their own peril. Better that they should examine Currie's battles and see in them the audacity, the attempt to incorporate maneuver and surprise that form the keystones of modern maneuver warfare doctrine.[14] Currie took advantage of the proficiency and experience of his Corps to develop battle situations that would achieve tactical surprise and local superiority, thereby helping to reduce the heavy casualties inevitably created by offensive actions during World War One. Currie's audacity and willingness to take calculated risks also helped to achieve tactical surprise.

Yet, although the Corps displayed a singular mastery of the "conventional" set-piece artillery-infantry attack, operational flexibility was shackled by inadequate C3 methods, often causing the Corps' attacks to bog down after the first 12 hours. As a result of both the tempo of operations and the deficiency of C3 means, battle procedure became disjointed, and lack of coordination destroyed the synergy which made the initial assault so effective. When this occurred Currie was often justified in stopping his attack, reorganizing, and then mounting another set-piece operation.

Modern proponents of "maneuver" warfare may sneer at the seemingly ponderous nature of the Canadian Corps operations, but given the conditions, it proved to be a highly effective approach. Currie and others in the Canadian Corps, such as Griesbach and Macdonell, showed a flair for taking calculated risks in order to gain a decisive advantage, a fact often overlooked by shallow examinations of the experience of the Canadian Corps because of the widespread belief that the strategic aim was attrition, and that this could only be accomplished by plodding generals making unimaginative plans for "mass and mutual massacres." At least in the case of the Canadian Corps during the final part of World War One, nothing could be further from the truth.

As the Canadian Army today moves toward adoption of a "maneuver warfare doctrine" (whatever that is deemed to be), it would do well to study its own past. The modern Canadian land force need not fall into the unfortunate trap of believing they need to look primarily at the experiences of a foreign armies, like the German, in order to find suitable examples of maneuver warfare in action. By doing so, the Canadian military today may only be learning from a second-hand source the same lessons, positive or otherwise, its own history can teach.

Finally, the Canadian experience should point to the danger of forgetfulness, and the awesome burden of memory. If nothing else, this examination of the Canadian Corps' crucial role in the Allied victory of 1918 should shatter the myth of Canadians as an "unmilitary" people.[15] Canada fielded one of the most potent formations on the Western Front during the Great War. Canadians were not, however, natural-born soldiers. In reality, Canadians became brutally efficient at the art of war only through the sacrifice, hard work, and dedication of the soldiers and their families, and the efforts of men like Currie, Griesbach, Odlum, McNaughton, Lindsay, Macdonell, and a pantheon of others. Canadian soldiers paid with their lives for the accomplishments of the Canadian Corps. By the end of World War One, Canada possessed an army, in the form of the Canadian Corps, that was second to none in terms of tactical doctrine and organization. The fact that its achievements and expertise were subsequently forgotten, almost willfully, was tragic. The burden of memory should have fallen primarily, but not exclusively on the shoulders of Canada's postwar military. But the responsibility also lay with the people of the nation as a whole, for it was in their name, by their elected officials, and for their benefit, that the soldiers of Canada were asked to kill and be killed in far-off foreign fields. Surely, the citizen-soldiers of Canada would have chosen to do otherwise.

If anything, the Canadian Corps' unique experience during the 100 Days reveals the futility and ugliness of war. The achievements of the Canadian Corps' campaign may seem glorious to the reader who examines them at 80 years' distance, but those who were there might see their accomplishments in a different light. Currie, and many of the Canadian and British soldiers who fought with him, the members of his "shock army," believed that they were fighting a "war to end all wars." By 1933, however, Currie again saw the gathering storm clouds over Europe threatening to pull Canadian men across the ocean. One of Arthur Currie's last wishes was to make Canadians understand both the heroism and the horror of war. In a speech written just before his death in 1933, he remarked:

Only those who suffered from gas, or saw their comrades writhing in that painful horror and fatal suffocation, can have any conception of the horror...in warfare. I wish I had the ability to make all Canadians see clearly one day of the gas battle in April 1915, or of the Passchendaele battle of 1917.[16]

Ironically enough, Currie's words reverberate with the sentiment of the Duke of Wellington, whose exhortation to "pound harder" opened this work and has formed a central theme throughout. It is perhaps fitting that the Iron Duke's thoughts on his brilliant victory at Waterloo close this account of the achievements of the Canadian Corps, words that no doubt would have been echoed by Currie and his soldiers: *"Nothing except a battle lost can be half so melancholy as a battle won."*[17]

Lest we forget.

NOTES

1. Travers, *How the War Was Won*, p. 177.
2. The Australian record is very close to the Canadian; according to Bean, the Australian Corps engaged 64 German divisions in 1918, the bulk of these during the 100 Days; see Bean, *AOH*, Vol. 6, Index, p. xliii-xliv.
3. *Aristeia* is a term used by Homeric scholars to describe a particularly special show of valour by a warrior. It is especially appropriate in this context because it acknowledges the temporary superiority or importance of one figure without necessarily denigrating the efforts and significance of all the others on the battlefield; see Richard Lattimore, trans. and ed., *The Iliad of Homer* (Chicago: University of Chicago Press, 1951), pp. 29-37.
4. The author fully realizes that many historians would take issue with this statement, pointing to the First Canadian Army's role in the liberation of Europe in 1944 as being the high point of Canadian arms. While the accomplishments of the First Canadian Army are indeed important, that formation was neither held in the same high esteem as was the Canadian Corps, nor was it given the same vitally important tasks.
5. For a discussion of the mind-set of Canadian doctrine, see Major C. S. Oliviero, "Maneuver Warfare: Smaller Can Be Better," *Canadian Defense Quarterly*, Vol. 18, No. 2 (Autumn 1988), p. 70.
6. See Granatstein, *The Generals*, pp. 3-178, 258-267.
7. Operations TRACTABLE and TOTALIZE were the First Canadian Army's battles to close the Falaise Gap in Normandy, 1944. For an examination of the First Canadian Army's performance, see English, *Normandy Campaign*; Max Hastings, *Overlord* (London: Simon and Schuster, 1984) pp. 293-320.
8. Brigadier W. Griesbach, Personal Diary, 1914-1919, entry 30-31 October 1918, Griesbach papers, NAC, MG 30 E15, Vol. 1, File 5.
9. Gudmundsson, has pointed out that the same phenomenon gripped the BEF, German and French Armies, creating a virtual "maelstrom" of ideas that eventually led to a breakdown in the utility of written "doctrine"; Bruce Gudmundsson, Lecture at the Royal Military College of Canada, Kingston, Ontario, 22 November 1994. See Griffith, *Battle Tactics*, for the British side of innovation and tactical adaption, and Lt. Col. Lucas, *L'Evolution Des Idees Tacticques en France et en Allemagne Pendant la Guerre de 1914-1918* (Paris: Berger-Levrault, 1923). Thanks to Bruce Gudmundsson for this last reference.
10. Robert Citino has said much the same thing about the development of the tank: "Tanks had not existed anywhere in 1914 outside a few fertile imaginations.... Less than four years later, war without them was virtually inconceivable... The history of warfare knows no comparable development in such a short period of time." (*Armoured Forces: History and Sourcebook*, [Westport, CT.: Greenwood, 1994], p. 45). Citino's comment would probably be even more valid if the development of a whole host of new and influential weapons systems and

techniques -- from true indirect fire artillery, tactical air support, chemical weapons, and dispersed infantry tactics -- were considered along with the development of the tank from 1914 to 1918. All of these new developments, and not just the tank, had irrevocably changed the face of battle forever. See also Stephen P. Rosen, *Winning the Next War: Innovation and the Modern Military* (Ithaca, NY: Cornell Universtiy Press, 1990), pp. 109-129; Bidwell and Graham, *Firepower*, Chapters 7-8.

11. This is precisely the argument made by Brown in "Not Glamorous, But Effective," pp. 421-443.

12. These concepts are outlined in the United States Army's Field Manual, FM 100-5, *Operations*, August 20, 1982, and the newer version, dated June 14, 1993. See also Richard Simpkin, *Race to the Swift : Thoughts on Twenty-First Century Warfare* (London: Brassey's, 1985); and Griffith, *Battle Tactics*, pp. 152-158.

13. English, *Normandy Campaign*, pp. 13-56.

14. The literature on maneuver warfare is growing at a phenomenal rate, and has generated a lively discussion in many western militaries; the best primer is Robert Leonhard's *Art Of Maneuver*, (Novato, Calif.: Presidio, 1991), and *Maneuver Warfare Anthology*, (Novato: Presidio, 1993); from the latter, see especially Richard Hooker, Jr., "The Mythology Surrounding Maneuver Warfare." The author would like to thank LCol. C. Oliviero at the Canadian Land Forces Command and Staff College for these references.

15. This term is taken from G.F.G. Stanley's *Canada's Soldiers: The Military History of an Unmilitary People*, 4th ed. (Toronto: Macmillan, 1974).

16. Arthur Currie, Speech to the Canadian Legion, 11 November 1933, from a draft in the Currie Papers, NAC, MG 30 E100, Vol. 41, File 185.

17. The Duke of Wellington wrote these thoughts while surveying the battlefield of Waterloo in the aftermath of his victory; quoted in *The Penguin Dictionary of Quotations*, ed. J.M. and M.J. Cohen (London: Penguin, 1960) p. 412.

APPENDIX: "POLICY AS TO COMMAND OF ARTILLERY UNITS DURING OFFENSIVE OPERATIONS"

S_E_C_R_E_T.

CANADIAN CORPS.
G.558/3-15G.
20th September, 1918.

```
1st Cdn. Division - 2 copies.
2nd Cdn. Division - 2 copies.
3rd Cdn. Division - 2 copies.
4th Cdn. Division - 2 copies.
G.O.C., R.A.       - 10 copies.
C.C.H.A.           - 10 copies.
-----------------------------------
```

POLICY AS TO COMMAND OF ARTILLERY UNITS

DURING OFFENSIVE OPERATIONS

1.   With a view to saving unnecessary repetition of orders and instructions with regard to the command of Artillery Units, the Corps Commander has decided to lay down the following policy which is designed to meet the various tactical conditions which arise during offensive operations.

2.   There will be three difffernt varieties of Command known respectively as:-

(a) Corps Control.

(b) Divisional Control.

(c) Normal Control.

3. CORPS CONTROL.

As soon as operations appear imminent, the order for Corps Control will be issued.

This means that all artillery Units in the Corps will be directly under the orders of the G.O.C., R.A., in order that he may co-ordinate barrages, bombardments and counter-battery work on the whole Corps front.

This phase will last normally until the conclusion of the set piece barrage. Cases may, however, arise in which the amount of Field Artillery at the disposal of the Corps is in excess of what is required for barrage purposes. In these cases the superfluous brigades will be distributed among the Divisions in front line, and will then come automatically under the orders of G.Os.c. Divisions 6 hours before ZERO, in order that they may be employed in close support of the infantry from Zero hour. As far as possible it will be arranged that these superfluous brigades belong to the Divisional Artillery of Divisions in the front line.

(Cont'd.)

- 2 -

4. <u>DIVISIONAL CONTROL</u>.

This will come into force automatically, as soon as the
set piece barrage is concluded.

It means that at least one Field Artillery Brigade, in
addition to the Divisional Artillery, and one Mobile Brigade
of Heavy Artillery are placed under the orders of each Divisional
Commander in front line, who will exercise command of these
units through his own C.R.A.; while each Division in Second
line assumes command of its own Divisional Artillery. All
remaining Field and Heavy Artillery will remain under orders of
G.O.C., R.A. as a Corps Reserve, which will be used either to
reinforce Divisions in front line or to move into position to
cover a selected defensive line.

As soon as a Division in second line leap-frogs a Division
in front line, the former will automatically assume command of
all artillery then supporting the latter, with the exception
of the Divisional Artillery of the original front line Division,
which will remain under the orders of its own Division.

Should it be necessary during the battle to arrange for
a co-ordinated advance and barrage along the whole Corps front,
as on September 2nd, the order for Corps Control will be re-
issued to enable the necessary co-ordination to be carried out.

<u>N.B.</u>- The 6-inch Howitzer Batteries only will be available at the
conclusion of the set piece Barrage.
The 60-pdrs. will remain under Corps Control for counter-
Battery work until the infantry advance forces them to stop
firing, when they will at once join the Mobile Brigade.

5. <u>NORMAL CONTROL</u>.

This will come into force as soon as the operations come to
a standstill and the front begins to stabilize.
This means that the Field Artillery in action covering Divisional fronts is under the orders of the G.Os.C. Divisions in
front line, that Divisional Artilleries' resting with their own
Divisions are under the orders of the G.O.C., Division so as to
be available for combined training, and that all Heavy Artillery,
and such other Field Artillery as is not in action, are under the
orders of the G.O.C., R.A.

One or more Bombardment Groups of Heavy Artillery will be
affiliated to each Division in the line and will carry out such
tasks as Divisional Commanders may require provided that these
tasks do not clash with any special shoots ordered by Corps H.Q.

In the event of any special shoots, such as gas bombardments
along the whole Corps front, which require the co-operation of
the Field Artillery, the G.O.C., R.A. will issue such orders as
may be necessary to Divisions, at the same time sending a copy of
the orders for information to the C.R.A.s concerned...

BIBLIOGRAPHY

A NOTE ON SOURCES

The past two decades have seen a resurgence in writing on the Great War, possibly because enough time has finally passed between the event and the analysis for historians to attempt an objective look at what remains an emotionally charged subject for many in the Western world. The notes contained herein are supplemented in the bibliography for selected works that merit special mention, positive or otherwise.

This work was based primarily on a reading of the documents contained in the National Archives of Canada Record Group Nine (RG 9) files, especially those documents collected by the Canadian War Narrative Section in Volumes 4789 to 4809. This collection constitutes a virtually complete and well-cataloged set of documents for the operations of every unit and formation, including British, that fought with the Canadian Corps during the 100 Days campaign. It includes unit and formation war diaries, operations orders and signals traffic, and, perhaps most important, excellent maps. In short, it is a gold mine for anyone writing on this period of the Great War, containing a much more complete collection of important documents than any Canadian collection of personal papers.

With respect to personal papers, the Currie papers at the NAC were by far the most helpful, but one is forced to wade through a deluge of personal correspondence to find "diamonds" of operational insight. Interestingly enough, the most voluminous collections were those of generals who remained in public life after the war, usually as politicians; Griesbach and Odlum are two of the best examples. For what it is worth, modern staff officers would do well to look at the Canadian formations' staff duties and military writing; it is of surprisingly high quality and thorough detail, and certainly not the work of "donkeys."

Special mention must be made of the Royal Military College Archives in Kingston, Ontario. This not only holds the papers of Brig. Gen. H. A. Panet, who was commander of the Second Division's Artillery, but also a great number of the original maps, airphotos, and terrain studies that the Corps and Divisional staffs used in planning their operations. These sources are in much better condition than similar ones in the NAC, and are far easier to access and make "hands on" use of. Many of the photographs and maps are leftovers from past battlefield study exercises. For anyone with an interest in the Great War, this collection is a dream come true.

Official histories of the Great War seem to be surrounded by controversy. Nevertheless, both Bean's *Official History of Australia in the War of 1914-1918*, and Edmond's *Official History of the Great War* are excellent, despite their respective biases. Nicholson's one volume work on the Canadian Expeditionary Force is an outstanding compromise between brevity and detail, and is also highly recommended. The German official history comes in nearly forty volumes, with an entire volume dedicated to the battle of Amiens alone. Anyone consulting this work with an even cursory knowledge of German will almost immediately sense the mood of despair and the psychological impact of 8 August 1918 on the Germans.

There are three other histories that should be singled out for their importance. The first is Arthur Currie's *Report on Corps Operations, 1918*, because it was written almost immediately after the period in question, and because it is the only published work on the period by Currie. His Australian counterpart, Sir John Monash, was much more prolific, and wrote an in-depth work entitled *The Australian Victories in France*. This work was especially useful for its detailed look at Amiens from the Australian perspective, and it is a tragedy that Currie never produced anything comparable. The third book that begs mentioning is Hahn's excellent work on *The Intelligence Service Within the Canadian Corps, 1914-1918*, because of its didactic tone and expert technical insight into the generation and use of tactical intelligence.

The most noteworthy secondary source works are those of a group that will be referred to as the "recent revisionists." These historians, including Tim Travers, Bruce Gudmundsson, Hubert Johnson, Paddy Griffith, David Trask, and Martin Samuels, have recently done some excellent scholarship in the area of the interaction of military strategy, tactics, and technology, and its impact on the Western Front. Despite differences, all work on the same underlying theme: the Great War generals were not all donkeys, and World War One was a very modern, technological struggle that spawned a "sea change" in modern warfare. The best books in this group are Paddy Griffith's *Battle Tactics of the Western Front* and Tim Travers' *How the War Was Won*, for the British side, and Bruce Gudmundsson's *Stormtroop Tactics* for the German.

There are three good biographies of Sir Arthur Currie. Hugh Urquhart's *Arthur Currie: The Biography of a Great Canadian*, was the first published, and remains a very good, if somewhat dated look at Currie's entire life. Daniel Dancocks' *Sir Arthur Currie: A Biography*, is very readable, but not as in-depth. A.M.J. Hyatt's work, *General Sir Arthur Currie: A Military Biography* is the best look at Currie as an operational commander, and also addresses some of the tactical problems and innovations encountered by the Canadian Corps.

Last, perhaps the best work specifically on the Canadian Corps during the final 100 Days is Daniel Dancocks' *Spearhead to Victory*. Although not a classic academic work, it is nonetheless a well-researched and compelling book. Dancocks has done an admirable job of placing the Corps' achievements in the context of the wider war. Its one flaw is a distinctly pro-Canadian bias, which the author clearly admits in the introduction. In short, *Spearhead* is a very good work of narrative military history, and was indispensable to this study.

PRIMARY SOURCES, UNPUBLISHED

Government Records, Personal Papers, and Manuscript Collections

1. National Archives of Canada, Ottawa.

Record Group (RG) 9 -- Canadian War Narrative Section -- RG 9, III, D, Vols. 4789-4809.

      These records are primarily orders, war diaries, after action reports, and official documents collected and used by the CWNS in its attempt to write an official narrative. It is an outstanding collection, primarily because all the most critical documents are collected in one place, and have an excellent finding aid guide to each file. This collection is better documented and easier to use than the other Record Group collections and personal papers. It includes dossiers on British and German formations that had contact with the Canadian Corps, as well as GHQ publications and translations of captured German documents. Highly recommended.

Manuscript Group (MG) 30 -- Personal Papers:

        Raymond Brutinel
        Henry Burstall
        Arthur Currie
        William Griesbach
        Archibald Macdonell
        Andrew McNaughton
        Victor Odlum
        David Watson

2. Archives, Royal Military College of Canada, Kingston Ontario.

Brig. Gen. H.A. Panet Papers
      Brigadier Panet had been GOCRA, 2nd Division from 1917 onward, and, after the war, became commandant of RMC, where he left his papers. It is a treasure trove of divisional reports and excellent maps, especially artillery barrage maps. Includes original barrage maps and artillery orders for Vimy onward. Also available are airphotos, maps, and detailed studies of the ground over which the Canadian Corps fought. These are now held by RMC, and but were originally used for post-war Staff College exercises.

PRIMARY SOURCES, PUBLISHED

Official Histories and Government Publications

Bean, C.E.W. *The Official History of Australia in the War of 1914-1918, Volume VI, The Australian Imperial Force in France During the Allied Offensive, 1918.* Sydney: University of Queensland Press, 1942, 1983.

Bean's history set the standard for official histories. It is an excellent work, almost unparalleled in its depth. Bean combined exhaustive research, inside knowledge, and a good sense of humor and proportion to create an excellent reference work. He must also be considered the chief architect of the "Australian myth," for his untiring efforts to claim glory for Monash and the Australian Corps. His contempt for the "chateau generals" is only barely hidden.

Currie, Lieut. Gen. Sir A.W. *Canadian Corps Operations During the Year 1918.* Ottawa: Department of Militia and Defence, 1919.

This work is Currie's official interim report, and is excellent for getting the operational perspective from the commander's viewpoint.

Edmonds, Brig. Gen. Sir James. *Official History of the Great War: Military Operations in France and Belgium, 1918.* Vols 3-5. London: H.M. Stationery Office, 1947.

Despite the controversy that surrounds both the author and his historical accuracy, this is nonetheless an extremely valuable book. Its narrative usually only goes down to battalion level, however, and it lacks a critical, analytical perspective that would make it more valuable for modern historians.

Nicholson, Col. G.W.L. *The Official History of the Canadian Army in the First World War: Canadian Expeditionary Force, 1914-1919.* Ottawa: Queen's Printer, 1962.

An excellent one volume official history of the CEF, though weak in its examination of the deeper significance of the events of the 100 Days. Nonetheless, this concise history proved to be invaluable for this topic.

Reichsarchiv, Germany. *Schlachten des Weltkreigs, Band 36: Die Katastrophe des 8. August 1918.* Berlin: Oldenberg, 1930.

This is the German side of the story, although it should be noted that, interestingly enough, it relies relatively heavily on British sources. Quite simply, it is a harrowing story of confusion and collapse, sprinkled with acts of desperate bravery. Even with a limited knowledge of German, the reader is struck by the bleak tone of the book. An excellent map is included.

Stacey, C.P. *The Canadian Army, 1939-1945: An Official Historical Summary*. Ottawa: King's Printer, 1948.
An outstanding one-volume history of the Canadian land forces during World War Two.

Various, *Report of the Ministry of Overseas Military Forces of Canada, 1918*. London: Ministry of Overseas Forces of Canada, 1919.
A large collection that outlines the functions of the Overseas Ministry, and the organization and terms of reference for each element of the CEF. Although it is not especially well written, it remains a vital source of background information on the Canadian Corps.

Semiofficial Publications

Brewsher, Maj. F.W. *The History of the 51st (Highland) Division, 1914-1918*. London: Blackwood and Sons, 1921.
Canada in the Great World War, Vol. 5: The Triumph of the Allies. Toronto: United Publishers, 1920.
Craig, J.D. *The 1st Canadian Division in the Battles of 1918*. London: Barrs and Co., 1919.
Grafton, Lt. Col. C.S. *The Canadian "Emma Gees": A History of the Canadian Machine Gun Corps*. London, Ont: Hunter Printing, 1938.
Hahn, Maj. J.E. *The Intelligence Service Within the Canadian Corps, 1914-1918*. Toronto: Macmillan, 1930.
Monash, Lieut. Gen. Sir John. *The Australian Victories in France*. Sydney: Angus and Robertson, 1936.
Montgomery, Maj. Gen. Archibald. *The Story of the Fourth Army in the Battles of the Hundred Days, August 8th to November 11th, 1918*. London: Hodder and Stoughton, 1919.

Monogaphs and Articles

Anderson, Maj.-General W.H. "The Breaking of the Queant-Drocourt Line by the Canadian Corps, First Army." *Canadian Defence Quarterly*, Vol. 4, No. 1 (January 1926).
_____. "The Crossing of the Canal du Nord." *Canadian Defence Quarterly*, Vol. 2, No. 1 (October 1924).
_____. "The Operations Round Valenciennes by the First Army, October-November, 1918." *Canadian Defence Quarterly*, Vol. 2, No. 3 (April 1925).
Broad, Lt. Col. C.N.F. "The Development of Artillery Tactics, 1914-1918." *Canadian Defence Quarterly*, three parts; Vol. 1, No. 1 (June-July 1922).
Junger, Ernst. *The Storm of Steel: From the Diary of a German Storm-troop Officer on the Western Front*. New York: Howard Fertig,1929, 1975.

Ludendorff, Gen. Erich. *My War Memories*. 2 Vols. London: Hutchinson and Co.,
    n.d.
Maurice, Maj. Gen. Sir F. *The Last Four Months: The End of The War in the West*.
    London: Cassell, 1919.
McNaughton, A.G.L. "The Capture of Valenciennes: A Study in Co-ordination."
    Canadian Defence Quarterly, Vol. 10, No. 3 (April 1933).
    "The Development of Artillery in the Great War." *Canadian Defence
    Quarterly*, Vol. 6, No. 2 (January, 1929).

SELECTED SECONDARY SOURCES

Anonymous. "The German Catastrophe of the 8th of August, 1918." *The Army
    Quarterly*, Vol. 25 (October 1932 - January 1933).
Bidwell, Shelford, and Dominick Graham. *Firepower: British Army Weapons and
    Theories of War 1904-1945*. London: George Allen and Unwin, 1982.
Blaxland, Gregory. *Amiens: 1918*. London: Frederick Muller, 1968.
Bond, Brian. *War and Society in Europe, 1870-1970*. London: Fontana, 1984.
Braim, Paul. "A Surge of Revisionism: Scholarship on The Great War." *Parameters*,
    Vol. 25, No. 1 (Spring, 1995).
Brown, Ian M. "Not Glamorous, But Effective: The Canadian Corps and the Set-piece
    Attack, 1917-1918." *Journal of Military History*, Vol 58 (July 1994).
Chappelle, Dean. "The Canadian Attack at Amiens, 8-11 August 1918." *Canadian
    Military History*, Vol. 2, No. 2 (April 1993).
Churchill, Sir Winston S. *The World Crisis, 1916-1918: Part 2*. London: Thornton
    Butterworth, 1927.
Citino, Robert. *Armoured Forces History and Sourcebook*. Westport, CT:
    Greenwood, 1994.
Clausewitz, Carl von. *On War*. Ed. and trans. Michael Howard and Peter Paret.
    Princeton, NJ: Princeton University Press, 1984.
Cooper, Duff. *Haig* 2 Vols. London: Faber, 1935-36.
Dancocks, Daniel G. *Spearhead to Victory: Canada and the Great War*. Edmonton:
    Hurtig, 1987.
_____. *Sir Arthur Currie: A Biography*. Toronto: Methuen, 1985.
De Groot, Gerard J. *Douglas Haig, 1861-1928*. London: Unwin Hyman, 1988.
Dewar, George A.B., and J.H. Boraston. *Sir Douglas Haig's Command*. Vol. 2.
    London: Constable and Co., 1922.
Doyle, Sir Arthur Conan. *The British Campaign in France and Flanders, July to
    November 1918*. London: Hodder and Stoughton, 1920.
English, John. *The Canadian Army and the Normandy Campaign: A Study in the
    Failure of High Command*. New York: Praeger, 1991.
_____. *On Infantry*. New York: Praeger, 1984.
_____ and Bruce Gudmundsson. *On Infantry: Revised Edition*. New York:
    Praeger, 1994.

Fuller, J.F.C. *A Military History of the Western World, Volume 3*. New York: Da Capo, 1956.

_____. *The Decisive Battles of the Western World and Their Influence Upon History, Volume 3*. London: Eyre and Spottiswoode, 1956. (Note: These two books are identical,but by different publishers.)

Gaffen, Fred. "The Canadian Corps' Greatest Battles," *Canadian Defence Quarterly*, Vol. 13, No. 3 (Winter 1983/84).

Gibbs, Phillip. *Open Warfare: The Way to Victory*. London: Willian Heinemann, 1919.

Granatstein, J.L. *The Generals: The Canadian Army's Senior Commanders in the Second World War*. Toronto: Stoddart, 1993.

Greenhous, Brereton. "'...It Was Chiefly a Canadian Battle': The Decision at Amiens, 8-11 August 1918." *Canadian Defence Quarterly*, Vol. 18, No. 2 (Autumn 1988).

Griffith, Paddy. *Battle Tactics of the Western Front: The British Army's Art of the Attack, 1916-1918*. New Haven: Yale University Press, 1994.

Guderian, Heinz. *Achtung-Panzer!* trans. Christopher Duffy. London: Arms and Armour, n.d.

Gudmundsson, Bruce. *Stromtroop Tactics: Innovation in the German Army, 1914-1918*. New York: Praeger, 1989.

House, Jonathan. *Toward Combined Arms Warfare: A Survey of 20th-Century Tactics, Doctrine, and Organization*. Fort Leavenworth, KS: U.S. Army Combat Studies Institute, 1984.

Hyatt, A.M.J. *General Sir Arthur Currie: A Military Biography*. Toronto: University of Toronto Press, 1987.

Johnson, Hubert C. *Breakthrough! Tactics, Technology, and the Search for Victory on the Western Front in World War 1*. Novato, CA: Presidio, 1994.

Keegan, John. *The Face of Battle*. London: Penguin, 1976.

Laffin, John. *British Butchers and Bunglers of World War One*. Gloucester: Alan Sutton, 1988.

Liddell-Hart, B. H. *A History of the World War, 1914-1918*. Boston: Little, Brown, 1935.

Livesay, J.F.B. *Canada's Hundred Days*. Toronto: Thomas Allen, 1919.

Lucas, Lt. Col. *L'Evolution Des Idees Tactiques en France et en Allemagne Pendant la Guerre de 1914-1918*. Paris: Berger-Levrault, 1923.

Lupfer, Timothy. *The Dynamics of Doctrine: The Changes in German Tactical Doctrine During the First World War*. Fort Leavenworth, KS: U.S. Army Combat Studies Institute, 1981.

Marshall-Cornwall, James. *Haig as Military Commander*. London: Batsford, 1973.

Morton, Desmond. *A Military History of Canada*, 3rd ed. Toronto: McClelland and Stewart, 1992.

_____. *When Your Number's Up: The Canadian Soldier in the First World War*. Toronto: Random House, 1993.

_____ and J.L. Granatstein. *Marching to Armageddon: Canadians and the Great War, 1914-1919*. Toronto: Lester and Orpen Dennys, 1989.

Nicholson, G.W.L. *The Gunners of Canada: The History of the Royal Regiment of Canadian Artillery, Volume 1, 1534-1919*. Toronto: McClelland and Stewart, 1967.

Paret, Peter, ed. *Makers of Modern Strategy*. (Princeton, NJ: Princeton University Press, 1986). See especially the excellent articles by Gordon Craig, "The Political Leader as Strategist," and Micheal Geyer, "German Strategy in the Age of Machine Warfare, 1914-1945."

Parkinson, Roger. *Tormented Warrior: Ludendorff and the Supreme Command*. London: Hodder and Stoughton, 1978.

Pitt, Barrie. *1918: The Last Act*. London: Cassell, 1962.

Prior, Robin, and Trevor Wilson. *Command on the Western Front: The Military Career of Sir Henry Rawlinson, 1914-1918*. Oxford: Blackwell, 1992.

Rawling, Bill. "Communications in the Canadian Corps, 1915-1918: Wartime Technological Progress Revisited." *Canadian Military History*, Vol. 3, No. 2 (Autumn 1994).

_____. *Surviving Trench Warfare: Technology and the Canadian Corps, 1914-1918*. Toronto: University of Toronto Press, 1992.

Richter, Donald. *Chemical Soldiers: British Gas Warfare in World War 1*. Lawrence, KS:University Press of Kansas, 1993.

Rosen, Stephen R. *Winning the Next War: Innovation and the Modern Military*. Ithaca, NY: Cornell University Press, 1990.

Samuels, Martin. *Doctrine and Dogma: German and British Infantry Tactics in the First World War*. Westport, CT: Greenwood Press, 1992.

Simpkin, Richard E. *Race to the Swift: Thoughts on Twenty-First Century Warfare*. London: Brassey's, 1985.

Sixsmith, E.K.G. *Douglas Haig*. London: Weidenfeld and Nicolson, 1976.

Smithers, A.J. *Sir John Monash*. London: Leo Cooper, 1973.

Stacey, C.P. *Canada and the Age of Conflict: A History of Canadian External Policy, Volume 1: 1867-1921*. Toronto: Macmillan, 1977.

_____. *Introduction to the Study of Military History for Canadian Students*. Ottawa: Queen's Printers, 1952.

_____. "The Staff Officer: A Footnote to Canadian Military History," *Canadian Defence Quarterly*, Vol. 5, No. 1 (Summer 1973).

Stewart, William. *Attack Doctrine in the Canadian Corps, 1916-1918*. Unpublished Thesis, Fredericton, NB: University of New Brunswick, 1980.

Swettenham, John. *McNaughton, Volume 1, 1887-1939*. Toronto: Ryerson, 1968.

_____. *To Seize the Victory: The Canadian Corps in World War War 1*. Toronto: Ryerson Press, 1965.

Sulzbach, Herbert. *With the German Guns*. London: Leo Cooper, 1973.

Terraine, John. *Douglas Haig: The Educated Soldier*. London: Hutchinson, 1963.

_____. *The First World War, 1914-1918*. London: Macmillan, 1965.

_____. *To Win a War: 1918, The Year of Victory*. London: Sidgwick and Jackson, 1978.

Trask, David. *The AEF and Coalition Warmaking, 1917-1918*. Lawrence, KS: University Press of Kansas, 1993.

Travers, Tim. *How the War Was Won: Command and Technology in the British Army on the Western Front, 1917-1918*. London: Routledge, 1992.

_____. "The Evolution of British Strategy and Tactics on the Western Front in 1918: GHQ, Manpower, and Technology." *The Journal of Military History*, Vol. 54 (April 1990).

Urquhart, Hugh M. *Arthur Currie: The Biography of a Great Canadian*. Toronto: Dent, 1950.

Warner, Philip. *Field Marshall Earl Haig*. London: Bodley Head, 1991.

Winter, Dennis. *Haig's Command: A Reassessment*. London: Viking, 1991.

Wray, Timothy. *Standing Fast: German Defensive Doctrine on the Russian Front During World War II*. Fort Leavenworth, KS: U.S. Army Combat Studies Institute, 1986.

Young, Peter. "August 8, 1918: Germany's Black Day." In *The Marshall Cavendish Encyclopedia of World War 1*. Toronto: Marshall Cavendish, 1976.

INDEX

About the Author

SHANE B. SCHREIBER, an infantry officer in the Canadian Army, is currently on regimental duty with the Third Battalion, Princess Patricia's Canadian Light Infantry, in Edmonton, Alberta.